MANAGING HIGH-TECHNOLOGY PROGRAMS

AND

PROJECTS

MANAGING HIGH-TECHNOLOGY PROGRAMS AND PROJECTS

Third Edition

Russell D. Archibald

John Wiley & Sons, Inc.

Published by John Wiley & Sons, Inc., Hoboken, New Jersey.
Published simultaneously in Canada.

For general information on our other products and services please contact our Customer Care Department within the United States at (800) 762-2974, outside the United States at (317) 572-3993 or fax (317) 572-4002.

Wiley also publishes its books in a variety of electronic formats. Some content that appears in print may not be available in electronic books. For more information about Wiley products, visit our Web site at www.wiley.com.

Library of Congress Cataloging-in-Publication Data:

Archibald, Russell D.
  Managing high-technology programs and projects / Russell D.
Archibald.— 3rd ed.
    p. cm.
  ISBN 0-471-26557-8 (CLOTH)
  1. Project management. 2. High technology. I. Title.
  T56.8 .A7 2003
  658.4′ 4—dc21

                                          2002155500

Printed in the United States of America.

10 9 8 7 6 5 4 3 2 1

Preface

In the 10 years since the publication of the second edition, the fundamental concepts of project management have not changed appreciably. However, there have been notable advances in the practice of project management in that decade, including:

- The advent of the Internet and the World Wide Web (Web) and their impact on all industries and governments, and on our ways of competing and collaborating on a global basis. "Internet speed" has increased the need for more effective project management methods and systems to continue to compete in the global marketplace. At the same time, the Internet and the Web have provided the means for achieving significant improvements in an organization's project management capabilities and performance.

- Increased emphasis on the application of systematic, disciplined project management methods to the early conceptual and definition life-cycle phases of projects, and linking these to the better known, more familiar execution phases.

- Recognition that projects are the primary means for implementing business strategies, and that projects must be managed within project portfolios and not simply as stand-alone projects or multiproject programs. The projects within each portfolio must support and help realize the growth strategies of the organization.

- Maturing of the project management function and the recognition of its growing importance within many organizations to the point where a senior executive is given responsibility for this function, together with the establishment of a Project Management Office.

- Maturing of the project management profession with the development of several different bodies of project management knowledge by competing professional associations in various parts of the world, a number of project management maturity models, and different approaches to certification of practitioners in the field.

- Continued development of more powerful and more integrated project management software applications that exploit the continued advances in information technology, the Internet, and the Web. Geographically dispersed projects and project teams (often called virtual teams) can now work together in real time no matter where in the world they are located using low-cost audio/video/digital teleconferencing on the Internet using broad-band satellite and cable modems.

- Where appropriate, movement toward enterprise-wide project management in which an enterprise is viewed as consisting of a collection of projects, or of several project portfolios, and managed accordingly.

- Greater recognition of the importance of resource constraints and resource management [the resource critical path (RCP), theory of constraints/TOC, and critical chain concepts] in establishing project plans and schedules and in monitoring progress.

- Further recognition that uncertainty in projects, rather than being a necessary evil, actually provides great opportunity for improvements and for taking actions to mitigate risks—if a proactive approach is taken toward risk and uncertainty.

- The wider use of more formalized risk analysis and tracking methods during both the conceptual and execution project life-cycle phases.

All of these developments add to the need for international understanding and use—within a single enterprise, within a project portfolio, or within a joint venture program or project—of similar, compatible planning, risk analysis and mitigation, scheduling, monitoring, controlling, and reporting—in a word, management—processes, methods, systems, and terminology. The most important objectives in gaining this understanding are to establish and maintain the commonality required to assure that the information can be integrated as needed on international joint venture and other complex programs and projects, and that the partners in such ventures can fully understand and integrate with each others' management methods and decision criteria. A primary purpose of this book is to continue to spread that needed understanding.

The additions and revisions incorporated in this third edition reflect these developments and include:

- The addition of three new chapters: Chapter 1, "Executive Overview of Project Management," emphasizes the linkage between strategic and project management, describes portfolio project management and the need for each organization to have a coherent project management process; Chapter 3: "Improving Project Management Capabilities," covers the cost and benefits of project management, a discussion of project management bodies of knowledge and maturity models, and recommends an approach to improving the project life-cycle management process and the organization's project management capabilities; and Chapter 5: "Integrative and Predictive Project Planning and Control," provides summary discussions of several categories of project management software and presents an approach to selecting and implementing software applications.

- Major revisions and extensions to five chapters:

    Chapter 2, "Programs and Projects," identifies ten recommended categories of projects, and for each project category discusses classifying criteria and provides numerous references for designing specific project life cycles and relating those to the project environment.

    Chapter 4, "Integrative Roles in Project Management," has been expanded to include the responsibilities of the project portfolio steering group, project sponsors, the person in charge of the project management office, and their interrelationships with each other and with program and project managers.

    Chapter 7, "Organizing the Project Management Function and Office," discusses the organizational alternatives that are in use in different organizations and the potential range of responsibilities that can be assigned to the project management office.

    Chapter 8, "Managing Project Portfolios, Programs, and Multiple Projects," explains how project portfolios are best managed and discusses proven ways to select and prioritize projects within portfolios, with several current references to the many different models used for these purposes. It discusses the need to manage projects at four levels in large organizations (portfolio, program, multiproject, and project) and describes a proven solution needed in many organizations for a multiproject operations planning and control system.

    Chapter 11, "Project Team Planning and Project Start-Up," contains an updated industry case study that reports the experience in a large telecommunications company in using this approach to get their projects off to a rapid, well-planned start over the past 18 years.

- Updating revisions to the remaining chapters.
- "CEO Demands" at the end each of the eight chapters in Part I presents summaries of what top executives must demand of their management team members relating to each chapter topic to achieve the full power of effective, integrated project management.

Together these demands comprise a road map for the continued improvement and development of the organization's project management capabilities. They represent reasonable demands that top executives can and must place on their management teams if they expect to compete and collaborate effectively in this Internet Age.

- Addition of an Appendix describing proven Russian methods for integrating scope, schedule, resource, financial, and risk management information for projects.

Part I, "Executive Guide to Program and Project Management," is of direct interest to senior executives including those responsible for the project management function and others to whom project managers report. It is also intended to inform program and project managers and project management specialists about the over-arching principles and practices that directly affect their responsibilities and performance. Part II, "Managing Specific Projects," is directed primarily to program, project, and other managers and project team members, and also to those holding overall responsibilities for the project management function within the organization.

Successful project management requires giving up some old management habits and attitudes and learning new ways to bring together many skills to select the right projects in the first place, and then to achieve the objectives on all projects: delivering the desired results on time and within budget. This in turn requires substantial management and organizational development and indoctrination at the executive levels, as well as indoctrination and training for project managers, functional managers and specialists, and project planning and control specialists. The book is designed to be used for these purposes. Experience with its use in the earlier editions within industry and government, and within universities at the graduate and undergraduate levels in many parts of the world, confirms the effectiveness of its design.

The seminar/workshop approach, bringing together teams of managers and contributors from one project, preferably, or from one organization, is by far the most effective way to get people to give up the old and embrace the new. Chapter 11, "Project Team Planning and Project Start-Up," presents specific, proven methods for project team training while simultaneously getting a project off to a rapid, well-planned start with a team committed to the project objectives and plan. By using real projects as the training vehicles, the seminar results are carried over directly into the current business of the organization.

RUSSELL D. ARCHIBALD

San Miguel de Allende, Guanajuato, Mexico

Acknowledgments

Iam indebted to many people for their ideas, inputs, and support in the preparation of the original edition of this book in 1976, the second edition in 1992, and in this third edition. I am grateful to Daniel P. Ono for his co-authorship of Chapter 11, "Project Team Planning and Project Start-Up," and to Vladimir Liberzon for his co-authorship of the Appendix, "Integrated Scope, Schedule, Resource, Financial, and Risk Management for Projects." Robert B. Youker has provided valuable contributions to all three editions. I also thank Sven Antvik, Shane C. Archibald, Martin Barnes, Robert Boivin, Dr. David I. Cleland, Ellodee A. Cloninger, Dr. Morten Fangel, Edward J. Fern, Quentin W. Fleming, Robert B. Gillis, Alan B. Harpham, Colin Hastings, Eric Jenett, Bill Kern, Dr. Steen Lichtenberg, Sandro Miscia, David L. Pells, Dr. Gerald R. Rossy, Cyndi Snyder, John Tuman, and R. Max Wideman for their contributions and their friendship over the years. I am grateful as well to the many authors whom I have quoted and cited in this third edition with whom I have not had the pleasure of working personally. Once again I must thank the persons I acknowledged in the preface to the first edition: Dr. David L. Wilemon, Chandra K. Jha, Marvin Flaks, Robert J. Braverman, and L. H. Brockman.

I thank my fellow members of the Project Management Institute and the International Project Management Association, as well as the many seminar participants and clients whose feedback has helped shape this book. I am also grateful to Jessie Noyes at John Wiley & Sons and the staff at Publications Development Company of Texas for their expert editorial assistance with the production of this book. Finally, once again I would like to publicly express my gratitude to my wife Marion for her continuing, never-failing love, interest, and support.

R.D.A.

Contents

PART

I

« »

Executive Guide to Program and Project Management

Part I is intended for top-level managers who are responsible for the strategic direction and growth of their organizations, as well as for those who hold responsibilities for project portfolios and the programs and projects they contain. Part I is also directed to managers and project management specialists at the program and project levels, to whom Part II is primarily addressed, to enable them to appreciate more fully how the discipline of project management has become an important factor in the continued success of all complex organizations.

Part I provides the senior executive and others with an in-depth understanding of:

- The role that projects play in the strategic direction of an organization and how project management is best integrated into the total corporate structure (Chapter 1);
- The nature and key characteristics of programs and projects (Chapter 2);
- The value and cost of, and ways to improve an organization's project management capabilities (Chapter 3);

1

- The three basic concepts that underlie modern project management: integrative roles, integrative and predictive planning and control, and project teamwork (Chapters 4 through 6);
- Organizing the project management office and function (Chapter 7); and
- Managing project portfolios, programs and multiple projects (Chapter 8).

At the end of each chapter in Part I several "CEO Demands" are presented relating to the main topics of the chapter. These demands—each one reasonable and achievable using today's state-of-the-art—provide a road map to top managers for moving their organizations toward achieving the full power of integrated strategic project management in this Internet Age.

1

‹ ›

Executive Overview of Project Management

1.1 IMPORTANCE OF EFFECTIVE PROJECT MANAGEMENT

Programs and projects are of great importance to all industrial, governmental, and other human organizations. They are the means by which companies, especially when delivering complex, advanced technology products or systems to their customers, earn a major share of their profit. Projects are also the means by which new products are conceived, developed, and brought to market. New or improved capital facilities and new information systems are acquired through projects. Broad scope management projects, such as restructuring or reorganizing, major cost reduction efforts, plant or office relocation, and the like, are vital to continued profitable operation and growth.

In governmental units from city to county, state, regional, and federal levels, projects are vehicles for growth and improvement. School systems, universities, hospital systems, and other institutional forms of organizations create and improve their services, products, and facilities through programs and projects. In all these various organizations—governmental, institutional, and industrial—there is a growing recognition that although many projects apparently exist within the organization they are often poorly understood and frequently not properly managed. The purpose of this book is to assist in the correction of this situation by presenting a concise, comprehensive, and practical understanding of the concepts, processes, methods, and tools of modern, professional project management and how these are successfully applied and continually improved in high-technology environments.

Projects Exist in All Organizations

A project is a complex effort to produce certain specified, unique results at a particular time and within an established budget for the resources that it will expend or consume. A program, as discussed in this book, is a group of two or more related projects. More detailed and definitive definitions of projects and programs are given in Chapter 2.

The concept of a project is not new. Projects exist in all human organizations. They come in many sizes and with widely varying degrees of complexity and risk and produce an infinite variety of end results. The principles and practices of modern project management apply to all these projects across the entire spectrum of human enterprise.

The Rapid Spread of Modern Project Management

In recent years application of project management principles and practices has spread rapidly to an increasingly broad range of human enterprise around the world. The numbers of project management books, magazines, e-zines, other Internet Web sites, seminars, conventions, and professional and popular magazine articles continue to grow. Membership in professional associations in the field also continues to grow at an impressive rate. The Project Management Institute (PMI®, www.pmi.org) has grown worldwide from 8,500 members in 1990 to over 100,000 in 2003, with chapters in 39 countries and members residing in 80 additional countries. The International Project Management Association (IPMA, www.ipma.ch) is an international network of 28 national project management societies. Other professional associations of interest include the Association of Project Management (APM, www.apm.org.uk) (a member of IPMA), the Product Development Management Association (PDMA, www.pdma.org), and the Association for the Advancement of Cost Engineering (AACE, www.aaci.org). The referenced Web sites of each of these organizations provide many links to other project management related organizations, forums, magazines, educators and trainers, and software and consulting service providers.

The Diversity and Categorization of Projects

The great diversity in the areas of application is illustrated by the many specific interest groups (SIGs) within the Project Management Institute (Table 1.1). Each of these groups brings together executives and project management practitioners who have related interests. Additionally there

Table 1.1   The 19 Specific Interest Groups (SIGs) within PMI® Related to Different Areas of Application

1. Aerospace/defense
2. Automation systems
3. Automotive
4. Design/procurement/construction (across all economic sectors)
5. Environmental management (pollution remediation and prevention)
6. Financial services (banking, investment)
7. Global communications technologies (management and movement of information)
8. Government
9. Hospitality (major events, such as the Olympic Games)
10. Information systems
11. International development (infrastructure, agriculture, education, health, etc.) in developing countries
12. Manufacturing
13. Marketing and sales
14. New product development
15. Oil/gas/petrochemical
16. Pharmaceutical
17. Retail
18. Service and outsourcing (buying rather than making)
19. Utility industry (generation and distribution of electric power, water, and gas).

are several other PMI® specific interest groups that deal with particular aspects of project management across all of these areas of application. The PMI® College of Performance Measurement is devoted to the military/aerospace area of application. The project management approach also has been found to be effective in reengineering and restructuring existing organizations and bureaucratic processes.

In spite of the diversity of the end products or results created by projects in these many areas, the project management approach is remarkably similar in each. A project is not the end result itself, be it a new product, facility, process plant, information system, reengineered process, new organization structure, document, or any other tangible result. Rather, *a project is the process of creating a new end result.* The same principles of project management are applicable to projects in all areas of application, although there are significant variations in emphasis and in the detailed planning and execution of projects within each application area and within various world cultures.

The globalization of trade, manufacturing, energy, space endeavors, information technology, services industries, and other areas of human activity is a powerful driver to develop and apply common approaches to the planning and execution of projects across industrial sector and international boundaries. International joint venture projects involving such deliverables as pipelines, process plants, space vehicles and platforms, aircraft, automobiles, and new information technology platforms and applications, to name just a few examples, require that all contributors to such projects—who are frequently located on different continents and operate in widely different cultures—use common or at least similar management systems. The collaboration (co-labor) needed to complete these projects successfully can only be achieved efficiently if all parties understand what the others are doing and how they are doing it, and if the plans and schedules for interrelated projects or programs are integrated and use commonly understood management methods and terminology.

Effective Project Management Is Important to All Organizations

All projects must be well conceived and then well managed during their planning and execution to achieve the desired results on schedule and within the specified cost (in money or other critical resources).

Failures in project selection, risk analysis, and conceptual planning have caused:

- The expenditure of scarce resources (money, skills, facilities, and time) on efforts that are doomed to failure.
- The organization to be exposed to unacceptable financial, technological, and competitive risks.

Failures in project planning and execution have caused:

- Expected profit on commercial contracts to become losses through excessive costs, delays, and penalties.
- New products to be introduced late with significant detrimental impact on established business plan objectives and market penetration opportunities.
- New product development projects to be completed too late to benefit the related product line or otherwise fail to produce the results expected.
- Capital facilities to be delayed, causing missed objectives in product lines that depend on the facilities.
- Information systems projects to exceed their planned cost and schedule, with negative impacts on administration and general costs and operating efficiencies. The "Chaos Study" (www.pm2go

.com/default.asp), conducted by The Standish Group, concluded that only about one software development project in six met quality, schedule, and cost objectives. Nearly half of the projects studied were terminated before completion.

Failure on one significant project can eradicate the profit of a dozen well-managed projects. Too frequently the monitoring and evaluation of high-exposure projects is ineffective, and the failures are not identified until it is too late to avoid undesirable results. It is important, therefore, that every organization holding responsibility for projects also has the capability to manage the projects effectively.

Project-Driven and Project-Dependent Organizations

Two broad classes of organizations can be identified: First, those *project-driven* organizations whose primary business is projects. Examples of this class include architect/engineer/constructor, general contractor, and specialty contractor firms; software development firms who sell their products or services on a contract basis; telecommunications systems suppliers; consultants and other professional services firms; and other organizations that bid for work on a project-by-project basis. Growth strategies in such organizations are reflected in the type, size, location, and nature of the projects selected for bidding, as well as the choices made in how the required resources will be provided (in-house or out-sourced) to carry out the projects, if and when a contract is awarded or the project is otherwise approved for execution.

The second class of organizations—those that are *project-dependent* for growth—includes all others that provide goods and services as their mainstream business. Projects within these organizations are primarily internally sponsored and funded. Examples include manufacturing (consumer products, pharmaceuticals, engineered products, etc.), banking, transportation, communications, governmental agencies, computer hardware and software developers and suppliers, universities and other institutions, among others. These organizations depend on projects to support their primary lines of business, but projects are not their principle offering to the marketplace. Many of these sponsors of internally funded projects are important buyers of projects from project-driven organizations.

1.2 PROJECTS: VEHICLES FOR STRATEGIC GROWTH

Strategically managing the growth of a company, agency, institution, or other human enterprise requires:

- *A vision of the future* of the organization at the top level.
- *Consensus and commitment* within the power structure of the organization on the mission and future direction of the organization.
- *Documentation* of the key objectives and strategies to fulfill the mission.
- *Planning and execution of specific projects* to carry out the stated strategies and reach the desired objectives.

Objectives are descriptions of where we want to go. *Strategies* are statements of how we are going to get there. Strategies are carried out and objectives are reached, when major growth steps are involved, through execution of projects and multiproject programs within the organization's project portfolios. Projects translate strategies into actions and objectives into realities.

Most organizations of any size have a strategic planning or growth management process in place, with at least annual efforts to develop their longer term plans, objectives, and strategies. It is important to recognize that objectives and strategies exist in a hierarchy—and not just at one level—in large organizations. A useful way to describe this hierarchy is to define three levels:

1. Policy.
2. Strategic.
3. Operational.

Figure 1.1 shows how the strategies become objectives at the next lower level in the hierarchy, until at the operational level projects are identified to achieve the operational objectives. Unless the higher level objectives and strategies are translated into actions through projects, the plans will simply sit unachieved on the shelf.

Sources of Growth

Two basic sources of organizational growth can be identified. These are:

- *Growth by accretion:* Slow, steady, layered growth of the basic products, services, markets, and people.
- *Stepwise growth:* Discrete steps—small, medium, and large—that go beyond growth by accretion.

Growth by accretion is relatively slow and most often observed in mature industries. Sales volume slowly builds, for example, perhaps as a result

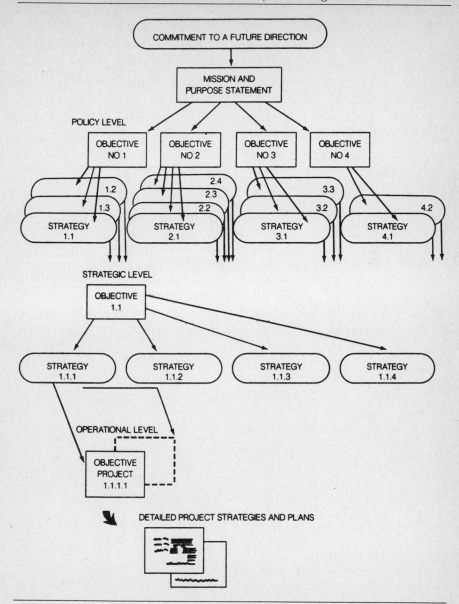

Figure 1.1   The hierarchy of objectives, strategies, and projects. *Source:* Russell D. Archibald, "Projects: Vehicles for Strategic Growth," *Project Management Journal, XIX, 4* (September 1988), p. 32. Used by permission.

of the existing salesforce getting better at their jobs individually, selling the production capacity that exists within the factory, possibly assisted by more effective marketing and advertising. At some point, when the factory capacity is limiting sales (and second and third shifts have already been added) further growth is dependent on a major or stepwise change: building a new factory, or expanding the old one.

Stepwise growth occurs when the organization goes beyond growth by accretion and initiates discrete actions to expand or improve: new products or services, new markets, new processes or production facilities, new information systems, new organizational patterns, new people. These growth steps are projects.

The Spectrum of Growth Projects

Table 1.2 shows a few representative examples of growth projects across the spectrum of different project magnitudes and serving different growth strategies. Larger and more risky projects require more formalized project management practices.

Programs and Projects Are the Vehicles for Growth

Stepwise growth involves a wide range of actions from low-risk baby steps to bet-the-company giant strides. It is not possible to draw a sharp line between growth by accretion and baby steps to expand, such as hiring an additional salesperson, or taking on a new distributor in a new state for an existing product line. But when the steps become significant in size, they clearly are recognizable as projects.

Table 1.2 Examples of Projects to Expand or Change

Project Size	Products or Services	Markets	Profits
Small	New package. Small product improvement.	Add new distributor. Local advertising campaign.	Substitute ingredients. Increase prices.
Major	Develop new product in existing line. Expand existing plant. Design/build new plant.	Enter new markets: Domestic Foreign: —Direct —License —Joint venture	New information system. Restructure organization. New policies and procedures.
Mega	Develop or acquire new product line.	Acquire major company.	Merge with competitor.

Major growth steps in any organization require projects for their realization—new facilities, systems, products, services, processes, technology, and/or markets. Acquisition of these by internal or joint ventures, acquiring or merging with another organization, licensing of technology or markets, or other methods always results in a project of some complexity. More organizations are now recognizing these facts, and more are approaching the management of these growth steps using proven project management principles and practices.

1.3 STRATEGIC PROJECT PORTFOLIO MANAGEMENT

Projects are major investments for most organizations. Investments must be managed on a portfolio basis. The characteristics and process of project portfolio management that have evolved over the past decade are described next.

Integrated Project Portfolio Management

Rather than attempt to manage individual projects as if they were stand-alone endeavors, executives have learned that every project is interrelated, primarily through the use of common resources but often in other ways and often with other projects in the organization. Linking selected projects within a *program* is the first step toward *project portfolio management.* Dye and Pennypacker (1999) provide a useful and comprehensive compilation of articles that reflect the growing awareness and maturity of the project portfolio management discipline in many organizations.

Multiproject versus Portfolio Project Management

The key differences between multiproject and portfolio project management are shown in Table 1.3. As indicated in Figure 1.2, a project portfolio consists of the programs and projects supporting a given higher level strategy. Although there could be only one overall corporate project portfolio, it generally makes more sense to define more than one portfolio on a strategic basis in large organizations to reflect product line, geographic, or technological divisions of the organization, industry, or market. Combe and Githens (1999) identify three general types of project portfolios:

- *Value-creating:* Strategic or enterprise projects.
- *Operational:* Projects that make the organization more efficient and satisfy some fundamental functional work.

Table 1.3   High-Level Comparison of Project Portfolio Management and Multiple Project Management

	Project Portfolio Management	Multiple Project Management
Purpose	Project selection and prioritization	Resource allocation
Focus	Strategic	Tactical
Planning emphasis	Long and medium-term (annual/quarterly)	Short-term (day-to-day)
Responsibility	Executive/senior management	Project/resource managers

Source: Lowell D. Dye and James S. Pennypacker, "Project Portfolio Managing and Managing Multiple Projects: Two Sides of the Same Coin?" *Proceedings of the 2000 PMI Seminars & Symposium,* Newtown Square, PA: Project Management Institute.

- *Compliance:* "Must-do" projects required to maintain regulatory compliance.

Combe (2000) reported that "Our senior management [of Northwestern Mutual, a major financial services company] was genuinely astonished at what they saw" when an analysis of their 1998 project budget of $85 million showed that only 20 percent ($17 million) was scheduled to be spent on strategic projects.

In organizations that are mature in their project management approach, a *Project Portfolio Steering Group* consisting of senior executives is responsible for the decisions that must be made concerning the programs and projects within the project portfolio(s) during the operation of that process. The responsibilities of the Project Portfolio Steering Group are discussed in Chapter 4 and Chapter 8.

The Project Portfolio Management Process

The *project portfolio management process* consists of the following twelve steps:

1. *Define the project portfolios required within the organization.* Examples of portfolio names include Product Line A, Information Technology Development, Corporate Information Systems, Division X, International, Strategic, Operational, and Compliance.

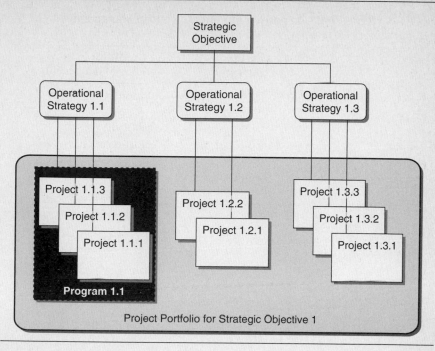

Figure 1.2   Schematic of strategies, projects, a program, and a project portfolio.

2. *Define the project categories within each portfolio based on uniform criteria for the entire organization.* Examples of project categories (or types) include capital facilities design and construction, information technology, new product/services development and launch, market development, acquisitions, e-commerce development (see Chapter 2).

3. *Identify and group all current and proposed projects within appropriate categories and programs.* Selection of new projects for inclusion in a specific portfolio, especially in the research and development of new products, is a complex process (Cooper et al., 1999, p. 23; Frame, 1999, p. 169). This step is more a function of the organization's strategic management than it is of project management, although both should be involved.

4. *Validate all projects with the organization's strategic objectives.* Does every project directly and clearly support an approved strategic objective? Is every strategic objective clearly supported by appropriate projects?

5. *Prioritize projects within programs and portfolios.* Reflect strategic considerations rather than internal politics in setting priorities. Again, this step is primarily the responsibility of senior strategic managers and the Project Portfolio Steering Group(s). For several project prioritization methods used by leading companies see Cooper et al. (1999, p. 9).

6. *Develop the Project Portfolio Master Schedule.* Include logical dependencies between projects. Project management methods and tools are appropriate for use with this and subsequent steps. The initial target master schedule is periodically revised to reflect current progress on active projects.

7. *Establish and maintain the key resources data bank.* From a practical standpoint it is necessary to limit the number of "key resources" to be allocated to the projects, even though today's information systems theoretically can handle many such resources.

8. *Allocate available key resources to programs and projects within portfolios.* Reflect resource constraints in the individual project priorities and schedules, and in the project portfolio master schedule (repeat Steps 5 through 8 as required).

9. *Compare financial needs (primarily cash flow) with availability.* Although money is usually more easily obtained than other key resources, such as people with specific skills and experience, there is always a limit to its availability.

10. *Decide how to respond to shortfalls in money or other key resources and approve the list of funded projects and priorities.* Revise individual project priorities, scope, and sequence within portfolios; cancel or delay lower priority projects; acquire additional resources if possible and desirable; repeat Steps 5 through 10 until available money and other key resources have been allocated on an optimum basis.

11. *Plan, authorize, and manage each program and project using the organization's project management process and supporting systems and tools for each project category.* Project managers and teams validate and elaborate the plans used to authorize each project as needed for successful project execution, and then manage the execution phases.

12. *Periodically reprioritize, reallocate resources, and reschedule all programs and projects as required within each portfolio.* Reflect changes in strategies, products, markets, competition, and technologies, as well as progress made to date on each project. Add newly proposed projects. Repeat Steps 1 through 12 as required, typically on a monthly basis. The Portfolio Steering Group gives strategic direction to each Project Sponsor who interprets that direction and communicates it to the affected Project Manager(s).

Project Portfolio Management Links Strategic and Project Management

Figures 1.1 and 1.2 illustrate how project portfolio management links strategic and project management. Senior line managers in the organization are the creators of the growth strategies and the "owners" of the projects that will carry them out, with a designated project sponsor with executive responsibility for each project, and a project manager as the focal point of integrated responsibility and accountability for planning and executing each one. Strategic management sets the future course of the organization and selects the projects to be added to the project portfolios. Project management plans, authorizes, and executes the specific efforts that implement the growth strategies. The managers of these projects are acting for and representing the project owners, and receive their direction through the project sponsor. These responsibilities are discussed in detail in Chapters 4 and 8.

The linkage that project portfolio management provides between strategic and project management is not simply a top-town connection. Combe describes the two-way flow that is needed to assure that projects effectively implement strategies, saying, "It's important that senior management view projects as a means to accomplish strategy, and institute practices that best position the company's projects to get their strategy implemented. But it's just as important that the organization's project managers understand the company's strategies. . . ." Only when the project-strategy linkage flows both ways does the organization get the real payoff . . . (Combe, 2000). Among the things Combe cites as necessary for ensuring this two-way flow are: having project managers who "maintain focus" and integrate the efforts of the people involved, and having a clearly-defined strategy and time-frame for implementation.

Enterprise Project Management

There has been movement in some areas of application toward *enterprise project management,* in which an enterprise is viewed as consisting totally of a collection of projects, or of one or several project portfolios, and managed accordingly. Dinsmore (1999) describes how an organization can be run by using project management as an organizational creed. He defines enterprise project management as:

> An organization-wide managerial philosophy based on the principle that company goals are achievable through a web of simultaneous projects, which calls for a systematic approach and includes corporate strategy projects, operational improvement, and organizational transformation, as well as traditional development projects. (p. 19)

This approach may continue to develop but at this time it appears to be appropriate only for some types of organizations.

1.4   INVENTORY OF PROJECTS: THE PROJECT REGISTER

An important recommended first step in any improvement effort, including the implementation of project portfolio management, is to prepare an inventory of programs and projects that are either in progress or in the planning or conceptual stages. Such an inventory can take the form of a *project register,* which should identify for each project within each portfolio:

- Project name and an identifying code number.
- Name of program/project manager, and percent of their time devoted to this effort.
- Assigned project sponsor, if any.
- Customer or client.
- Value in dollars or other currency (contract value, investment cost, or other monetary measure of size).
- Project category and whether it is a "major" or "minor" project (see Chapter 2).
- Total key human resource investment (work-months, work-years by skill).
- Possible exposure, dollars or other currency (penalties, loss of market, competitive gain, performance guarantees, other).
- Most critical risks (economic, environmental, political, competitive, technological).
- Key start, milestone, and finish dates (contract award, occupancy, completion, or other).
- Associated projects (facilities construction, research and development, product development, other contracts).
- If part of a program, identification of the program.
- Identification of the specific project portfolio that the project is a part of.
- Identification of approving authorities, dates of top management review, and approval to proceed.
- Other pertinent information.

Project Overload

Senior managers are often surprised by the number of projects that are identified in a rigorous preparation of such a project register. This listing of all authorized projects as well as all projects underway or planned for which formal authorization has somehow been overlooked will provide a direct indication of whether or not the organization is overloaded considering currently available resources. When too many projects have been started without careful resource planning, all projects will probably suffer delays. Without formalized project management policies and planning procedures, an overload condition can occur without higher level management's being aware. It may be necessary to do some digging in the functional departments to find all the projects in larger organizations.

The basic responsibility of top management in this regard is to:

- Set criteria defining categories and sizes of projects.
- Require establishment and maintenance of a project register.
- Establish and revise priorities among programs and projects as required.

These actions, discussed in more detail in Chapters 4 and 8, will set the stage for effective application of the 12 steps in the project portfolio management process.

1.5   THE ORGANIZATION'S PROJECT MANAGEMENT PROCESS

The objectives of modern project management are two-fold:

1. To assure that each project when initially conceived and authorized supports the organization's approved higher level strategic objectives and contains acceptable risks—competitive, economic, political, technical, cost, and schedule—regarding the project's objectives.
2. To plan, control, and lead each project simultaneously with all other projects effectively and efficiently so that each will achieve its approved objectives: Meeting the related strategic objective by producing the specified results on schedule and within budget.

The first of these objectives is closely linked to the strategic management of the organization. Application of systematic project management practices during the early strategic planning and project concept phases has been introduced in many organizations within the past few years, with beneficial results. Too frequently, project failures can be traced directly to unrealistic original technical, cost, or schedule targets considering the resources available to the organization, and inadequate risk analysis and risk management.

Total Life Cycle Project Management Plus Risk Management

In the early decades of modern project management, the primary focus was on the second of the two objectives listed earlier. Somehow a project was conceived and authorized and then it was handed to a project manager to plan, schedule, execute, monitor, and control through its execution phases. Even the most effective planning and control methods and the most dedicated project manager and project team cannot avoid or prevent failure when the initial objectives are impossible to achieve, or when unacceptable risks are taken. Repeated failures in achieving project objectives has led to the realization that systematic project management disciplines must also be applied during the conceptual phases of a project as well as during its execution. We now recognize that *total life-cycle project management* coupled with adequate *risk management* is necessary for success.

As systematic project management methods were applied to the conceptual phases, the need for improved risk analysis, mitigation and management became more apparent. Today this first objective of project management is very widely recognized and improved methods, tools, and systems are continually being developed to assure that both of these basic objectives are achieved for every project.

Documenting the Organization's Project Management Process

In order to achieve the full benefits of modern project management each company or agency must have a documented picture of its overall *project management process*. This process:

- Describes how the organization's project portfolios are related to the organization's growth strategies.
- Identifies and defines the basic types or categories of projects that exist or are planned (see Chapter 2).
- Defines the project life cycle and the detailed project management process ("the Project Life Cycle Management System—PLCMS" as described in Chapter 3) for each project category.

- Defines, for each project category, the corporate guidelines for risk analysis, planning, and control, with provision for appropriate adaptation for specific situations.

- Specifies the documents and related levels of approval authority for initiating and authorizing new projects and major changes to authorized projects.

- Identifies the key roles and defines their responsibilities and authority as related to strategic, project, and functional management.

- Specifies and describes the methods, procedures, and tools (including the project management software applications) to be used for each project category.

- Specifies the procedures for escalating the inevitable conflicts (competition for scarce resources, priorities between projects, and others) and unresolved issues to the appropriate level for their prompt resolution.

This process is usually documented as a flow chart with supporting narrative descriptions together with appropriate references to pertinent corporate policies, procedures, and forms. When this is done properly, the result is *integrated* project management. Only when the project management process is properly documented can effective improvement actions be planned and implemented, as described in Chapter 3.

Because of the diversity in the many areas of application and in the categories or types of projects that exist, and because of the detail involved, it is not feasible to provide a useful example of a well-documented project management process. The remainder of this book conveys a sufficient understanding of the building blocks (concepts, methods, and tools) so that readers can develop, implement, and continually improve an effective project management process for their situation.

1.6 TRIAD OF PROJECT MANAGEMENT CONCEPTS

The three basic concepts that underlie professional project management are:

1. Identified points of integrative project responsibility.
2. Integrative and predictive project planning and control.
3. Identifying, managing, and leading the *project team* to integrate the efforts of all contributors to the project.

1. Identified Points of Integrative Project Responsibility

There are several levels within each organization involved with projects where persons must be identified that hold integrative responsibilities for projects. The most important of these are:

- The executive level:
  - —Chief Operating Officer/General Manager.
  - —Project Portfolio Steering Group(s).
  - —Project Sponsors.
  - —Manager/Director/Vice President of Project Management (Project Management Office).
- The program/project managers.
- The functional department managers and project leaders.

The program/project manager role has been the focus of attention in much of the project management literature, but the other integrative roles listed are equally important to achieving truly effective project management. These roles and their related responsibilities are discussed in detail in Chapter 4 and in Part II.

2. Integrative and Predictive Project Planning and Control

The second concept of the project management triad requires that each project be planned and controlled on an integrated basis, including all contributing functional areas or organizations, through the entire project life cycle, including all the elements of information (schedule, cost, technical, risk) pertinent to the situation. Most organizations are faced with the need to plan and execute many projects simultaneously using common resource pools, creating the need to use one common project planning and control system for all projects so that all can be appropriately integrated and coordinated. Chapter 5, "Integrative and Predictive Project Planning and Control," presents an overview of this important topic and several chapters in Part II discuss it in detail.

3. The Project Team

The third of the project management triad of concepts is that of designating and managing the project team to integrate the efforts of all contributors to the project. Projects consist of many diverse tasks (or "work packages" in the established usage in many areas of application) that require the expertise and resources of a number of different specialties. These tasks are assigned to various people, usually both from within and outside the organization, who hold primary responsibility for the project. Other persons hold decision-making, regulatory, and approval authority over certain aspects of a project. Every individual contributing to a given project is considered a member of that project team. The most effective project management is achieved when all such contributors collaborate and work together as a well-trained team under the integrative leadership of the project manager. Chapter 6 and Chapter 11 discuss various aspects of project teams and team working.

1.7 CHALLENGES POSED BY THE INTERNET

The Internet is posing serious challenges to industry, business, and government. A survey of the CEOs of 506 major companies (sales over $5 billion) listed "Impact of the Internet" as their second top challenge in 2001 (Table 1.4).

The most basic challenge is to determine in which of two situations your company, agency, or organization finds itself:

- *Transform or perish.* For many organizations, the changes brought on by the Internet and its related technologies are truly a life or death matter. Either the company or agency transforms itself to compete in this new environment or accepts the fact that its days are numbered.

- *Exploit the Internet to grow and compete.* All those for whom the Internet is not a life or death matter have the choice either to capitalize on the opportunities presented by the Internet or not. However, even those who are not today faced with the transform-or-perish option may well find themselves confronted with that option tomorrow. The developments in the global arena are moving so fast that it is impossible to predict which industries, companies, and agencies are invulnerable to the challenges of the Internet phenomena.

Table 1.4   CEOs of 506 Companies with Sales over
$5 Billion List Their Greatest Challenges for 2001

1. Changes in type and level of competition	41%
2. Impact of the Internet	38%
3. Industry consolidation	37%
4. Downward pressure on prices	33%
5. Skill shortages	32%

Source: PC Magazine Internet Business, June 12, 2001, p. 18.

Within this context, the specific questions posed by the Internet for senior executives include:

- What must I do to transform my organization to assure that it will survive and prosper?
- What changes can/must I introduce into my organization to participate appropriately in the new e-business communities and the "customer-led revolution"—within this new economy?
- How can my company compete effectively when much of our previously proprietary intellectual property has been made available on the Internet?
- How can we adequately protect our proprietary interests and intellectual capital and at the same time enter into strategic partnerships with companies that can easily become direct competitors?
- How can I promote, foster, and support the means to enable the broad collaboration that is now necessary both within my organization and with our strategic partners?
- What can I do to be sure that we can develop and launch our new products and services rapidly enough to compete in this high-speed environment?
- How can/do I prioritize and manage strategies, projects within strategic programs and within my project portfolios, and activities within projects in this new environment?
- For the shareholder and prospective investor, how can I differentiate my organization from all the others so that our financial fortunes in the stock market do not rise and fall with the herd?

The principles of program and project management, effectively applied, provide powerful answers to at least some of these challenges.

Using the Internet to Respond to Its Challenges

"Internet speed" refers to the recent drastic reductions in both (1) the time required to launch a new product or service, and (2) the time available to competitively respond to market opportunities. The Internet both causes this situation and enables the competitive response. Using the Internet to help deliver completed projects in shorter times requires a concerted effort, starting with the CEO.

There are a number of powerful, commercially available, Web-enabled project management software systems using client servers and desktop/notebook/handheld computers that bring Internet speed to the project planning and control arena. These systems, when properly coupled with systematic project management as described in this book:

- Enable improved collaboration and communication for project teams no matter where the members are located geographically, with everyone working from the same currently updated information.

- Provide risk and issue tracking, and effective escalation processes.

- Empower project team and staff members through access to central information repositories, with suitable controls on who can change the information.

- Automate much if not most of the project management process and related documentation and record keeping.

- Enable key resource assignments within and between projects, programs, and project portfolios, and facilitate corporate resource planning and acquisition.

- Enable tracking and evaluation of changes in project scope, schedule, cost, and risk.

- Allow integration of project management processes with all other business systems.

- Capture the "lessons learned" on every project for incorporation into and continued improvement of the project management process and related data repositories.

The selection and implementation of such systems is in itself a complex management project that requires application of the principles and practices discussed in this book.

WHAT CEOs MUST DEMAND

Unleashing the Full Power of Project Management to Compete and Collaborate

To gain the full power of project management the CEO must demand that:

1. Strategic and project management disciplines be fully integrated.
2. Project portfolio management fully supports the organization's growth strategies.
3. A coherent project management process exists and is fully understood.

(continued)

4. The project management process recognizes the appropriate project categories that exist within the organization and provides detailed guidance for the planning and control of projects in each category.

5. This process and the supporting systems and tools are fully implemented and integrated with corporate policies, procedures, and systems.

6. The Internet and Web are used properly in the daily project management operations.

More detailed CEO demands that must be made to achieve effective project management are identified at the end of each of the chapters in Part I.

2

‹ ›

Programs and Projects

Project management encompasses the conceptualization, selection, authorization, planning, and execution of efforts called *projects*. The concepts and systems employed to manage projects—as well as the related difficulties—flow from the nature of the projects themselves. Therefore, it is important that executives, managers, and specialists involved with programs and projects have a good understanding of their unique characteristics and how they can best be categorized.

2.1 PROGRAMS, PROJECTS, AND TASKS

Some confusion exists regarding these terms, which are sometimes used ambiguously and even interchangeably. (See Wideman, 2002, for an extensive, useful Web-available glossary of project management terms with alternative definitions from a variety of sources. The PMI® PMBOK®, 2000, pp. 195–209, also contains an extensive glossary of such terms.)

Generally accepted practice in a number of industries has established the following common usage for these terms:

Program: A long-term undertaking that includes two or more projects that require close coordination.

Project: A complex effort, usually less than three years in duration, made up of interrelated tasks, performed by various functional organizations, with a well-defined objective, schedule, and budget.

Task: A short-term effort (a few weeks to a few months) performed by one functional organization, which may combine with other tasks to form a project. Tasks are usually composed of interrelated shorter duration activities.

There is no universal agreement on the use or definition of these terms. The term *work package* is used in much of the project management literature to mean the same thing as a task, referring to a defined piece of work that is the common linkage point for estimating, budgeting, scheduling, reporting and controlling time, cost, other resources, and results (technical or other).

As a program or project is broken down into its constituent elements, there is a tendency for each organization to apply the name *project* to its portion of the overall effort. This can cause confusion, much as the terms *system, subsystem,* and so on do in the technical area. There is probably no viable alternative in most situations, other than carefully establishing the project name in each case and emphasizing the interrelationships that exist.

The project management approach as presented in this book is applicable to programs, projects, or tasks. However, the primary concern is at the program and project levels. Although the term *project* is used primarily, application of the concepts to programs will be apparent.

Understanding these key words is the first hurdle to be crossed in achieving good program or project management. In some organizations, the word *program* can refer to a continuous effort (such as a long-term training program). This is a different use of the word than is intended in this book.

2.2   WHAT PROJECTS ARE

Projects share certain fundamental characteristics. The important characteristics from the management viewpoint are summarized next.

Projects Are Unique Complex Efforts That Start and End

Projects are intended to produce certain specified results at a particular point in time and within an established budget. They cut across organizational lines. They are unique endeavors, not completely repetitious of any previous effort.

A Project Is the Process of Creating Specific Results

A project may be viewed as the entire process required to create a new product, new plant, new system, or other specified results. The product to be created often receives more attention than the process by which it is created, but both the product and the process—together, the project— require effective management. The end result is not the project.

Unfortunately, there is a tendency in some areas of application to continue to refer to the *project* long after the actual project has been completed, especially when a fixed facility has been designed and constructed. For example, a World Bank funded project resulted in the design and construction of the largest earth-filled dam in the world plus a large hydro-electric power generation and distribution facility on the Indus River at Tarbella in the Northwest Frontier Province of Pakistan. Some managers and engineers in the Pakistan Water and Power Development Authority still call the facility the "Tarbella Project," and there still is a sign with that name on it as you enter the facility. This ambiguous usage can also lead to confusion regarding the phrase "project start-up," since in project management terms that phrase refers to the starting up of the project itself, while in some construction project management literature start-up refers to commissioning and starting up the operation of the resulting facility. The facility start-up phase is very different than starting up a new project, or a new phase of an on-going project, as discussed in Chapter 11.

Project Life Cycle

The project's life cycle has identifiable start and end points that are associated with a time scale. A project passes through several distinct phases as it matures (see Table 2.1). The life cycle includes all phases from point of inception to final termination of the project. The interfaces between phases are rarely clearly separated, except in cases where proposal acceptance or formal authorization to proceed separates two phases. However, it is often difficult to pin down the precise moment in the early part of the conceptual phase when a project can be identified as a *project,* especially for new product or service projects.

Project Character Changes

In each succeeding phase of a project, new and different intermediate products (deliverables or results) are created, with the product of one phase forming a major input to the next phase. Figure 2.1 illustrates the overall process. Approval is usually required to proceed from one phase to the next, with the major funding approval usually occurring between the "definition" and "design" phases.

The rate of expenditure of resources changes, usually increasing with succeeding phases until there is a rapid decrease at completion. The people, skills, organizations, and other resources involved in the project often change in each life-cycle phase. Overlapping of phases,

Table 2.1 Typical Life Cycle Phases of Various Types of Projects

Project Type	Project Phase						
	1 Concept	2 Definition	3 Design	4 Development/ Manufacture	5 Application or Installation	6 Project Close-Out	Post Completion
Telecommunication equipment contract	Preproposal: identify opportunity; decide to bid	Prepare proposal; submit, receive award	Engineering design	Procure materials; fabricate, assemble, install and test	Concentration and acceptance testing	Confirm contractual compliance; obtain customer sign-off; receive final payment; issue project evaluation report	Create new projects for follow-up contracts; provide spares and field support
New product or service development project	Identify opportunity or need; establish basic feasibility	Prepare new product proposal, product plan, review and approval sheet, R&D case, project appropriation request	Design product or service; build and test prototype	Design production article; build and test tooling; produce initial production articles	Distribute and sell initial product or service; verify performance	Hand over product or service to on-going operations; obtain sign-off; issue final project evaluation report	Create new projects to improve product or service
R&D project for manufacturing development	Identify opportunity or need; establish basic feasibility	Prepare R&D case	Conduct studies; analysis and design work	Conduct pilot tests; analyze and document results	Conduct full-scale tests; analyze and document results	Issue final project evaluation report	Create new project to implement results
Capital facilities project	Identify opportunity or need; establish basic feasibility	Investment analysis; prepare budget and project appropriation request	Process design, engineering for construction, equipment design and/or specification	Procure equipment; construct civil works; install and check out equipment	Start-up and commission operating facility	Hand over to operations; obtain sign-off; issue final evaluation report	Create new design and construct projects
Systems project	Identify opportunity or need; establish basic feasibility	Investment analysis; prepare budget and project appropriation request	Systems analysis and detailed design	System coding; compiling, testing and documentation	Install and test system under production conditions	Hand over to user organization; issue final evaluation report	Create new projects

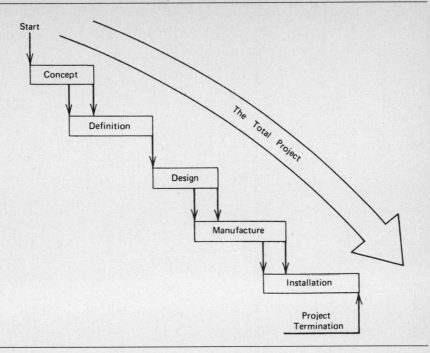

Figure 2.1   The total project integrates all life-cycle phases.

called "fast-tracking" in engineering/construction projects and "concurrency" in military/aerospace projects, frequently occurs. This complicates the planning and coordination needs, and places even more importance on the project manager role. Key decision points occur at the completion of each project phase. Major review of the entire project occurs (or should occur) at the end of each phase, resulting in authorization to proceed with the next phase, cancellation of the project, or repetition of part or all of a previous phase.

Uncertainty Related to Time and Cost Diminishes as the Project Matures

The specified result and the time and cost to achieve it are inseparable. The uncertainty related to each factor is reduced with completion of each succeeding life-cycle phase (Figure 2.2).

In phase 1, the area of uncertainty (largest circle) is reduced with each succeeding phase until the actual point of completion is reached. The requirement for project planning and control systems and methods capable of predicting the final end point as early and as accurately as possible comes directly from this general characteristic of projects.

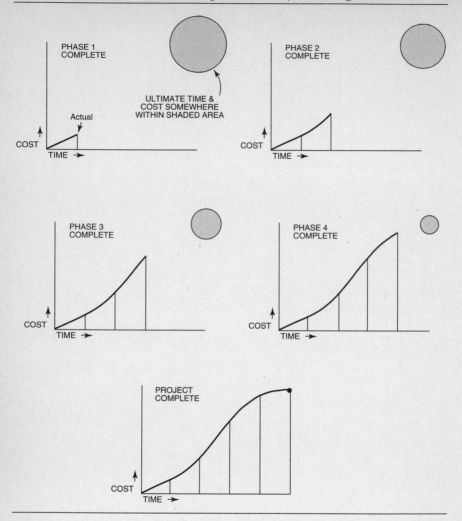

Figure 2.2   Relative uncertainty of ultimate time and cost by life-cycle phases.

Without effective project accounting methods, it may be impossible to know how much the final results actually cost even long after the project's completion.

Many Projects Do Not Survive the Concept or Definition Phases

In almost all categories of projects in various industries, many more ideas enter the conceptual phase than emerge as fully executed projects.

New product projects are canceled as they fail to meet screening criteria; proposals to design and construct new facilities are rejected or awarded to a competitor. The seeds for success or failure are frequently sown in these early phases, but the outcome often is not known until the project nears completion or has been completed.

It is usually at the end of the definition phase, or its equivalent, when approval to spend significant amounts of money is given, and the project is reasonably assured of passing through all remaining phases. This is when the proposal is approved and a contract is awarded, or the product development funds are released, for example. It is at this time that a full-time project manager, if justified, is most often appointed (as discussed later), although many organizations are now realizing that it is false economy not to appoint a project manager (even if not full time) during the conceptual phase of a project so that continuity of responsibility in one person is achieved.

Cost of Accelerating a Project Rises Exponentially as Completion Nears

Recovery of lost time usually becomes increasingly more expensive for each succeeding project phase (Figure 2.3). This characteristic places emphasis on the need for integrated control through all phases, with particular attention to project start-up and the earlier phases to avoid delay and shorten the project schedule.

Management Implications

From these characteristics of projects, certain important implications may be drawn:

- Projects must be managed on a life-cycle basis, with maximum continuity of responsibility and integrated planning and control from start to finish.
- Equal attention must be paid to managing both the *product* of a project and the overall process of creating that product—the *project* itself.
- Creation of a separate, self-supporting organization for each project generally is not feasible or practical, as discussed later, because of the rapidly changing situation from phase to phase.
- Decisions made in early phases of a project usually have a greater leverage on its ultimate time and cost than those made in later phases.

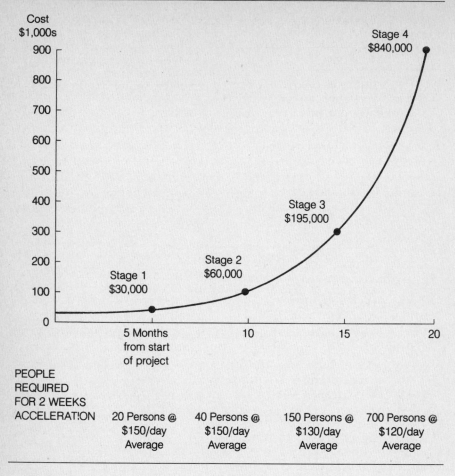

Figure 2.3   Cost of two weeks' acceleration at various project stages.

Comparison of Projects with Departments and Operations

A project is a complex, unique effort that cuts across organizational lines; has a definite start and finish point; and has specific schedule, cost, and technical objectives. A project, therefore, has important management differences when compared to a typical functional department handling repetitive work on essentially a never-ending basis (Table 2.2). Galbreath (1987, p. 6) states that:

Uniqueness of effort and result are the hallmarks of project situations. Consistency and uniformity are typical of operations. . . . Operations are geared

Table 2.2   Characteristics of a Project Compared with a Functional
Department

Project	Accounting Department
1. Specific life cycle: conception; design; fabrication, assembly or construction; test; initial utilization.	1. Continuous life from year to year.
2. Definite start and completion points, with calendar dates.	2. No specific characteristics tied to calendar dates, other than fiscal year budgets and reports.
3. Subject to abrupt termination if goals cannot be achieved; always terminated when project is complete.	3. Continued existence of the function usually assured, even in major reorganization.
4. Often unique, not done before.	4. Usually performing well-known function and tasks only slightly different from previous efforts.
5. Total effort must be completed within fixed budget and schedule.	5. Maximum work is performed within annual budget ceiling.
6. Prediction of ultimate time and cost is difficult.	6. Prediction of annual expenditures relatively simple.
7. Involves many skills and disciplines located in many organizations that may change from one life-cycle phase to the next.	7. Involves one or a few closely related skills and disciplines within one well-defined and stable organization.
8. Rate and type of expenditures constantly changing.	8. Relatively constant rate and type of expenditure.
9. Basically dynamic in nature.	9. Basically steady-state in nature.

to maintain and exploit, while projects are conceived to create and make exploitations available. Projects, therefore, typically precede operations in the normal business cycle. . . . If successful operation can be imagined as a continuous, uninterrupted stream of effort yielding a predictable collection of similar results, we must view each project as a temporary pulse of activity yielding a unique, singular result. . . . Operations may outlive their results, but projects expire when their result is achieved.

Management Implications

Methods and systems developed for planning and control of resource expenditures within functional departments are usually ineffective when applied to projects.

The relatively new concepts and systems developed to meet project needs do not in themselves create conflicts and problems, but rather they reveal the existing differences, conflicts, and incompatibilities between projects and functional organizations. A major challenge to top managers is presented by this situation: How to manage all projects effectively while maintaining the efficient operation of the functional organization. The concepts and practices of integrated project management have been developed in response to this challenge.

2.3   PROJECT CATEGORIES

A wide variety of projects exist within business, industrial, and governmental organizations. Properly defining the categories of projects within a given organization is useful for several reasons. The project life-cycle management process will vary considerably from one category to the next, and the most appropriate process must be applied to each project. By developing and continually improving the process for each project category, managers can assure some degree of standardization will be applied to the management of their projects.

There are many ways to categorize projects; for example: size, complexity, geography, technology, risk (economic, technological, political), nature of the end product or result, the business or industrial sector, the economic or political sector involved, and others.

Basic Project Categories with Similar Project Management Processes

Ten recommended basic project categories are listed in Table 2.3. Projects within each of these categories have very similar life-cycle phases and utilize very similar authorization, planning, budgeting, scheduling, monitoring and control procedures, and tools throughout their life cycles. Subcategories are also identified within most of the 10 basic categories. There will be differences—in some cases, significant—between the project life-cycle management process for the basic category and its subcategories. Others may wish to add subcategories where none are shown in Table 2.3, or to add additional subcategories to those that are listed.

These categories are not necessarily mutually exclusive: Many projects will include aspects of two or more categories. For example, most communications systems projects include at least the adaptation of information system software. Many facilities projects also include communication systems, and vice versa. In such cases, the project probably should be classified in the more dominant category, or—if justified by

Table 2.3   Recommended Project Categories, with Each Category (or Subcategory) Having Similar Project Life Cycle Phases and Each Having a Unique Process Management Process

Project Categories	Examples
1. Aerospace/Defense Projects	
1.1 Defense systems	New weapon system; major system upgrade.
1.2 Space	Satellite development/launch; space station mod.
1.3 Military operations	Task force invasion.
2. Business and Organization Change Projects	
2.1 Acquisition/Merger	Acquire and integrate competing company.
2.2 Management process improvement	Major improvement in project management.
2.3 New business venture	Form and launch new company.
2.4 Organization restructuring	Consolidate divisions and downsize company.
2.5 Legal proceeding	Major litigation case.
3. Communication Systems Projects	
3.1 Network communications systems	Microwave communications network.
3.2 Switching communications systems	Third generation wireless communication system.
4. Event Projects	
4.1 International events	2004 Summer Olympics; 2006 World Cup Match.
4.2 National events	2005 U.S. Super Bowl; 2004 Democratic and Republican Political Conventions.
5. Facilities Projects	
5.1 Facility decommissioning	Closure of nuclear power station.
5.2 Facility demolition	Demolition of high rise building.
5.3 Facility maintenance and modification	Process plant maintenance turnaround. Conversion of plant for new products/markets.
5.4 Facility design/ procurement/construction	
Civil	Flood control dam; highway interchange.
Energy	New gas-fired power generation plant; pipeline.
Environmental	Chemical waste cleanup.
High rise	
Industrial	New manufacturing plant.
Commercial	New shopping center; office building.
Residential	New housing subdivision.
6. Information Systems (Software) Projects	New project management information system. (Information system hardware is considered to be in the product development category.)

(continued)

Table 2.3   *(Continued)*

Project Categories	Examples
7. International Development Projects	
7.1 Agriculture/rural development	*People and process intensive projects* in developing countries funded by The World Bank, regional development banks, US AID, UNIDO, other UN, and government agencies; and
7.2 Education	
7.3 Health	
7.4 Nutrition	
7.5 Population	
7.6 Small-scale enterprise	
7.7 Infrastructure: energy (oil, gas, coal, power generation and distribution), industrial, telecommunications, transportation, urbanization, water supply and sewage, irrigation)	*Capital/civil works intensive projects*—often somewhat different from 5. *Facility Projects* as they may include, as part of the project, creating an organizational entity to operate and maintain the facility, and lending agencies impose their project life cycle and reporting requirements.
8. Media and Entertainment Projects	
8.1 Motion picture	New motion picture (film or digital).
8.2 TV segment	New TV episode.
8.2 Live play or music event	New opera premiere.
9. Product and Service Development Projects	
9.1 Information technology hardware	New desk-top computer.
9.2 Industrial product/process	New earth-moving machine.
9.3 Consumer product/process	New automobile; new food product.
9.4 Pharmaceutical product/ process	New cholesterol-lowering drug.
9.5 Service (financial, other)	New life insurance/annuity offering.
10. Research and Development Projects	
10.1 Environmental	Measure changes in the ozone layer.
10.2 Industrial	How to reduce pollutant emission.
10.3 Economic development	Determine best crop for sub-Sahara Africa.
10.4 Medical	Test new treatment for breast cancer.
10.5 Scientific	Determine the possibility of life on Mars.
11. Other Categories?	

their size, complexity, or risk—defined as two or more projects (of different categories) within a program.

Multiproject Program Categorization

Programs often contain projects from two or more of these basic categories. A major communication system program, for example, will usually include projects in the communications, facilities, aerospace, and information systems categories. Each project must be planned and managed using its individual project management process, with integration at the program level using a process that links the individual processes at the appropriate interface event points. See Chapters 8 and 13 for further discussion of this topic.

2.4 CLASSIFYING PROJECTS WITHIN A CATEGORY

There will often be a wide range of projects within each project category in large organizations. The management methods required for a multimillion dollar new manufacturing plant facility are more elaborate than for the classic bicycle shed project immortalized by Parkinson (1957), even though they are both new facilities projects. The project management process for each project category must provide for the flexibility to choose the proper level of planning and control for large, complex, high-risk, "new territory" projects compared to smaller or "old hat" projects.

Project Size

Project size can be measured in several dimensions: money, amount of other scarce resources (people, skills, or facilities), scope, and geography are the most tangible and obvious. Larger projects in any of these dimensions usually carry greater risks—but not always.

Project Complexity

The complexity of a project is indicated by the diversity inherent in the project objectives and scope, and by the number of different internal and external organizations involved, which is usually an indication of the number of required specialized skills, sources of technology, or sources of funding. A project that requires only the skills and other resources of one operating division is usually less complex from a management viewpoint than a joint venture project supported by two separate corporations. Complexity rises exponentially with the number of organizations involved. Interaction of the project with ongoing operations is a common source of complexity, especially for facilities projects closely involved with current manufacturing, assembly, or process plant operations. Projects that are carried out under the surveillance of one or more regulatory agencies are usually more complex than those without such surveillance.

External or Internal Customer

If a project is to be performed under a formal contract with an external customer, it will pose different management challenges than if it is to satisfy an internal customer and need. The contractual terms will directly affect the degree of risk associated with a contractual project; if they are well drafted, the terms can beneficially mitigate risks. A project for an internal customer requires authorization and control (using work orders and other internal contractual documents and agreements) similar to a project under a formal contract with an external customer. The legal restraints and recourses may not be available on a project for an internal customer, so in that case the tendency may be not to exert as diligent an effort in project planning and control. This adds to the risk that the project will not meet its desired objectives.

The relative importance of a given project customer will often have a great effect on how a particular project is prioritized and managed.

Degree of Customer Involvement in the Project

In many projects, the customer must perform significant work, make important decisions, and provide key deliverables on schedule if the project is to be completed on schedule. Customer delays are frequent causes of delay and added cost on projects. It is imperative that the customer portions of the project be planned and scheduled on an integrated basis with the rest of the project, that the customer project manager participate actively in the project evaluation and review meetings, and take responsibility for actions assigned to that project manager. The customer's project management process must be integrated appropriately with that of the project in question.

Risk Levels in Projects

The risks involved in projects vary between and within project categories. Some of the major factors affecting risk are:

- Degree of newness of the project type to the organization.
- Size, as discussed previously.
- Duration and urgency of completion: Higher risk if short duration with fixed end date or if long duration with likely unpredictable economic or political changes.
- Complexity, as discussed previously.
- Technology: degree of innovation and uncertainty regarding the product technology or its production process.

- External customer (project under contract) or internal customer, as discussed previously, and their overall importance to the organization.

- Contractual terms: penalties, guarantees, foreign exchange.

- Regulatory surveillance and approvals required.

- Degree of customer involvement in the project.

- Market volatility.

- Availability of scarce resources: skilled, experienced people, specialized facilities.

Major and Minor Projects within a Category

It is useful to identify at least two classes of projects within each category. We will call these major and minor projects, although each organization probably uses more descriptive names. Some organizations may find it more appropriate to define three such classes (e.g., A, B, and C). The distinction between these major and minor classes will be noted in the following definitions:

- *Major projects* are those whose large size, great complexity, and/or high risk require:

  —Designation of an executive *project sponsor.*

  —Assignment of a full-time *project* (or *program*) *manager.*

  —The full application of the project management process specified for the particular project category for major projects (all specified forms, approvals, plans, schedules, budgets, controls, reports, frequent project review meetings, with substantial levels of detail in each).

- *Minor projects* are those whose size, simplicity and low risk allow:

  —One project manager to manage two or more minor projects simultaneously (it should be noted that such projects should not simply be assigned to a functional manager as an additional duty, as discussed in more detail in Chapter 4).

  —Less than the full application of the complete project management process for the project category (selected basic forms, approvals, plans, schedules, budgets, controls, reports, less frequent project review meetings, with less detail required in each).

  —No formal assignment of an executive *project sponsor.*

If the organization wishes to achieve enterprise-wide project management, all projects, both major and minor, must have their plans, schedules and budgets entered into the overall project management information system so that all required (or "controlled") resources are forecast and can be allocated properly to reflect the current priorities of the individual projects. Short of including all resources in the overall system, the organization can focus only on a selected smaller list of critically scarce resources. Knowing that if these are properly allocated, the remaining resources can be provided as needed.

Managing multiple projects, whether they are major or minor as defined previously, is discussed throughout Part I of the book and particularly in Chapters 3 and 8.

In addition to these major and minor projects, some organizations are responsible for what have become known as *mega* projects. These are extremely large projects that usually involve a large number of companies and/or agencies. International joint ventures in space, transportation, energy, and other areas are examples of such mega projects. They may be funded from a variety of sources: governmental, private and international development banks, and they usually cross a number of international boundaries. Mega projects are beyond the scope of the major project classification described previously, and it is rare for one organization to be involved in more than one of these at a time.

2.5 LIFE CYCLES FOR HIGH-TECHNOLOGY PROJECTS

As discussed in Section 1.3, to achieve the full benefits of modern project management, each company or agency must have a documented picture of its overall project management process. This process identifies the basic types or categories of projects that exist or are planned and describes the project management philosophy and approach of the organization. But this overall process cannot be applied without modification to all of the categories of projects that exist within the organization.

The detailed project management life-cycle process for each identified project category (or subcategory as appropriate) must:

- Define the project life-cycle (phases, subphases, and decision/ approval points) and describe the methods, procedures, forms, documents, tools, systems, and other practices for authorizing, planning, risk analysis and mitigation, budgeting, scheduling, monitoring, and controlling all projects within the category.

- Specify the documents and related levels of approval authority for initiating and authorizing new projects and major changes to authorized projects.

- Identify the key project roles and define their responsibilities and authority.

- Specify the procedures for escalating the inevitable conflicts (competition for scarce resources, priorities between projects, and others) and unresolved issues to the appropriate level for their prompt resolution.

The detailed project management process for a given category must also include provisions for handling projects of different sizes, complexities, risks, durations, sources and types of funding, and serving different customers.

Importance of Designing and Documenting Project Life-Cycle Processes

Designing and documenting project life-cycle processes will:

- Enable all concerned with creating, planning, and executing projects to understand the process to be followed during the life of the project.

- Capture the best experience within the organization so that the life-cycle process can be improved continually and duplicated on future projects.

- Enable all the project roles and responsibilities and the project planning, estimating, scheduling, monitoring, and control methods and tools to be appropriately related to the overall project life-cycle management process.

Unless a well-documented, understandable picture of the life-cycle process for each project category exists, it will be impossible to achieve the full benefits of modern, systematic project management.

High-Technology Project Categories

Of the ten recommended project categories listed in Table 2.3, we focus primarily on four project categories:

1. **Communication Systems Projects.**
2. Information Systems Projects.
3. **Product and Service Development Projects:**
   - **Industrial product.**
   - Consumer product.
   - Pharmaceutical product.
   - Service.

4. Research and Development Projects:

- Environmental.
- Industrial.
- Economic development.
- Medical.
- Scientific.

Although they often involve high-technology components and in some cases are entirely involved in high-technology efforts, the remaining six categories listed in Table 2.3 are not the primary focus of this book. While the concepts and practices discussed in Part I of the book are applicable to all project categories, the more detailed methods presented in Part II are primarily applicable to the categories highlighted in bold in the previous list and the examples provided are drawn from those categories.

Military/aerospace programs and projects. This category of projects has a long history related to project management. In fact, the discipline of project management comes directly from both the facilities design and construction and the military/aerospace arenas in both the Western and the Eastern hemispheres. Military and aerospace programs and projects are at the forefront of high-technology endeavors in most cases. However, they are not the primary focus of this book since their life cycles and management processes are unique in most countries to the requirements imposed by governmental system acquisition policies and standards, and most of these programs and projects are funded by national governments. References to complete and up-to-date literature on project management practices in the United States for military/aerospace programs and projects can be obtained from the PMI® College of Performance Management (CPM, www.pmi .org/collegeinfo).

In spite of this disclaimer, most of the concepts and practices presented here are applicable to the majority of military/aerospace programs and projects at the level of the private contractor in most Western countries. A number of the practices described and examples given in this book are derived from such programs and projects.

Since earth satellites play such a predominant role today in communications and information systems, many projects in these two high-technology categories include such space projects and are now funded by nongovernmental companies and agencies. Such high-technology programs and projects are considered to be within the scope of this book, and the methods and practices described in the following chapters are certainly applicable to them.

Facilities projects. Like the military/aerospace category the facilities projects category, involving the design/procurement/construction of all kinds of structures and the installation of all kinds of equipment, has a long history in project management and a very substantial body of literature devoted specifically to that category. Although many of these facilities projects involve high-technology components, this book does not attempt to duplicate or even summarize the very effective methods and systems that exist and are widely applied to this important category of projects.

Most organizations have well-established policies and procedures for controlling projects requiring investment of capital funds. These policies and procedures provide detailed definitions of various types of capital projects. Generally, these involve expenditures to acquire land, buildings, and capital equipment, whether by purchase, construction, or lease; and extraordinary expenditures for major alterations and rearrangements of existing facilities.

When a capital facilities project is indispensable to or forms a part of a project for a new product, information system, communication system, a research effort, or other type of project, it should be managed as an element of the total program or project. Additional financial controls usually are required for capital projects to assure that the proper costs are capitalized as desired by management and required by accepted accounting practices and tax laws.

International development projects. These also frequently include high-technology as well as fixed facilities components, but these projects are sufficiently different in their project life cycles and detailed project management processes that they too are not the primary focus here. The lending agencies for international development have implemented extensive procedures and defined the life cycles of these projects in some detail, and usually require that these recommended practices be followed on the projects that they are financing. The World Bank Institute has produced a comprehensive, 12-module training course (whose primary author is Robert Youker) on managing international development projects of all types. This course reflects over 20 years of training people from and in all parts of the world in the disciplines of project management and is available in electronic format for purchase by anyone interested in these important projects (World Bank Institute, 2002).

Designing and Documenting Life Cycles for High-Technology Project Categories

It is not possible or appropriate to define a specific life cycle that will be useful and practical for all projects within a particular category—or probably even a particular subcategory. Instead, our intention is to present the basic life-cycle concepts and building blocks so they can be assembled into the most appropriate life-cycle process design for a given organization and project category (or subcategory), size (major or minor), duration, complexity, and degree of risk.

Definition of the generic project life-cycle phases for a category is relatively straightforward. There is general agreement that these broad, generic project phases are (common alternative terms are shown in parentheses):

- Concept (initiation, identification, selection).
- Definition (feasibility, development, demonstration, design prototype, quantification).
- Execution (implementation, production, and deployment, design/construct/commission, install and test).
- Closeout (termination and postcompletion evaluation).

However, these phases are so broad and the titles so generic that they are of little value in documenting the life-cycle process so that it can be widely understood, reproduced, and continually improved. What is needed is the definition of perhaps five to ten basic phases for each project category, usually with several subphases defined within each basic phase. Table 2.1 shows six generic phases plus one "postcompletion" phase for various types of projects. Phases 3, 4, and 5 in Table 2.1 are subphases of the overall generic "execution" phase.

In designing and documenting a life-cycle process (or model) for a given project category there are three basic parameters to work with:

1. The number of basic phases and the number of subphases within each, together with the definition of each of these.
2. Which of the basic phases (and the subphases) will be strictly sequential, which will overlap, and for those that overlap how much overlap can be tolerated.
3. The number and placement of decision points (approval, go/kill, go/hold) in the process.

Table 2.4 lists a number of various life-cycle models with references for some of the categories and subcategories listed in Table 2.3, reflecting the results of an incomplete literature search.

The Stage-Gate™ New Product Development Life-Cycle Process

Figure 2.4 shows an overview of a widely used life-cycle process for new product development.

Table 2.4 Project Life Cycle Models and References: Generic and for Various Project Categories

Project Categories*	Life Cycle Models and References
Generic Project Models: All (or many) project categories below.	Belanger 1998, pp. 62–72: Generic, Waterfall, Parallel-Work, Evolutionary Models. Morris 1994, pp. 245–248: Standard, Waterfall, Cyclical, Spiral Models.

1. Aerospace/Defense Projects
  1.1 Defense systems
  1.2 Space
  1.3 Military operations
	DOD 2000: Defense Acquisition Model.
	NASA 2002: Process Based Mission Assurance (PMBA) Program Life Cycle, 8 phases: 1. Program Mgt, 2. Concept Development, 3. Acquisition, 4. Hardware Design, 5. Software Design, 6. Manufacturing, 7. Pre-Operations Integration and Test, 8. Operations.

2. Business and Organization Change Projects
  2.1 Acquisition/Merger
  2.2 Management process improvement
  2.3 New business venture
  2.4 Organization restructuring
  2.5 Legal proceeding
	See generic models (above).
	
	See Chapter 5, Table 5.4.

3. Communication Systems Projects
  3.1 Network communications systems
  3.2 Switching communications systems
	See Table 2.1 and above generic models.

4. Event Projects
  4.1 International events
  4.2 National events
	See above generic models.

5. Facilities Projects
  5.1 Facility decommissioning
  5.2 Facility demolition
  5.3 Facility maintenance and modification
  5.4 Facility design/ procurement/construction
	See Table 2.1 and above generic models.

6. Information Systems (Software) Projects	Desaulniers and Anderson 2002: Predictive (Waterfall, Prototyping, RAD, Incremental Build, Spiral) and Adaptive (ASD, XP, SCRUM) Models. Whitten 1995, pp. 19–22: Code and Fix, Waterfall, Incremental, Iterative Model. Muench 1994: Spiral Software Development Model.

*Each having similar life cycle phases and one unique project management process.

(continued)

Table 2.4   *(Continued)*

Project Categories	Life Cycle Models and References
6. Information Systems (Software) Projects *(continued)*	Lewin 2002, p. 47: "V" Software Development Model; p. 50: Formula-IT Development Model. Kezsbom and Edward 2001, p. 122: Refined Process Spiral Model.

7. International Development Projects
  7.1 Agriculture/rural development
  7.2 Education
  7.3 Health
  7.4 Nutrition
  7.5 Population
  7.6 Small-scale enterprise
  7.7 Infrastructure: energy (oil, gas, coal, power generation and distribution), industrial, telecommunications, transportation, urbanization, water supply and sewage, irrigation)
	World Bank Institute 2002, Module 1.
	People and process intensive projects in developing countries funded by The World Bank, regional development banks, US AID, UNIDO, other UN, and government agencies; and
	
	Capital/civil works intensive projects—often somewhat different from *5. Facility Projects* as they may include, as part of the project, creating an organizational entity to operate and maintain the facility, and lending agencies impose their project life cycle and reporting requirements.

8. Media and Entertainment Projects
  8.1 Motion picture
  8.2 TV segment
  8.2 Live play or music event	

9. Product and Service Development Projects	Cooper and Kleinschmidt 1993: Stage-Gate® Process Model. Kezsbom and Edward 2001, pp. 108: Stage/Gate Product Development Model. Thamhain 2000: Phase-Gate Process Model.

9.1 Information technology hardware
  9.2 Industrial product/process
  9.3 Consumer product/process
  9.4 Pharmaceutical product/process
  9.5 Service (financial, other)
	Murphy 1989: Pharmaceutical Model.

10. Research and Development Projects
  10.1 Environmental
  10.2 Industrial
  10.3 Economic development
  10.4 Medical
  10.5 Scientific
	Eskelin 2002, p. 46: Technical Acquisition: Basic Model, Phased Model, Multi-Solution Model.

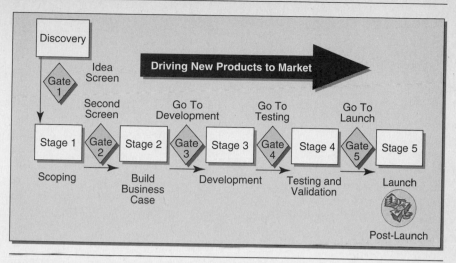

Figure 2.4   Overview of a typical Stage-Gate™ process. *Source:* Robert G. Cooper, Scott J. Edgert, and Elko J. Kleinschmidt. *Portfolio Management for New Products* (Cambridge, MA, 2001), p. 272. Contact: www.perseuspublishing .com. Used with permission. Stage-Gate is a registered trademark of R. G. Cooper & Associates Consultant, Inc., a member company of the Product Development Institute. See www.prod-dev.com.

Project Life Cycles, Project Definition, and Project Schedules

All project life cycles are viewed on a time scale, usually from left to right, although some flow from top to bottom on a page. Some include repetitive subphases that can be portrayed as recycling in time or they can simply be repeated on the time scale. The spiral model sometimes used for software development is one exception to this time scale rule. However, even the most elaborate life-cycle diagrams are not sufficient for fully defining the project (as discussed in Chapter 10) or for developing an adequate project master schedule and supporting detailed schedules (also discussed in Chapter 10).

A well-defined life cycle can, however, be of great assistance when systematically defining a project using the project/work breakdown structure (P/WBS) methodology, described in Chapter 10. The project manager/planner has the choice of (1) developing a P/WBS by placing the major life-cycle phases at the second level of the structure (together with other overarching project elements such as "project management"), (2) developing a stand-alone P/WBS for each of the major life-cycle phases, or (3) using a combination of these approaches. The project deliverables are quite different for each major project life-cycle phase, and this will become evident as the P/WBS for each phase is developed. The P/WBS then becomes the framework for developing the project master schedule and the lower level hierarchy of schedules, as discussed in Chapter 10.

Project Life Cycles and the Environment

Desaulniers and Anderson (2002) present a strong case for adaptation of the project life cycle to the current environment of a project. Although they refer specifically to software development projects, the point can be equally important to some product/service development and research projects. As they say, "The organizational characteristics, the degree of familiarity with the technologies to be used, and the competitive demands for initiating the project are just some of the environmental factors that can differ from project to project." Furthermore, because the environment can have a significant effect on the project, the authors say that ". . . care and consideration need to be given to the selection of the development life cycle to be employed."

These authors then describe the differences between "Predictive" and "Adaptive" project life cycles. "The Predictive life cycles favor optimization over adaptability. . . . Adaptive life cycles accept and embrace change during the development process and resist detailed planning" (Desaulniers and Anderson, 2002). They list and describe the following types of life cycles in each of these two life-cycle categories:

1. Predictive Life Cycles:
   —Waterfall (also known as Traditional or Top Down): Linear ordering of the major software development activities; each phase is usually completed before the next phase begins and no phase is repeated.
   —Prototyping: Functional requirements and physical design specifications are generated simultaneously.
   —Rapid Application Development (RAD): These employ an evolving prototype that is not thrown away.
   —Incremental Build: Decomposition of a large development effort into a succession of smaller components.
   —Spiral: Repetition of the same set of life-cycle phases of plan, design, build, and evaluate until development is complete.
2. Adaptive Life Cycles:
   —Adaptive Software Development (ASD): Mission driven, component based, iterative cycles, time boxed cycles, risk-driven, and change-tolerant.

—Extreme Programming (XP): Teams of developers, managers, and users, programming done in pairs, iterative process, collective code ownership.

—SCRUM: Similar to the above Adaptive life cycles with iterations called "sprints" that typically last 30 days with defined functionality to be achieved in each sprint; active management role throughout.

Design and documentation of the life-cycle model for each project category or subcategory must reflect the important characteristics of the project environment.

2.6 PROJECT ENVIRONMENT

Every project must be understood and managed within the particular environment in which it exists. What works well for a specific project within one environment may be ineffective in a different environment. Many projects have difficulties and are less successful than desired because their objectives, organizational design, and management approaches are incompatible or in conflict with key environmental elements.

Project success will be determined in many situations not so much by the most logical or efficient arrangement of roles, responsibilities, and resources, but by the most workable co-alignment of the various internal parts of the project with external agencies. In addition to the factors discussed earlier for software development projects, these could also include local, regional, and national government agencies; suppliers of goods and services; users of the project results; and, most importantly, those who benefit the most (or are most affected by) project success: the project beneficiaries. All of these parties are often referred to as "project stakeholders" in much of the project management literature. This alignment is particularly important in international development projects that are designed to raise the standard of living of masses of people.

It is important for the project manager first to understand the project environment, and second to link the project with the key actors and factors in the environment in such a way that project success is enhanced to the greatest extent possible. Finally, the type and magnitude of change that will occur within the environment during the life of the project and as a result of its completion must be anticipated, and sufficient flexibility provided in the management approach to accommodate these changes.

Beyond adapting the project life cycle to the environment, as described earlier, other important methods are available to identify the key environmental actors and factors and then link the project to the as appropriate to the situation.

Environmental Scans

Not all elements in a project's environment will be crucial to its success. Systematic scanning of the environment to identify the key actors and factors that are crucial to success is an important part of the project sponsor's, the project manager's, and indeed the entire project team's, responsibilities. Such scanning can vary from an undirected, fortuitous, and subconscious observation to a purposeful, predetermined, and highly structured inspection. Figure 2.5 presents a format that has proven useful for this purpose.

In using this approach, a fairly large number of potentially crucial environmental actors and factors are first identified and recorded in the appropriate sector and ring. Then, usually through project team consensus, the few most critical actors and factors are highlighted as shown by outlining either with a square box or an oval (or some other set of symbols). *Actors* are defined as individuals, groups, institutions, organizations, agencies, and so on, who can take action (or fail to do so) affecting the project. *Factors* are elements such as attitudes, laws, regulations, customs, habits, trends, physical or economic conditions, and so on, which, although they cannot take actions, nevertheless exert great influence on project by their very existence.

Links between the Project and Its Environment

To be successful, the project must be linked wherever possible to its environment. In addition to reflecting the environmental factors through design of the life-cycle process model, this is accomplished through specific linkages with the key actors and factors that have been identified in the environmental scanning. These linkages can be made through organization structures and management processes.

Examples of organizational linkage include:

- Formal steering committees.
- Electing key actors to the board of directors or advisors to the project or its sponsoring organization.
- Arranging for the project manager or project team members to serve on the boards or on committees of the key actor's organizations.
- Teaming up project people with the key actors in third-party organizations.
- Ad hoc committees for coordination or planning, with key actor participation.
- Appointing liaison managers with responsibilities to interact with the key actors, or having the project manager perform this function.

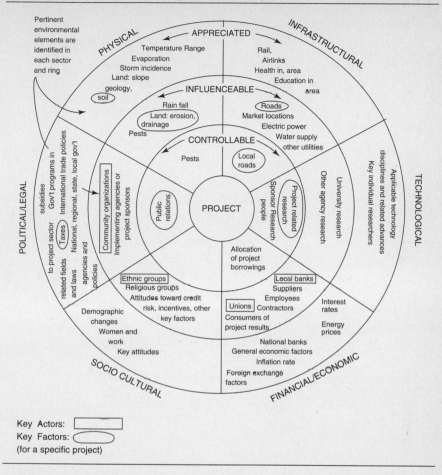

Figure 2.5   A method for documenting an environmental scan. Adapted from Nicholas R. Burnett and Robert Youker, "Analyzing the Project Environment," CN-848, July 1980, The World Bank Institute Course Note Series. Washington, DC: The World Bank Institute.

Here are some examples of management process linkages:

Actors

- Invite key actors to participate in project review meetings, especially when developing plans that affect them.
- Invite key actors to tour the project offices and field sites, and introduce them to project team members and visiting dignitaries.
- Provide them with copies of appropriate reports.

Factors

- Assure that the identified key factors are properly considered when selecting and prioritizing projects, when designing the project life-cycle model, and when developing project plans, budgets, schedules, and so on.
- Establish reporting systems so that the impact of changes in these factors can be reflected in project plans.
- Establish systems to monitor assumptions and alert the project manager to significant changes in the factors.

Table 2.5   Examples of Linkages Between the Project and Its Environmental Actors and Factors

Project Management Tasks	Key Environmental	
Project Phase	Actors	Factors
1. Define the project.	Get them involved in the definition process; use their ideas if possible; explain the project to them; identify problems and negative reactions.	Assure that key factors are included in planning assumptions; identify limits imposed by key factors which affect project definition.
2. Organize and build the project team.	Establish formal, ad hoc, and informal relationships with key actors; consider actors as members of the project team; include where possible in meetings.	Incorporate the influence in organization design; make all team members aware of the key factors and their effects on project success.
3. Plan, schedule, and budget the work.	Involve actors in preparation of plans, schedules, and budgets, as possible; assure that plans reflect realities imposed by key actors.	Incorporate information relating to key factors into plans, budgets, and schedules.
4. Authorize the work and start up the execution activities.	Keep actors informed, especially when activities will have a direct impact on them.	Monitor factors to avoid direct conflicts and generation of problems whenever possible.
5. Control the work, schedule, and costs.	As above.	As above.
6. Evaluate progress and direct the project.	Include actors in evaluation process where possible; give advance information on major changes.	Periodically update data on each key factor and include in progress evaluation process.
7. Close out the project.	Involve actors in close-out planning and activities; keep informed as appropriate.	Continue to monitor factors and reflect changes in close-out plans.

Table 2.5 presents some further examples of how the project can be linked to its environment during seven generic project management phases or tasks.

Dynamics of the Project Environment

Just as the project itself is changing in character as it moves through its life-cycle phases, so too is the project environment changing. Project sponsors and managers must reexamine their key environmental elements periodically to reaffirm the identity of the key actors and factors that relate to their projects.

Although this type of environmental scanning was developed for use on international development projects in developing countries it is a powerful method for increasing the probability of project success in high-technology projects—especially those with complex interactions with outside regulatory agencies and with the local population, such as environmental remedial projects, or nuclear power plant decommissioning projects.

CEO DEMANDS: PROGRAMS AND PROJECTS

Regarding this discussion of programs and projects, the CEO must demand that:

1. The appropriate project categories be defined encompassing all programs and projects within the organization.
2. A detailed project management process be defined for each project category, with alternative provisions for any subcategories that require variations in that process.
3. Provision be made in each category project management process definition to simplify the requirements for the planning and control of "minor" projects while satisfying the overall needs of the organization's enterprise resource management systems.
4. Systematic environmental scans be employed on all major projects and that appropriate links be established between those projects and the key actors and factors in the environment that could have significant influence on project success.

3

‹ ›

Improving Project
Management Capabilities

Before looking at ways to improve an organization's project management capabilities, we will first discuss the benefits and costs of using an integrated, systematic approach to project management, the bodies of knowledge in project management, and maturity models for organizations using project management.

These topics provide the needed frameworks for discussing the various ways to improve the effectiveness of an organization's project management capabilities.

3.1 BENEFITS AND COSTS OF SYSTEMATIC PROJECT MANAGEMENT

Advantages of Modern Project Management

The formalized, systematic project management approach presented in this book has several advantages and benefits when compared to the alternative approach of relying on the functional managers to coordinate project activities informally, using procedures and methods designed for managing their functional departments. The fundamental reason that the approach described here is used, and its use continues to expand, is that it produces a substantial increase in the probability that each and every project will be successful: achieving its strategic objectives by producing the specified results on time and within the approved budget. This in turn directly increases the success of the total organization.

The basic reasons for this increased success—when the principles and practices described here are properly applied—are:

- Projects are selected and authorized only when they clearly support the organization's growth strategies, their risks have been sufficiently evaluated and understood, they have been priority ranked with other competing projects, and the key limited resources (people, money, and facilities) have been allocated to each project as required for successful execution.

- Project commitments are made only to achievable technical, cost, and schedule goals.

- Portfolio, program, and project responsibilities are well defined and properly carried out.

- Every project is planned, scheduled, and controlled so that its commitments are achieved.

- Project teams work together with commitment to the project objectives, plans, and schedules.

The advantages gained by defining and assigning the *integrative project responsibilities* as described, including appointing a project manager for each major project, are:

- Placing accountability on one person (the project manager) for the overall results of the project while clearly making accountable the other key persons at the executive and functional levels for their responsibilities on the project.

- Assuring that decisions are made on the basis of the overall good of both the project and the organization, rather than for the good of one or another contributing functional department.

- More effectively coordinating all functional contributors to the project.

- Properly using integrated planning and control methods, systems and tools, and the information they produce.

The advantages of *integrated planning and predictive control* of all projects include:

- Assuring that the activities of each functional area are being planned and carried out to meet the overall needs of the project in full coordination with all other projects.

- Assuring that the effects of favoring one project over another are known (e.g., in allocation of critical resources).

- Identifying problems early that may jeopardize successful project completion, to enable timely and effective corrective action to prevent or resolve the problems.

The advantages of effective *team-working*, especially in conjunction with the other two primary concepts of project management—focused, integrative responsibilities and integrative predictive planning and control—include:

- Bringing needed multiple disciplines together from diverse organizations to collaborate creatively to achieve project objectives.
- Creating strong commitment and understanding to the project and its objectives.
- Developing as a team jointly agreed plans, schedules, and budgets for executing the project, with resulting commitment to achieving the specified results within the target schedule and cost.
- Achieving outstanding team performance on each project.

The Goals and Benefits of Project Portfolio Management

The three broad goals of project portfolio management are:

1. *Maximization of value:* To most firms, the principal goal is to allocate resources so as to maximize the value of the portfolio in terms of the major company objective (e.g., long-term profitability, return on investment, or likelihood of success).
2. *Balance:* Here the main concern is to develop a balanced portfolio—to achieve a desired balance of projects in terms of a number of parameters.
3. *Strategic alignment:* The main focus here is to ensure that, regardless of all other considerations, the final portfolio of projects is strategically aligned and truly reflects the business strategy (Cooper et al., 2001, pp. 26–27).

Beyond the benefits of systematic management of projects, the organization that moves on to portfolio project management will realize additional returns.

"The benefits of portfolio management are tremendous. After establishing their new portfolio process, top management of SmithKline Beechman felt their new portfolio was 30 percent more valuable than the old one without any additional investment. They saw the marginal return on additional investment triple from 5:1 to 15:1. These achievements prompted the company to eventually increase development spending by more than 50 percent" (Bridges, 1999, p. 53; citing Sharpe, 1998, p. 10).

Cost of Project Management

The sources of the costs related directly to the application and continual development and improvement of the project management discipline are summarized in Table 3.1. As noted there, many of the costs associated with this discipline are commonly included in the direct budget for each project. The costs related to managing the project portfolios and the project management office (PMO) are usually included in the organization's overhead and/or general and administrative expenses.

The magnitude of the total cost of project management varies widely, depending on the type, size, and number of the projects, and the project management maturity level of the organization. Ibbs and Kwak (1997, p. 20) report that a survey of 20 companies shows that "Eighty percent of the companies answered that they spend less than 10 percent of total project cost for utilizing project management services." The range of reported costs in that survey was from 0.3 percent to 15 percent of total project cost. Salaries and related costs for the various people involved are the largest single item involved. Licensing of project management and related software applications, consulting assistance, and training in project management are also usually significant costs.

Ibbs and Kwak (1997, p. 59) present the organizational and financial benefits of implementing project management tools, processes, and practices. They look at return on investment in project management and provide a vehicle for estimating the returns to be expected from increasing an organization's project management maturity.

Measurement of Project Management ROI

Knutson (1999) describes a useful approach to measure the return on investment in the project management discipline. She proposes using four measurement plateaus:

Measurement Plateau 1: Comprehension and Acceptance. What is the level of comprehension and acceptance of project management within the organization?

Measurement Plateau 2: Application. What is the frequency and accuracy with which the technical and sociological components of project management are applied?

Table 3.1   Sources of Costs for Application and Development of the Project Management Discipline

	People (Salary plus Overhead)	PM Software Applications (Acquisition and Maintenance)	PM Planning, Computing, and Communications (PCs and ISP*)	PM Travel, Training, and Consultants
Project Portfolio Management (see Chapters 1, 4, and 8)	Portfolio steering group. Support staff (if required).	Supported by PMO.	Supported by PMO.	Minimal PM travel. Consultant may be needed for first implementation.
Project Management Office (PMO) (see Chapters 4 and 7)	PMO Director. Support staff.	Acquire and maintain PM software for total organization.	Acquire/administer Intranet/Internet/Web server and support for PM discipline. Acquire PCs.	Training for continual PM improvement. Consultant for PMO start-up.
Program/Project Office (PO) (for each program or project). Costs are included in direct project budget. (see Chapter 9)	Program or project manager. Planning and control staff.	Tailor and use PM SW for each project's needs.	Use PCs. Use Intranet/Internet/Web as required. Enter data as required for project planning and control.	Project start-up team planning. Other training as required. Travel for project as required. Consultant needed perhaps.
All affected functions (see Chapter 4)	Managers. Functional project leaders. Work package leaders.	Supported by PMO and all project offices and project managers.	Provide: —Planning inputs. —Progress info. —Time sheets.	PM Training as required.

*Internet Service Provider.

Measurement Plateau 3: Influence on the Business. What business results have been produced by the existence of the discipline of project management?

Measurement Plateau 4: Return on Investment (ROI). What is the calculated ROI on the direct investment in the project management discipline?

Knutson says:

> To attempt to measure the success of project management—rather than of projects—we need to focus on initiatives within the realm of project management, such as methodologies, automated support, organizational structure, information creation and dissemination, and so on. In this paper, the focus is not only on using the techniques to determine the success of a single project, but more importantly, on how these same techniques can be used to address multiple initiatives that comprise the business and cultural discipline of project management.

Knutson then presents techniques for evaluating and measuring the results of project management on each of these four plateaus and lists six possible criteria upon which the discipline of project management might be evaluated that are similar to some of the project management maturity models discussed later in this chapter.

Application of her approach within any organization will produce a reasonable and defendable calculation of the return on investment in modern project management.

The Value of Project Management: Beyond ROI

Crawford and Pennybacker (2000) say that calculating the ROI in project management is not sufficient. On the contrary, they argue that the true value of project management lies in intangibles, and they advocate a balanced scorecard approach. They cite a survey of 100 senior-level project managers by PM Solutions' research arm, the Center for Business Practices (2001), which found that 94 percent of those surveyed felt that "implementing project management added value to their organizations." Among the organizations surveyed, they reported significant gains following implementation of project management initiatives, including 50 percent improvement with project/process execution, 36 percent improvement in customer satisfaction, 54 percent improvement in financial performance, and 30 percent improvement in overall employee satisfaction. "The survey revealed that most companies rely on multiple coordinated project management improvement initiatives rather than just one or two" (Crawford and Pennypacker, 2001).

3.2   FORMALIZED BODIES OF KNOWLEDGE IN PROJECT MANAGEMENT

As project management has developed into a profession over the years, there have been several concerted efforts to document and describe the "body of knowledge" for that profession. The two most widely known versions of this have been developed and promulgated by the Project Management Institute (PMI®, the *PMBOK® Guide;* PMI, 2000) and the Association for Project Management (APM, 2000) in the United Kingdom. The PMI® *PMBOK® Guide* has been approved in the United States by ANSI as an American National Standard (ANSI, PMI 99-001-2000). These bodies of knowledge are the subject of continuing debate and development within the profession (Morris, 2001, p. 21). For example, Vargas (2001) proposes restructuring the PMI® *PMBOK® Guide* and reports a 20 percent increase in the PMI PMP certification test scores in students who were taught using the restructured *Guide* when compared to those taught using the existing structure. An Adobe Acrobat file can be found at the site www.aec.com.br/newpmbok, which contains all 39 processes conforming to the conventional *PMBOK® Guide,* but in the order proposed by this article.

The PMI® *PMBOK® Guide* identifies five "process groups," with 39 detailed management processes within them, and eight "knowledge areas" in the project management field. Table 3.2 shows the titles of these groups, processes, and knowledge areas and their relationships to each other. This listing is not meant to be exclusive, but to indicate generally where the project management processes fit into both the project management process groups and the project management knowledge areas.

The general relationship of the five process groups and their relative levels of activity over a typical project life cycle are shown in Figure 3.1.

The differing structure of the APM Body of Knowledge is shown in Table 3.3. Morris describes fairly recent attempts to rectify this situation of having two fundamentally differing models of the project management body of knowledge that is "somewhere between being intellectually and professionally inadequate and, at best, being in need of urgent revision" (Morris, 2001, p. 22). A group of 33 experts from a number of countries began the effort in 1999 to develop a global project management body of knowledge. The primary result of this effort to date is the recognition of the extreme difficulties that lie in the path of developing such a global body of knowledge that is acceptable to all concerned.

Liberzon (2000) says "we have redesigned accepted PM standards (*A PMBOK® Guide*) for usage in Russia . . ." to reflect the extensive project management experience during and after the USSR years in that heavily industrialized country. He proposes that a sixth process, Analysis, be added to the five processes covered in the PMI *Guide* to reflect the

Table 3.2 Mapping of Project Management Processes to the Process Groups and Knowledge Areas as Identified in the *PMI PMBOK® Guide*

Knowledge Areas	Process Groups				
	Initiating	Planning	Executing	Controlling	Closing
Project Integration Management		Project plan development.	Project plan execution.	Integrated change management.	
Project Scope Management	Initiation	Scope planning. Scope definition.		Scope verification. Scope change control.	
Project Time Management		Activity definition. Activity sequencing. Activity duration estimating. Schedule development.		Schedule control.	
Project Cost Management		Resource planning. Cost estimating. Cost budgeting.		Cost control.	
Project Quality Management		Quality planning.	Quality assurance.	Quality control.	
Project Human Resource Management		Organizational planning. Staff acquisition.	Team development.		
Project Communications Management		Communications planning.	Information distribution.	Performance reporting.	Administrative closure.
Project Risk Management		Risk management planning. Risk identification. Qualitative risk analysis. Quantitative risk analysis. Risk response planning.		Risk monitoring and control.	
Project Procurement Management		Procurement planning. Solicitation planning.	Solicitation. Source selection. Contract administration.		Contract closeout.

Source: PMI PMBOK® Guide 2000. Adapted from Figure 3-9, p. 38.

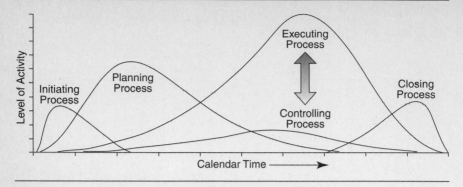

Figure 3.1   Levels of activity in project management process groups over the project life cycle. Adapted from Figure 3-2, p. 31, PMI PMBOK® Guide 2000.

importance of that activity, plus more emphasis on resource management as reflected in Russian project management practices.

This book does not attempt to cover all of the topics listed in either of these bodies of knowledge. However, it does cover those topics that have been found to be most in need of more widespread, improved understanding based on the author's experience in managing projects and consulting with clients in many industrial and governmental sectors in a number of countries.

3.3   PROJECT MANAGEMENT MATURITY MODELS

In recent years, the use of maturity models has grown in popularity for evaluating where a given organization stands in comparison to its potential and to other organizations in particular areas of management. Improving an organization's project management capabilities generally involves moving up the ladder of whatever maturity model best suits the needs of that organization. Such improvement, however, involves looking at the specific areas of project management and introducing improvements where the greatest payoff exists, while keeping in mind the total picture of integrated project management principles and practices.

Maturity models are not a new concept, despite their recent rise in popularity. The most famous of these models, the Capability Maturity Model (CMM) from the Software Engineering Institute (SEI)—a model that was first developed to measure the maturity of software development practices—first emerged in 1987 (see Figure 3.2). The CMM model has become the standard for measuring capabilities in the software development industry, which generally embraces standards quickly, and the

Table 3.3   The British Association of Project Management/APM Body of Knowledge Structure, rev. 3rd. ed.

Project	Organization and People	Techniques and Procedures	General Management
Systems management	Organization design	Work definition	Operational/Technical
Program management	Control and coordination	Planning	Management
Project management	Communication	Scheduling	Marketing and sales
Project life cycle	Leadership	Estimating	Finance
Project environment	Delegation	Cost control	Information technology
Project strategy	Team building	Performance measurement	Law procurement
Project appraisal	Conflict management	Risk management	Quality
Project success/ failure criteria	Negotiation	Value management	Safety
Integration	Management development	Change control	Industrial relations
Systems and procedures		Mobilization	
Closeout			
Postproject appraisal			

Source: Peter W. G. Morris, "Updating the Project Management Bodies of Knowledge." *Project Management Journal,* 32, 3 (September 2001), p. 23.

structure of the CMM has been reused for the development of many other maturity models, including Project Management Maturity Models. But the field of project management has not settled on a standard, and the future for such a standard is uncertain (Rosenstock et al., 2000).

Two Examples of Project Management Maturity Models

PM Solutions, Inc. has developed a detailed maturity model with eight levels that "can be used in assessing the maturity of your organization in managing projects enterprise wide—in other words, your project management culture . . ."(Crawford and Pennypacker, 2000).

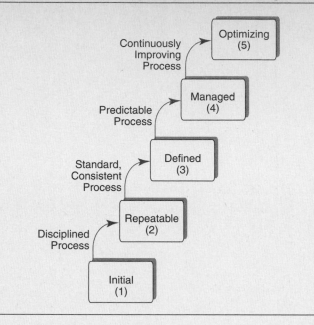

Figure 3.2   The Software Engineering Institute Capabilities Maturity model.

Brief descriptions of each level of the PM Solutions' maturity model are given in Table 3.4.

The Berkeley PM Process Maturity Model

"The five-step Berkeley PM Process Maturity Model is used to establish an organization's current PM maturity level. This model demonstrates sequential steps that map the organization's incremental improvements in its PM processes. . . . The model progresses from functionally-driven organizational practices to project-driven organizations that incorporate continued PM learning. An organization's position within the model signals their position relative to the other organizations in their industry class or otherwise that have been addressed" (Ibbs et al., 2001).

The five steps in the Berkeley model are:

1. *Level 1: Ad Hoc:* There are no formal procedures or plans to execute a project.
2. *Level 2: Planned:* Informal and incomplete processes are used to manage a project.
3. *Level 3: Managed at the Project Level:* PM exhibits systematic planning and control systems that are implemented for individual projects.

Table 3.4 Description of Levels in the PM Solutions' Project Management Maturity Model (PMMM)

			PMMM Level				
Level I	Level II	Level III	Level IV	Level V	Level VI	Level VII	Level VIII
	Basic Processes		Enhanced and Standardized Processes			Optimal Processes	
			Management Maturity				
Nonawareness	Initial Process	Basic Process	Repeatable Process	Advanced Process	Well-Defined Process	Managed Process	Optimizing Process
Description of Each Level							
Nothing.	Ad hoc processes. Some awareness.	Basic processes. Summary level information. Project focus.	Most processes standard on large, visible projects. Detailed level information. Project focus.	All processes standard on all projects. Program focus.	Processes integrated with corporate processes. Organizational focus.	Project management information used to support strategic decisions.	Continuous improvement.

Source: J. Kent Crawford and James S. Pennypacker, "The Value of Project Management: Why Every Twenty-First Century Company Must Have an Effective Project Management Culture," *Proceedings of the PMI 2000 Seminars & Symposium.* Houston, TX, September 7–16, 2000, Newtown Square, PA: Project Management Institute.

4. *Level 4: Managed at the Corporate Level:* PM processes are formal while information and processes are documented informally.

5. *Level 5: Learning:* The key characteristic of companies that operate at the Learning Stage is that they continuously improve their PM processes and practices (Ibbs et al., 2001).

PMI®'s Organizational Project Management Maturity Model Program (OPM3)

Some 200 volunteers have been working since 1998 (see www.pmi.org /opm3) to create an organizational project management maturity model as a PMI standard. "Unfortunately, there is no consensus as to the contents of an organizational project management maturity model, or even the principles on which such a standard is constructed. Some 30 existing models serve the market, with more appearing all the time. Books on the subject are now beginning to appear (e.g., Kerzer, 2001; Knutson, 2001)" (Cooke-Davies et al., 2001). "Based on market research surveys to over 30,000 professionals, the design of the model is now complete, incorporating 180 best practices and over 2,400 capabilities, outcomes, and key performance indicators. The target date for delivering the OPM3 to PMI for publishing is June 2003" (Schlichter, 2002).

3.4 RECOMMENDED IMPROVEMENT APPROACH

The recommended approach consists of the following steps:

- Identify the symptoms of ineffective project management.
- Relate the symptoms to probable causes through (1) review of this book and other sources, (2) performance audits of on-going projects, and (3) postcompletion analysis of completed projects.
- Identify and rank the opportunities for improvement.
- Define an improvement program to correct the probable causes.
- Execute the improvement program, evaluate the results, and look for additional areas of improvement.

Project management practices are recommended to plan and execute such improvement projects. Crawford and Pennypacker reported that an extensive survey of over 100 senior-level project management practitioners (also referred to earlier in this chapter) showed that "Over 70 percent of the organizations implemented three or more initiatives within the past three years" (Crawford and Pennypacker, 2001). These included implementing a project management office, a project management methodology, project management software, integrating project management into key company processes, training staff in project management tools and techniques, and deploying a development program for the project staff.

Identifying Opportunities and Need for Improvement

The need for improving project management capabilities can be determined by realistically answering these fundamental questions within a specific organization:

- Do projects exist within the organization?
- Does each project support an approved corporate strategy?
- Have the risks associated with each project been effectively determined and managed?
- Have these projects been completed, or are they going to be completed, in accordance with the original (or revised with justification) schedules, budgets, contract prices, and so on, specified in the contracts or other authorizing documents?
- Have the original profit objectives been achieved on commercial projects? Have penalties been paid?
- Can the present management structure and planning and control systems be expected to manage effectively the larger, more numerous, or different projects required to achieve the organization's growth strategies or other long-range goals in the near and longer term?

If the answers to these questions are affirmative, the organization's capabilities in project management are exceptionally good. If not, various improvements are in order. These could require changes in the knowledge and skills of people; organization of responsibilities; policies, processes, procedures, systems, tools, and methods for project management; or in all three of these areas.

Symptoms and Probable Causes of Poor Performance on Projects

Some symptoms of poor project performance are:

- *Schedule performance:* Late completions and delays with attendant cost overruns and contract penalties.

- *People performance:* High project staff turnover, high stress levels, low morale.
- *Cost performance:* Actual costs frequently exceeding budgets.
- *Management performance:* Excessive involvement of top management in project execution details.
- *Resource management performance:* Excessive multitasking (start and stop work on tasks), duplication of effort, inefficient use of functional specialists.

Identifying and correcting the causes of these typical problems usually requires rather intensive effort by knowledgeable project management practitioners.

Identifying Problems, Risks, and Pitfalls

The Project Management Center of Excellence for AT&T designed and implemented a formal project management review process to establish "a practical way of putting Project Management (concepts) into widespread practice . . . assessing how we are doing . . . and identifying targets for improvement" (Schneidmuller and Balaban, 2001). These authors report excellent results and wide acceptance of the review process by project managers and their staffs.

Ondov reports that "The Technical Assessments Group at AT&T Labs, formerly a part of Bell Labs, has been evaluating software projects across the AT&T companies for over 10 years, covering hundreds of projects of all types" (Ondov, 2001).

While the results reported by Ondov relate to IT/software projects, they can also be applied to many other categories of projects without undue risk of misinterpretation. The assessments actually covered many additional areas, but those relating specifically to the *PMBOK® Guide* are summarized in Table 3.5.

Ondov (2001) also describes a number of improvements that have been noted during these project assessments and lists the project management challenges and critical success factors that the AT&T Labs Technical Assessments Group have identified over its lifetime.

Typical causes of poor project performance, in addition to those identified above, include:

- The Project Life Cycle Management System (PLCMS) and the underlying processes are not understood or documented as integrated wholes—or do not exist.
- Too many projects are under way at one time for the available resources; the organization is overcommitted.

Table 3.5   Problems Identified through Formal Evaluation of Software Projects at A&T Labs

Project Initiation	Project Execution	Project Tracking and Control	Project Closeout
Unclear business problem and/or success criteria.	Communication and information flow is limited.	Tracking but no control.	Success not evaluated (but may be "declared"!).
Lack of an executive sponsor or champion.	Little focus or expertise in vendor management.	Ineffective progress monitoring.	Project is not closed—and never dies.
Multiple people as project manager (or no real project manager at all).	Inadequate resources.	Status reporting is misleading or infrequent.	Learnings not captured or used for subsequent efforts.
Scope/size of effort under-estimated.	Process violated (e.g., quality gates ignored).		
Unrealistic expectations of COTS (commercial off the shelf) system.	Not enough attention to external interfaces, deployment, and support.		
End date predetermined without recognizing implications.	Testing interval is squeezed.		
Project plan is missing or is only the schedule.	Ineffective prioritization.		
Inadequate requirements.			
Unrealistic schedules.			
The *real* risks are not acknowledged.			

Source: Rhoda Ondov, "Managing Software Projects at AT&T: Common Risks and Pitfalls." *Proceedings of the Project Management Institute Annual Seminars & Symposium,* November 1–10, 2001, Nashville, TN. Newtown Square, PA: Project Management Institute.

- Original project schedules, cost commitments, or technical objectives are impossible to achieve.
- Key integrative roles (see Chapter 4) are not assigned or understood.
- No one is responsible for overall integration of each project.

- The project manager job is poorly understood; the assigned person is not effective.
- Project managers report to the wrong part of the organization.
- Wrong type of person is assigned as project manager.
- Excessive conflict exists between project and functional managers.
- No integrated and predictive planning and control exists.
- Project plans and schedules are not realistic.
- Estimates of time and cost include contingencies at every level.
- No project cost accounting ability exists.
- Project priorities are rapidly changing and conflicting; decisions do not reflect the current priorities.
- There is poor control over customer changes.
- There is poor control of design changes and no configuration management.
- Project scope is not controlled.
- Project offices are improperly organized and staffed.
- Excessive "multitasking" is allowed or forced, where individuals frequently jump from one project task to another.
- Project management software is used only as "window dressing."
- Project teams are not committed to the approved plans and schedules.

This list is illustrative only and does not attempt to include all of the myriad causes of poor project performance.

Possible Improvement Efforts

To achieve significant improvement in an area as complex as project management, it is necessary to introduce changes in all areas—people, organization, processes, systems, and procedures—in a well-coordinated manner. Some typical improvement projects and tasks in each of these areas are identified here, reflecting the detailed discussions throughout the book. Additional efforts no doubt can be defined for specific situations.

1. Strategic project portfolio management.   Carry out improvement projects to:

- Design and implement an appropriate project portfolio management process for the organization (as discussed in Chapter 8).
- Formalize the selection of new projects and prioritization of all projects in each portfolio (Chapter 8).

- Proactively exploit and manage risk and uncertainty in programs and projects (see Chapter 10, especially Section 10.7).

2. Management development and training. Establish development and training efforts to:

- Improve the understanding and acceptance of project management concepts and practices at all levels.
- Develop the planning, control, and other related skills required by project managers and project support specialists.
- Develop the leadership skills of program and project managers.
- Create the necessary understanding of new project management policies, systems, tools, and methods.
- Improve the understanding and practice of teamwork.
- Develop policies and procedures related to:

  —Selection criteria for project managers by type and size of project.

  —Career development of persons working in project management assignments.

  —Performance evaluation of and rewards to project managers and others assigned to or contributing to projects.

3. Organization of responsibilities. Carry out the following improvement projects as appropriate to the situation:

- Establish at a reasonably high level in the organization a Program/Project Management Office (PMO) holding responsibilities for implementation and continued improvement of project management processes, practices, and tools (discussed in Chapter 7).
- Establish an operations planning and control office to provide integrated planning and control support for multiple small project situations (see Chapter 8).
- Define the integrative responsibilities for project portfolios, programs, and projects at every level of the organization and assure that all persons holding these responsibilities fully understand and accept them (see Chapter 4).
- Improve the understanding and practice of teamwork (Chapters 6 and 11).
- Establish appropriate policies regarding the roles of the project portfolio steering group, project sponsors, program and project managers, and functional managers and project leaders (Chapters 4, 7, 8, and 9).

- Develop responsibility matrices based on the project/work breakdown structures to clarify the relationships of all managers and contributors involved in projects (see Chapters 10 and 11).

- Develop position descriptions for the roles, described in Chapters 8 and 9, appropriate to various types and sizes of projects.

- Formalize the project-functional matrix organization of responsibilities and take the actions needed to make the matrix work.

4. Integrative systems, tools, methods, and procedures.   Initiate improvement projects to:

- Identify and define the project categories for the organization and document the integrated Project Life Cycle Management System (PLCMS) for each project category (discussed in Chapter 2).

- Improve the PLCMS for each project category (see further discussion in Section 3.5).

- Establish procedures to assure coordination of plans and actions between all functions (marketing, engineering, purchasing, manufacturing, field operations, others): (1) prior to commitment, during submittal of a project proposal or acceptance of a contract change and (2) during execution of the project.

- Introduce new or revised planning and control procedures (see Chapters 10 through 15).

- Implement integrative, multiproject information systems that capitalize appropriately on the Internet and all available communication means (Chapter 5).

- Establish a project control room for major programs and projects with related support procedures (Chapter 14).

In a given situation the responsible manager should select the appropriate improvement tasks, establish their interdependencies and relative priorities, and lay out the resulting improvement program to reflect the resources available for the effort. More specific recommendations for implementing new or upgraded project management planning and control software systems are presented in Chapter 5.

The Pilot Improvement Project Approach

The nature of project-oriented situations gives a unique opportunity to develop and test a particular group of changes on a pilot test or prototype basis, using a carefully selected project, prior to full-scale commitment to the changes. The pilot project can serve not only as a vehicle for introducing and testing new practices and methods but, also, as a case study for use in management development and training efforts.

If this approach is used, care must be exercised in choosing a program or project that is:

- Not too far along in its life cycle.
- Representative of other projects within the organization.
- Not so beset with inherent problems (i.e., already committed to unattainable schedules) that the benefits of any improvement cannot save it.

There is always the danger that the pilot project will receive such special attention by all concerned and, therefore, be so successful that the usefulness of the changes being tested cannot be determined. In this case another result may be that other projects suffer significantly because all resources and attention have been devoted to the pilot project.

A number of improvements cannot, however, be introduced on a single project but must affect all active projects if maximum benefits are to be obtained. Implementation of a project portfolio management process obviously requires the incorporation of a number of projects in the initial application. Implementation of a computer-based planning and control system for multiple projects is another example that cannot be tested with only one project.

Using Real and Case Study Projects for Management Development and Training

For a detailed description of how to develop and train project teams using real projects see Chapter 11.

3.5 IMPROVING THE PROJECT LIFE-CYCLE MANAGEMENT SYSTEM (PLCMS)

Once the life cycles have been designed and documented for each category or subcategory of projects, as discussed in Chapter 2, Section 2.5, it is then possible to define and document the project life-cycle management system for each appropriate category. Only when such documentation exists can the system be improved on a systematic basis.

To establish a total quality management (TQM) approach to an organization's project management capabilities and to avoid suboptimal improvements being introduced on a disjointed, piece-meal basis, the following approach is recommended:

1. Document and describe the *Project Life-Cycle Management System* (PLCMS) for each project category (as defined in Chapter 2) within the organization.
2. Define the life-cycle phases for the project category.
3. Identify the gates or decision/approval points between the life-cycle phases.
4. Describe and define the process flow within each project phase and identify the intermediate and final deliverables for each phase.
5. Identify and interrelate the existing risk analysis, planning and control processes, and related documents and approvals within each phase.

Reengineer the Integrated Process

6. Apply appropriate reengineering methods to each category's PLCMS to:
   a. Identify system constraints, gaps, and weaknesses.
   b. Relate the undesirable project results and possible causes to the PLMSC wherever possible.
   c. Redesign the PLMSC beginning with the most obvious constraints, gaps, and weaknesses and document the results.
7. Obtain needed agreements and conduct appropriate tests or analyzes to prove out the validity and feasibility of the proposed system revisions.
8. Plan, approve, and execute the improvement project to implement the revised PLMSC.
9. Repeat the steps as required until an optimum achievable PLMSC has been implemented.

Improving the New Product Life-Cycle Process

Cooper et al. (2001, Appendix A, "Overhauling the New Product Process: Stage-Gate™ Methods—A Synopsis," pp. 333–339) describe a useful approach to improving the new product development process based on their extensive experience with many client companies in a number of industries. Their Stage-Gate™ process is shown in Chapter 2, Figure 2-5. These authors provide complete and authoritative information on how to design, implement, and improve these processes (Cooper et al., 2001,

Chapter 11, "Designing and Implementing the Portfolio Management Process: Some Thoughts Before You Charge In," pp. 303–332).

Consider Applying the Theory of Constraints (TOC) to Improve the PLCMS

The theory of constraints (TOC) developed by Goldratt and its application to project management, critical chain project management (CCPM) (Goldratt, 1997), have generated considerable enthusiasm among many practitioners and consultants in the past few years in the project management field:

> Basically, TOC is a commonsense way to understand a system. TOC says, "Any system must have a constraint that limits its output."
>
> . . . The purpose of using TOC is to improve a business system. In *What Is This Thing Called Theory of Constraint, and How Should It Be Implemented?* Goldratt (1997) stated:
>   . . . before we can deal with the improvement of any section of a system, we must first define the system's global goal; and the measurements that will enable us to judge the impact of any subsystem and any local decision, on this global goal. (Leach, 2000, pp. 52, 53)

The global goal of any PLCMS is to proceed from the start of the concept phase through to completion of the project execution and closeout phases as quickly as possible while consuming minimum resources (human, money, materials, and facilities). Application of TOC to the improvement of a PLCMS is summarized in Figure 3.3. Leach (2001) provides a detailed explanation of the theory, tools, and techniques for applying TOC together with the total quality management approach to improving project management systems. He also describes how TOC and critical-chain project planning and control can improve schedule and cost performance on projects, as discussed later in Chapters 11 and 13.

3.6 OVERCOMING THE BARRIERS TO PROJECT MANAGEMENT

Introducing integrated project management practices and the related formalization of the project management function usually require significant adjustments in attitudes, understanding, responsibilities, methods, and reporting relationships throughout the involved organizations. These changes affect the parent organization and all organizations represented on the project team.

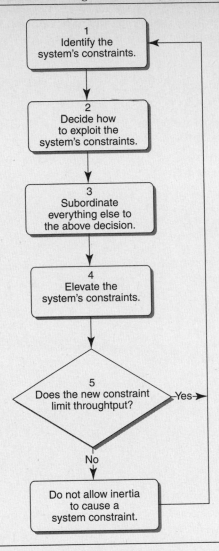

Figure 3.3   The five focusing steps that represent the TOC approach to on-going improvement. *Source:* Lawrence P. Leach, *Critical Chain Project Management* (Norwood, MA: Artech House, 2000), p. 64. Used with permission.

Cultural and other factors—within the project environment, the involved organizations, the industry, the geographic region, and the involved nations—create barriers to these required changes. These barriers can require substantial effort to overcome or mitigate, and, if they are not overcome, will reduce the effectiveness of the project management efforts.

A five-phase strategy is recommended to implement changes required for effective project management and to help overcome the barriers that will be encountered:

1. Identify and understand the barriers anticipated in regard to a proposed change.

2. Create awareness of the need for change and identify and harness the motivating forces that will help to overcome the barriers.

3. Educate and train all affected people using the knowledge gained in the first two steps.

4. Define "change projects" to implement new project management practices and use good project management practices to plan and execute them.

5. Modify and evolve the project management practices and/or the manner of their implementation to accommodate the current or anticipated cultural and other barriers.

Identifying the Barriers

To overcome barriers to change, each organization needs first to *identify and prioritize* the key changes that are required to progress toward fully effective project management. Then, the barriers to each of these changes can be identified so that strategies for mitigating them can be developed and executed. Eight key changes that have been found to generate barriers are identified here; others will no doubt be identified within specific organizations:

1. Integrative roles below the general manager.
2. Shared responsibilities for projects.
3. Direction from two bosses: functional and project.
4. Integrative, predictive planning and control.
5. Computer-supported information systems for management purposes.
6. Project objectives over department objectives.
7. Working, and being rewarded, as a team rather than as individuals.
8. Temporary assignments on projects.

Other Sources of Barriers

In addition to these specific project management-derived barriers, cross-cultural lack of understanding or long-standing animosities (national or ethnic) bring with them additional barriers. These can be found in joint-venture projects bringing together two corporate cultures in the same country, or projects involving two industries, or multinational projects involving two or more nationalities and languages. Additional cultural factors that create barriers to effective project management no doubt can be identified by the experienced reader.

Forces Helping to Overcome the Barriers

A number of forces will usually be present in a given situation that, if properly harnessed, can assist in overcoming the barriers. Pressures from the organization's competitors, failures that show that the existing methods are not adequate, the interchange of people with different experiences from other organizations, the desire within many people to improve and do a better job, the need to prepare the organization for the future, dissatisfaction with the present situation—all of these plus others are sources of energy that can be harnessed.

Of critical importance is the need to create an *awareness of the need for the change* in question. This awareness is often the result of a project disaster, either within the company or the industry, that brings home to all concerned that products and markets are changing, environments are changing, competition is becoming global and, if we want our organization to survive, it is necessary for us to change also. Creating the awareness of need for a given change requires demonstration, education, and communication. Once the awareness of need exists, the barriers will be less formidable and can be surmounted or mitigated more easily. In laying out a strategy for dealing with change, the priorities must be set considering both the importance of each factor and the feasibility of making the change.

Education and Training

Having identified the expected barriers, and having gained an understanding of the forces that are present that will assist in making a change, one can design an education and training program to support the implementation of the change. The nature of project management, which involves discrete projects, allows the use of selected projects as the education and training vehicles. Such projects can be thought of as prototypes from the management viewpoint—testing the new practice or method, and demonstrating to the project team and the entire organization what the role of the project manager really is and how the changes being introduced in the project planning and control system really work.

However, some of the required changes—such as implementation of portfolio project management—will involve a number of projects. In the case of portfolio project management, a prototype division or product line can be used for the initial implementation, rather than attempting to convert an entire corporation overnight.

Team planning workshops, described in Chapter 11, have been widely recognized as an effective method of (1) introducing new project management practices; (2) educating, training, and developing the project teams; and (3) overcoming the barriers that may block the total effectiveness of the project management approach. One group of experienced professionals recommended four types of workshops at the start of cross-cultural projects: Workshops at both the management and project team levels, and—for each level—two workshops, one dealing with the cultural aspects and factors, and the second dealing with the project objectives, scope, content, and plans (Archibald and Harpham, 1990).

It is not effective simply to announce the adoption of the project portfolio-management process, the appointment of a project manager, or the acquisition of a new planning and control system, as examples. A well-designed education and training program is required, anticipating the barriers to be expected, and capitalizing on the motivating factors that will assist in the acceptance of the change. Middle-level managers generally resist the introduction of project management practices most strongly, so they must be included in the education and training program.

Taking Appropriate Actions to Implement the Change

Either in conjunction with or following the proper education and training, management actions are required to introduce and put into practice the project management concepts described in this book. Senior managers themselves must learn about, understand, and support the new practices and demonstrate through their communications and behavior that these are important to the future of the company. Senior managers must recognize that they are role models in the organization, and that their actions and attitudes speak far louder than their words.

The introduction of new integrative processes, new integrative roles, new planning and control methods or tools, and new ways of working together as teams must be viewed as projects in themselves. We can "let the medium be the message" in this regard. These change projects must be carefully planned and must include supporting education and training efforts designed around the anticipated barriers. Recognizing these efforts as "management research and development projects" can be a useful way of positioning them and gaining greater acceptance and support throughout the organization.

Modifying and Evolving Project Management Practices

In all organizations that manage projects, their practices have evolved over a period of time. It is not possible, or even desirable, to attempt to leap from no formal project management to the full-blown ultimate that can be envisioned or that some organizations have actually achieved over a number of years. Many of the cultural and other barriers are formidable and will not be overcome in a short time. In each of the three basic concept areas (integrative roles, integrative planning and control systems, project teams), it will be necessary to introduce changes on a step-by-step basis. Compromises will often be required between the ideal and what can be made to work this year. Experience will be needed in absorbing one level of change before the organization is ready for the next. For example, an organization may elect to start out with assignment of a project coordinator with a more limited integrative role, rather than a project manager, due to cultural barriers involved in the "manager" title or in acceptance of the full integrative role. In such cases, the manager to whom the project coordinator reports will probably carry out the role of the project manager, in addition to their normal duties.

Summary

Success in overcoming the cultural barriers to effective project management can be enhanced by using the five-phase strategy described here:

1. Define the changes required and identify the anticipated barriers.
2. Create an awareness of the need for change and identify and harness the motivating forces that will help to overcome the barriers.
3. Educate and train all affected people using the knowledge gained in the previous steps.
4. Define "change projects" to implement new project management practices and use good project management practices to plan and execute them.
5. Modify and evolve the project management practices to accommodate the barriers.

Project management is the management of change. Improving project management capabilities requires change. Therefore, implementing or improving project management itself requires the use of effective project management practices, and must be viewed from a long-term perspective. There is no one best answer that fits all situations. The concepts of project management must be tailored to the situation and culture, including the cultural mix of the project team.

CEO DEMANDS: PROJECT MANAGEMENT IMPROVEMENT

To achieve significant improvements in project management, the CEO must demand that:

1. A complete inventory of projects be prepared and maintained as a project register within each defined project portfolio of the organization.

2. An objective analysis of past and current performance on all projects be carried out to determine whether improvements in the project management capabilities are required and to identify and rank the potential areas for improvement.

3. Specific project management areas that need improvement be identified using the most appropriate project management maturity model and comparing the organization's project performance with other comparable organizations.

4. The Project Life-Cycle Management System (PLCMS) for each project category within the organization be documented and reengineered to relieve all constraints to the maximum extent.

5. The implementation of improvements in project management be conceived, planned, and managed using the project management concepts and methods described in this book.

6. The project management improvement program be supported with ongoing education and training throughout all affected parts of the organization at all levels.

4

« »

Integrative Roles in Project Management

4.1 KEY INTEGRATIVE ROLES AND THEIR PURPOSES

The role of the project manager is a central one that has received considerable attention in the project management literature over the years. Other equally important integrative roles in project management that have frequently been ignored are briefly described here, and their responsibilities and authority are discussed in the following sections.

Executive Level

The *General Manager* integrates the strategic direction of all projects with the corporate strategic plans, primarily through the Portfolio Steering Group or through the designated project sponsors. Such direction is also given by approval of the allocation of the organization's financial and other resources to the project portfolios.

The *Portfolio Steering Group* integrates and validates the organization's strategic objectives with the programs and projects within the project portfolios over which the group has cognizance, and establishes and approves the relative priorities of projects within each portfolio.

The *Project Sponsor* integrates the on-going strategic direction of the assigned project(s), given to and through the program or project manager, with the on-going operations of the organization.

The *Manager of Project Management* integrates the operational aspects of the work being done on all projects assigned to the project management office (PMO); and integrates the development and use of the organization's project management processes, methods, and tools on all projects with the rest of the organization. This manager also holds responsibility for the Project Management Office (PMO) (or equivalent) of the organization. (See Chapter 7.)

Program and Multiproject Level

Program Managers integrate the efforts of all project contributors on their assigned projects. *Multiproject Project Managers* integrate the priorities and issues for their assigned projects, and carry out the integrative responsibilities of a project manager for each project. These may be a group of minor projects (as defined in Chapter 2) that are not related closely enough to be considered a program.

Project Level

Project Managers integrate the efforts of all project contributors for their individual projects, with emphasis on *what* must be done (scope of work), *when* it must be done to meet the project schedule, and accomplishing the work within the approved project budget.

Functional Department and Project Contributor Level

Functional Department Managers integrate the efforts of project contributors on all projects within their individual departments or disciplines, primarily through the allocation of resources available within the department to the approved, active portfolio of projects. The functional direction emphasis is on *how* the work is done (technical discipline), *how well* it will be done (quality), and *who* will do the specific project tasks or work packages (assignment of individual resources).

 Functional Project Leaders integrate the work of all contributors to their specific assigned projects within each of their respective functions or disciplines. These project leaders are the primary points of contact for the project manager within each function.

 Work Package Leaders integrate the work of individual contributors to each of their assigned work control packages within each project.

Other Important Roles in Project Management

Other important roles relating to projects also exist, including:

- *Project customer:* The person or organization who has authorized and usually pays for the project.

- *Project champion:* The person who promotes and keeps the project alive, who may or may not be the general manager or the project sponsor.
- *Owner* of the results of the project, who may or may not be the project customer.
- *User or operator* of the project results, who may or may not be the owner.

While all of these additional roles are important they do not carry the same level of *integrative* responsibility as the key roles listed earlier. However, if the project customer organization is a major contributor to the project, performing important tasks on which project completion is dependent, then there is a need to identify the integrative roles within the customer's organization as well. The same can be said for all outside organizations that contribute significantly to the project in question.

Generic Relationship Model of These Integrative Roles

Figure 4.1 illustrates the generic relationships between these integrative roles. The key integrative roles must be identified and defined by the organization's project management policies, directives processes, and procedures. Appropriate titles will be given to each, reflecting the established usage for the type of organization and the nature of the business or public service it is involved in. The responsibilities and authority of each of these key roles is discussed in more detail in the following section.

4.2   RESPONSIBILITIES AND AUTHORITY OF THE INTEGRATIVE ROLES

Responsibilities for initiating, planning, executing, controlling, and terminating programs and projects are allocated among the persons assigned to the roles described earlier. Assigning authority commensurate with these responsibilities is often problematic, especially when the integrative nature of these roles is not well understood. The manner in which these responsibilities and the related authority are allocated will depend on:

- The size and nature of the organization: project driven or project dependent, as discussed in Chapter 1.
- The relative importance of programs and projects compared to the total organization and its on-going operations.
- The industrial or governmental sector in which it operates.

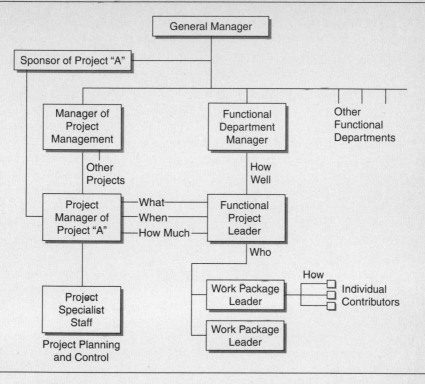

Figure 4.1   Generic relationships of key integrative roles.

- The number and nature of the project portfolios and project categories that exist within the organization, and the number of programs and projects under way at any given time.
- The maturity of the project management discipline within the organization.
- The size, nature, and priority of a given program or project and its current life cycle phase.
- The experience and capabilities of the persons involved.

The following sections present generally accepted descriptions of the responsibilities associated with each of these integrative roles, together with comments as appropriate regarding the associated authority of each role. More detailed discussion of the portfolio steering group, the manager of project management, and project and functional managers' roles and responsibilities and the alternative ways to assign and organize them is given in Chapters 7, 8, and 9.

4.3   GENERAL MANAGER

The role of the *general manager* (a title used here to denote the person with overall operational responsibility for a multifunctional division or an entire company) in project management is focused on:

- How the organization's portfolio of projects supports the overall business strategies of the organization.
- The organization's overall project management process.
- How this process is integrated with all other aspects of the organization.
- Assuring that sufficient money, human, and other resources are available to support all of the approved projects.

Although all of the responsibilities given to the other integrative roles are delegated by the general manager there are certain project responsibilities that cannot be truly delegated. Except in rare circumstances, the general manager is not involved directly with the planning and execution of any one program or project. Generally, the responsibilities retained by the general manager include:

- Assuring that the right projects are selected and created in the first place to support the growth strategies of the organization.
- Providing adequate resources to carry out the approved projects.
- Assuring that the project management practices in use within the organization are appropriate.
- Monitoring the overall performance on projects and integrating that performance with the other operations of the organization.
- Resolving project related conflicts involving senior managers that have not been resolved by them.
- Evaluating project performance of those managers reporting to the general manager.
- Periodically evaluating progress on major projects (major milestone accomplishments, forecast of cost and profit at completion, etc.).

The general manager holds the ultimate authority (as delegated to that position by the board of directors or other higher level authority) for all aspects of his organization. The authority of this position to carry out the responsibilities on projects listed above is rarely if ever questioned.

4.4 PROJECT PORTFOLIO STEERING GROUP

The *project portfolio steering group* is a key element in the successful application of the project portfolio management concept. Because of the scope of responsibilities involved it is generally not appropriate to entrust these responsibilities to a single manager or executive. A number of different perspectives are required to properly balance out the conflicting possibilities and make the best decisions when selecting, prioritizing, and allocating key resources to the diverse projects within each portfolio.

The overall responsibilities of the steering group are:

- Approving the design of the project portfolio management process during its initial implementation, and any significant subsequent changes to it.
- Active participation in the operation of the project portfolio management process.
- Recommending to the CEO and other cognizant senior managers the acquisition of additional financial and other resources when required to plan and execute the projects needed to achieve the strategic objectives of the organization on a timely basis.
- Identifying opportunities for improvement and recommending improvements in the project portfolio management process and the other project management processes, systems and tools.

These responsibilities and this process are discussed in more detail in Chapter 8.

4.5 PROJECT SPONSORS

The *project sponsor* role is usually held by a senior manager acting for the top management of the sponsoring or project executing organization. This role may be held by the general manager, by a high-level executive, or it may be delegated to someone who reports to the general manager. For a very major project, the sponsor role may be held by a steering group or a "plural executive" comprised of key people from various parts of the organization.

The project sponsor role differs from the project portfolio steering group role in several respects. The portfolio steering group is responsible for the entire group of projects in its portfolio, as discussed above. The project sponsor, usually held by one person, is the primary conduit for strategic direction of the project and provides direct contact and communication to the responsible program or project manager regardless of that manager's location in the organization structure.

A team of experienced project management professionals concluded that:

> The absence of a specifically assigned project sponsor with well defined and understood responsibilities is the cause of many difficulties for projects and project managers. By focusing more attention on this vital role, the effectiveness of project management practices could be improved in most organizations. (Archibald and Harpham, 1990)

When a project sponsor has not been identified the project manager often has difficulty in knowing who to go to, other than the general manager (to whom access is often difficult or inhibited) for the required decisions that are beyond the project manager's assigned authority. Also, when no project sponsor is assigned, some managers (including the project manager at times) may assume that the project manager should act also as the project sponsor, with the result that the project manager causes problems and conflicts by reaching beyond her assigned authority. It is possible to assign one person to both the roles of project sponsor and project manager, but in most circumstances these roles should be separated.

The project sponsor is the focal point for project decisions that are beyond the scope of authority of the project manager. Typical responsibilities of the project sponsor are to:

- Hold accountability for the project investment.
- Define and make the business case for the project.
- Approve the project scope and objectives, including schedule and budget, and changes thereto.
- Issue project directives as appropriate.
- Appoint or approve the appointment of the project manager and approve that person's organizational charter and reporting location.
- Monitor the project environment (economic, political, competitive, technological) and advise the project manager of pertinent changes.
- Make and approve major project changes and decisions on project requirements.
- Review project progress periodically and provide strategic direction to the project manager.
- Set strategic priorities and resolve conflicts escalated by the project manager or other project team members.
- Assure that the products of the project will satisfy the original justification for the project, in light of economic, competitive, and market

changes in the environment during the project execution, in close cooperation with the project manager.

The charter of the project sponsor should delegate appropriate authority to the person or group of persons assigned to this role to carry out these responsibilities. As previously mentioned, on large, complex and high-risk projects the best solution may be to name three or more senior people to act as a plural executive in this role, unless the general manager is willing and able to act as the project sponsor. This role is usually not a full-time assignment, whether one or several persons are assigned to it.

4.6 MANAGER OF PROJECT MANAGEMENT

The *manager (or vice president, director, etc.) of project management* has emerged in many organizations as they mature in their project management capabilities. This position is a recognition of the project management function as an important capability of the organization, along with the more traditional functions of marketing, engineering, procurement, manufacturing, construction/field operations, finance and accounting, legal, and so on. The manager of project management may also be the project sponsor for specific projects, in some situations.

Some practitioners have predicted that there will soon be a *Chief Projects Officer* (Dinsmore, 1999, p. 72) in some organizations on a par with the fairly recent position of Chief Information Officer. This position might combine aspects of the project sponsor and manager of project management roles.

The manager of project management is typically responsible for:

- Providing professional direction and training to the program, project and multiproject managers—whether or not they report directly to this manager. This is usually directed primarily to developing the program/project managers' skills and the use and application of the organization's project management methods and information systems.

- Developing and improving the organization's project management processes, policies, procedures, and practices, including the acquisition and development of needed computer software applications, and assuring that adequate indoctrination and training in all of these areas is provided throughout the organization.

- Providing appropriate project planning, scheduling, estimating, monitoring, and reporting assistance to the project and multiproject managers. What is "appropriate" assistance varies considerably: at one extreme, some organizations have established totally centralized support for all projects; at the other extreme each project manager and project office is self-sufficient in this area.

- Resolving interproject conflicts, in full coordination with the responsible project sponsors and project managers, consistent with the scope of authority delegated to this position and to the project sponsors by the general manager.

- Assuring project compliance with contractual and regulatory commitments.

The authority delegated to the manager of project management will vary considerably, depending on the maturity of the project management function within the organization and how self-sufficient each project manager is, and how each individual project office is staffed. The manager of project management must be a full-time assignment in any organization of reasonable size and complexity. See Chapter 8 for more detailed discussion of this important role and of the project management office.

4.7   PROJECT, PROGRAM, AND MULTIPROJECT MANAGERS

The *project* and *program manager* roles are more operational in nature compared to the strategic role of the project sponsor. The project manager plans and directs the execution of the project to meet the time, cost and performance (scope and quality) objectives as established by the project sponsor and/or by the documents that authorize the project.

The general manager may delegate very limited or very broad responsibilities and authority to one person to integrate all the work on one project. If very limited responsibility and authority are delegated, that person acts primarily as a project coordinator or expeditor, and the general manager retains the role of the real project manager.

The project manager, to deserve this title, must be delegated the basic responsibility of overall planning, direction, and control of the project through all of its phases to achieve the desired results within the approved budget and schedule. The project manager is the general manager of the project in terms of responsibility, accountability for final profit and loss on the project, and for meeting the established completion date. The project manager's primary task is the integration of the efforts of all persons contributing to the project. This responsibility does not supplant the responsibility of each functional manager whose people are contributing to the project, but rather overlaps the functional responsibilities, with emphasis on the total project.

The project manager is delegated *project authority:* the authority to give direction to the functional project leaders, or in their absence to the appropriate functional managers, that is required to plan, execute, monitor, evaluate, and control the work to be done on his or her assigned project. As shown in Figure 4.1, this project direction relates to *what* needs to be done, *when* it must be accomplished, and *how much money* and *how many work hours* are to be expended. These are established by negotiation between the project manager and the various functional managers or functional project leaders. Project direction also includes *obtaining the needed information* to plan, monitor, evaluate, and control the overall project. The functional manager or project leader, on the other hand, gives direction concerning *how well* the work is to be done (quality), *who* specifically will do the work, and *how* the work will be accomplished (technical methods). When the project manager tries to give direction on *how well, who,* and *how,* she will probably generate significant conflicts with the functional people.

The project manager's authority depends to a large degree on her ability to earn it, rather than depending entirely on delegated legal authority. The sources of these two types of authority are:

Legal Authority Sources	Earned Authority Sources
Organizational charter	Technical and organizational knowledge
Organizational position	Management experience
Position or job specification	Maintenance of rapport
Executive rank	Negotiation with peers and associates
Policy documents	Building and maintaining alliances
Superior's right to command	Project manager's focal position
Delegated power	The deliberate conflict
The hierarchical flow of authority	The resolution of conflict
Control of funds	Being right

Since the project manager must elicit performance from others who are not under her direct control, she must rely on interpersonal influence bases other than formal, legal authority. Wilemon and Gemmill (1971, p. 319) have identified three influence bases that are of major importance to project managers: expert power, referent power, and reward and punishment power. *Expert power* refers to the ability of the project manager to get project contributors to do what he or she wants them to do because they attribute greater knowledge to that person and believe that he or she is more qualified to evaluate the consequences of certain project actions or decisions. *Referrent power* refers to the responsiveness of project contributors because they are, for some reason or another, personally attracted to the project manager and value both their relationship to him or her and the project manager's opinion of them. *Reward and punishment* power refers to what the project manager can do directly or indirectly to block or facilitate attainment of personal goals of people who balk at his or her requests.

Considerable more detail is presented in Chapter 9 regarding the responsibilities and duties of project managers.

The program manager role is essentially the same as that of the project manager plus the added dimension of integrating and coordinating the work being done on two or more projects simultaneously. On major programs there will usually be a project manager assigned for each project within the program, and the program manager gives direction to each of those project manager. The above comments regarding the responsibilities and authority of a project manager also apply to the program manager role.

The program manager often takes on the responsibilities of the project sponsor for each of the projects within a program. Depending on the organizational rank of the program manager it may not be necessary to assign another person as the program sponsor.

The multiproject manager performs the duties of the project manager on several projects at the same time. These may be several small projects, or a project manager near the end of one project may also be assigned to another project that is in its initial conception phase, for example.

Multiproject managers hold the same responsibilities for their assigned projects as that of the manager of a single project, and are delegated similar authority as a project manager.

Chapter 8 discusses the program and multiproject manager roles in more detail.

4.8 FUNCTIONAL MANAGERS, FUNCTIONAL PROJECT LEADERS, AND WORK PACKAGE LEADERS

Since it is usually not feasible to create a totally self-sustaining organization with all the needed specialized skills for any one project, essentially all projects are supported by some kind of functionally specialized or departmentalized organization. Most organizations are planning and executing a number of projects simultaneously. The result of this matrix management situation is that each specialized department has people assigned to perform various tasks on each of the many current projects.

As previously mentioned, three levels of integrative responsibility exist within each of the contributing functional departments:

1. The functional manager.
2. The functional project leaders.
3. The work package (or task) leaders.

Each functional department manager must first provide the needed resources (people and facilities) to support every project on a timely basis, and then to integrate the often conflicting demands of all active projects within his department. The functional department manager integrates the work on all projects by working through the assigned functional project leaders assigned to each active project. These functional project leaders in turn take project direction from each project manager.

Functional Manager Responsibilities and Authority

Each functional manager holds overall responsibility for planning and executing the specific work (tasks, work packages, activities) to be performed within that function to create the resulting project deliverables (hardware, software, documents, facilities, services) for each active project. The basic technical and management specifications of each work package (result to be achieved, quality, deliverables, schedule, budget) must be established in a negotiating process between the project manager and the functional manager or her representative, namely the functional project leader. Within the limits of these specifications, the functional manager has the responsibility of detailed planning, functional policy and procedure direction, functional quality, and developing and providing an adequately skilled staff.

The authority of the functional department manager is more traditional and better understood, since the people within his department are under the direct control of this manager. However, many functional managers have difficulty becoming accustomed to sharing their responsibilities and authority with project managers, and allowing the project managers to exert project direction within their functional departments.

Functional Project Leaders Responsibilities and Authority

On any given project, there will be several functional project leaders whose role is to integrate the project work within their particular functions or subfunctions (marketing, engineering, test operations, manufacturing, production, other). Each functional project leader integrates the work being done and the activities of the project team members within her specific function. The project manager integrates the work of all functions at the project level, and the functional managers integrate the work on all projects being supported within their functions through their day-to-day direction of the functional project leaders.

The functional project leader (other titles may be used for this position) is key to successful operation within a matrix organization. This person is the focal point of all activity on his assigned project within the functional organization. The functional project leader is the alter ego of his supervisor, usually the department manager, and performs all subfunctional tasking. His responsibilities cut across all subfunctional lines for the total functional effort on that project, and include actively planning and controlling the functional organization's efforts on the project. In effect, this person is a mini project manager within his department.

The authority of the functional project leader is delegated from the department manager and is derived from the organization's project management process documentation. The functional project leader gives project direction to the work package (or task) leaders within the function in question.

Some examples of specific job titles that are functional project leader positions are:

- *Project Engineer,* integrating all engineering aspects of all or an assigned part of the project.
- *Project Controller* (not comptroller), handling project planning, scheduling, budgeting, monitoring, and reporting.
- *Project Accountant,* handling financial and resource usage reporting.
- *Project Cost Engineer,* handling project cost control.
- *Project Contract Administrator.*
- *Project Purchasing Agent.*
- *Project Manufacturing Coordinator.*
- *Project Field Superintendent,* handling field operations.

Work Package Leader Responsibilities and Authority

Each work package (or task) leader integrates the work of the individuals assigned to his work package (the lowest element of work that is normally planned and controlled within the integrated, overall project plan). Work package leaders (other titles may of course also be used) are responsible for:

- Developing and maintaining work package plans for accomplishments.

- Establishing work package technical guidance.

- Establishing work package detailed schedules and operating budgets that are properly integrated with the overall project plans, schedules, and budgets.

- Controlling and reporting on work package performance.

The authority of work package leaders is delegated from the cognizant functional department manager to carry out these responsibilities.

4.9 ALTERNATE WAYS OF FILLING THE PROJECT MANAGER ROLE

The most effective project management results from the assignment of one person to fill the total role of the project manager, and for this person to carry out the responsibilities from the earliest possible moment in the conception of the project to its ultimate completion. However, for a number of reasons it is frequently not possible to achieve this objective. For example, many more projects pass through the conceptual and definition phases than go on to final completion. Several times as many proposals are usually submitted to potential customers than are accepted and funded by the customers. It is not always possible to assign a project manager to every proposal and know that this person will be available to carry through the project if the award is made. Also, when projects have a relatively long duration (more than 18 months), the needs of the organization (and of the person) often demand that the project manager be promoted to larger or different responsibilities before the project is completed. Sometimes because of the lack of a clear understanding or acceptance of the requirements of the project manager, this role is often arbitrarily or unknowingly divided among various individuals who may be scattered throughout the organization. The most commonly encountered difficulties in this regard, and the most effective solutions, are discussed in the following sections.

Continuity of the Project Manager Assignment

The effectiveness of a project manager is directly related to the continuity of responsibility through the life cycle of the project. The difficulties in assuring this continuity have previously been discussed. When the continuity of project manager responsibility is broken and the current project manager knows that at a certain point she will hand over the project to someone else, then the project manager will very likely cover up problems and defer difficult issues and hand them off to the new project manager. The final project manager at the end of the chain inherits all of the tough, unmade decisions that would have been much easier to resolve earlier in the project.

Possible steps to minimize these difficulties include:

- As early as possible, alert the potential project manager to an embryo project and have that person monitor the activity as time permits until a firm assignment is feasible.

- Where a project management department exists, assign a project manager to represent the department on all major proposals. This person will at least evaluate the proposals from the project management viewpoint, and will also provide needed background information to the specific project manager assigned to a contract if and when it is awarded.

- When selecting a project manager, establish a clear understanding with the selectee and upper management levels that the person will be expected to remain in the assignment until the project is complete.

- Avoid the practice of "passing the baton" for project responsibility from department to department as a project passes from phase to phase. If the project manager is actually transferred from department to department, then the continuity of personal responsibility is preserved.

- Establish, through the Project File (see Chapter 10), a well-documented history, including a set of plans and performance against the plans, to become the "turnover file" should it be necessary to change the project manager prior to completion.

- Attempt to overlap project assignments, where possible, by assigning a project manager whose project is nearing completion, and therefore may demand less time, to a new project which can be followed part time during the early conceptual phase and then on a full-time basis when the first project is complete.

Full-Time versus Part-Time Assignment

Large projects will require one person to be assigned full-time to the role of project manager. Smaller projects do not require and cannot justify such a full-time assignment, but the need remains to fill the role, nevertheless.

Several commonly encountered causes of ineffective project management relate to the part-time assignment of project managers. Frequently, the required number of project managers are not readily available, and various compromises result.

Projects Assigned to Functional Managers

A manager who has a full-time functional responsibility may be given the added burden of acting as the project manager for one or more projects. This is generally ineffective, unless 80 to 90 percent of the work to be done on the project will be performed by people reporting to this manager through the organization structure. Given additional duty, either the functional or the project responsibility will suffer due to lack of time. Also, the manager's primary allegiance will be to the department and not the project and when conflicts occur the project will probably suffer. Additionally, when other functional managers are enlisted to aid the project they are caught between the realization that if they help to make the project very successful they are bolstering the chances of a rival functional manager being promoted instead of themselves; and that if, on the other hand, the project can be caused to fail at least partially, then the competitive edge of the manager running the project has been reduced. When this part-time assignment is combined with the "pass-the-baton" approach previously discussed, rivalry is intensified by the (sometimes very justified) feeling that each manager is passing along many unsolved problems. The last person to receive the project assignment may have inherited an impossible task, and it is usually very difficult to pinpoint the person responsible for failure of the project.

Finally, because the characteristics of projects are different from those of a functional organization, as discussed in Chapter 2, most managers find it difficult to switch alternatively every day from managing a project to managing a function. This can create unusually high stress in the manager and the project team members.

Several Projects Assigned to One Full-Time Project Manager

A more effective solution in situations where not enough project managers are available for full-time assignment one to a project, or where a number of minor projects exist, none requiring a full-time manager, is to assign several projects to one full-time project manager. This approach has the advantage that the person is continually acting in the same role, that of a project manager, and is not distracted or encumbered by functional responsibilities. His primary allegiance is to his projects, and his skills as a project manager can be more rapidly developed.

In the process of planning, controlling, evaluating, and directing one project, the project manager can frequently cover his other projects

when in contact with functional managers and team leaders, thus mini-
mizing the time expended by the functional managers for this purpose.
Interproject priorities and conflicts can often be resolved directly by the
multiproject manager for his assigned projects. Rivalry between functional managers is reduced as a result.

Division of the Project Manager's Responsibilities

The responsibilities of the project manager are frequently inappropri-
ately divided among several persons. Who is the real project manager?
Usually, the real project manager is the person to whom all those carrying out portions of the project manager role report. It is often a surprise
to this manager to discover that he is, in fact, the real project manager,
as he may be several levels up the reporting structure.

The most frequently found method of dividing project responsibilities
is to assign one person the technical (product) responsibilities, another
the schedule, and a third the cost. Many times a fourth person holds the
contract administration responsibilities, perhaps another serves as the
prime customer contact point, and still another is concerned with
the manufacturing aspects.

Such division of the project manager's responsibilities is probably one
of the most common cause of projects not achieving their objectives. Unless one person integrates the efforts of the project engineer, the project
planner and controller, the project cost engineer, the project contract
administrator, and so on, it is not possible to evaluate the project effectively to identify current or future problems and initiate corrective action in time to assure that the objectives will be met.

The project manager cannot actually perform all of the planning,
controlling, and evaluation activities needed, any more than he can perform all of the technical specialty activities required. Project management support services must be provided, and the project manager must
direct and control these support activities. The hazard is that the support activities may exist, but in the absence of an assigned project manager, they are not properly used.

Retention of the Project Manager Role by the
General Manager

In certain situations, such as with one major project of extreme importance to the company or division, the general manager may properly
elect to retain the role of project manager. This may also be appropriate with multiple small projects, as discussed in Chapter 9. In such
cases, it is usually desirable to appoint a project coordinator to perform much of the planning and communicating related to the project

for the general manager. The project coordinator should report directly to the general manager in this role and should integrate the needed project management support functions.

Filling the Project Manager Role in Multiple Project Situations

A number of organizations are responsible for few major projects but many smaller ones. In such situations, the project manager role may remain with the appropriate level of line management, but responsibility must be clearly established for integrated planning and predictive control of all projects to support and coordinate the efforts of all functional managers. This responsibility may be assigned to a position with various titles such as planning manager, operations control manager, projects coordinator, projects controller, and so on. (See Chapter 8.)

4.10 CHARACTERISTICS, SOURCES, AND SELECTION OF PROJECT MANAGERS

The effectiveness of a project manager depends heavily on her personal experience and characteristics, more so than in many other management positions below the general manager level. The ability to function effectively in a relatively unstructured relationship to other managers, to earn authority, to integrate the efforts of many people, and to resolve conflicts appropriately are very important to the project manager's success.

Project Manager's Key Personal Characteristics

Some of the key personal characteristics of effective project managers are:

- Flexibility and adaptability.
- Preference for significant initiative and leadership.
- Aggressiveness, confidence, persuasiveness, verbal fluency, ambitious, active, forceful.
- Effectiveness as a communicator and integrator.
- Broad scope of personal interests, is a generalist rather than a specialist.
- Poise, enthusiasm, imagination, spontaneity.
- Able to balance technical solutions with time, cost, and human factors.
- Well organized and disciplined.

- Able and willing to devote most of their time to planning and controlling.
- Able to identify problems and willing to make decisions.
- Able to maintain proper balance in the use of their time.

Project Manager's Skills

A team of experienced project management professionals developed a profile of the project manager's skills and knowledge and concluded that the project manager's integrative skills are the most important for project success (Archibald and Harpham, 1990, p. 10). Figure 4.2 shows a summary profile of the project manager and the central importance of the integrative skills.

The integrative skills of most importance and use to the project manager include:

- Holistic thinking.
- Using a systems approach.
- Being flexible, adaptable, open-minded.
- Ability to set and balance priorities.
- Cross-cultural abilities (macro and micro).

The remaining four skill areas shown in Figure 4.2 are:

1. *Skills in project management methods and tools:* These represent the classic practices in project management that are described throughout the book, and elsewhere in the project management literature. These relate to planning, organizing, monitoring, and controlling the project.
2. *Team and people skills:* These include the interpersonal skills that are required to lead, communicate, coordinate, facilitate, motivate, and build the project team.
3. *Technical (specialized discipline) skills:* These are the engineering, scientific, economic, mathematical, or other skills related to the particular discipline that forms the predominant experience bank of the project manager.
4. *Basic business and management skills:* This area covers the basic understanding of how the business or industry operates, how companies and other organizations are managed, and fundamental methods of planning, budgeting, financing, and operating organizations.

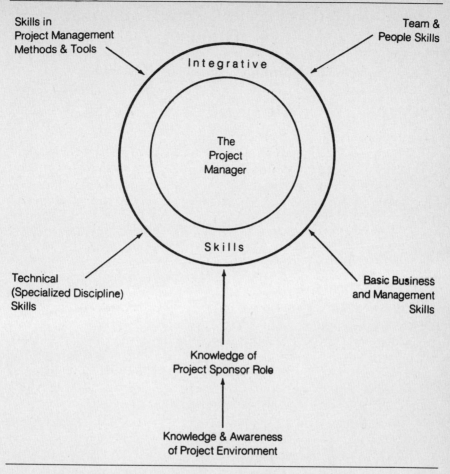

Figure 4.2   Project manager skills profile. *Source:* Russell D. Archibald and Alan Harpham, "Project Managers Profiles and Certification Workshop Report," *Proceedings of the 14th International Expert Seminar,* March 15–17, 1990. Zurich, Switzerland: International Project Management Association/IPMA, p. 10. Used by permission.

A certain minimum level of knowledge and skill in the last two areas, technical and basic business and management, are considered to be prerequisites for any person to be considered for the job of project manager. The other three skill areas—team and people, project management methods and tools, and integration—are often learned on the job. Identification of these five skill areas can be useful in structuring the subject matter to be used in training project managers and their teams.

Education and Certification of Project Managers and Project Management Specialists

Many universities, training institutions, professional associations, and consulting firms provide seminars, workshops and courses on campus, on-site, online through the Internet, in many aspects of project management. These offerings are directed to program and project managers and the various specialists who work in the project management field. Current information on these offerings can be obtained from the Web sites given earlier in Chapter 1 and by searching the Internet. A number of universities around the world now offer certificates and degrees in project management.

The Project Management Institute (PMI®), the national members of the International Project Management Association (IPMA), and other associations provide certification programs in project management. For example, PMI® certifies a person who qualifies as *project management professional* (PMP) who meets specified criteria in education, experience and service to the profession and then passes a comprehensive exam based on the PMI PMBOK® (PMI, 2000). The British Association of Project Management (APM) provides a rather different type of certification in project management that relates more to the person's capability rather than his knowledge. In spite of the current limitations regarding these certifications, many organizations have made such certification a prerequisite for advancement in their project management career paths. Details of these certification procedures can be obtained from the associations' Web sites given in Chapter 1.

Sources of Project Managers

The prime sources of project managers (either from within or outside of the parent organization) are: other projects, product line managers, functional managers, and functional specialists.

The best source is from other projects—provided the projects and the project managers have been successful. However, there is an ever-increasing demand for project managers, and it is very difficult to find a project manager who has just completed a project at the right time for each new project.

Probably the second major source of new project managers is from the staff of planning, estimating, scheduling, and control specialists that provide support services to the project managers. These specialists know first-hand what the project planning and control requirements are, and work closely with program and projects managers and therefore know what those positions involve. Not every specialist has the personal attributes to make a successful project manager, but many do. These specialists know the project planning and control software and how to best use it, which is a major plus factor if they are given the project manager role.

Functional managers are sometimes given a full-time project manager assignment. If someone has been a first-level or middle manager, the project environment may be strange to him and unless he has the proper personality traits and is provided with proper training and guidance they may have a difficult time carrying out their responsibilities.

Functional specialists are often given a project manager assignment and may become quite effective in such an assignment. The greatest difficulty usually relates to the changeover from *doing* a specific type of work to *managing* the efforts of others. To be most effective it is necessary for the specialist to become a generalist and not try to continue his specialty on a major project for which he is also the project manager. On small projects this is often unavoidable, and requires good understanding of the differences between the two roles.

Selection of Project Managers

Selection of a person to be a project manager should not be a unilateral procedure performed by the general manager or other senior manager. The position and the project should be described frankly to the candidate, who should be given the freedom to accept or reject it without prejudice. Unless she is personally motivated by the opportunity and the nature of the challenge, she will probably not become an effective project manager. Every effort should be made to select a person who has a reasonable chance to stay with the project to its completion.

4.11 CAREER DEVELOPMENT IN PROJECT MANAGEMENT

As recognition grows of the nature and importance of project manager assignments the need becomes more apparent for more formalized career development in project management. Because projects begin and end, project management assignments are less secure than functional assignments. Frequently, the best qualified people cannot be attracted to projects because they must leave the security of a functional department for an unknown future when the project ends.

In an increasing number of organizations, the project management function has been established as a part of the fairly permanent organizational structure. This provides a base on which to build continuity of project assignments, long-term security for project-oriented employees, and more effective career development programs.

Development of Project Managers

The integrative skills required by project managers can best be developed through actual experience on projects. However, this development can be accelerated and the effectiveness of the manager increased through appropriate development and training seminars and workshops, and through direct exposure to the methods employed by other successful project managers. Since projects exist in all sizes, it is possible to assign a less experienced person to a smaller or less complex project. If successful with that, the person can then be assigned to larger projects.

The project planning and control specialist staff is a primary source of candidates for the project manager assignment. If such a specialist can be assigned as a deputy project manager for a period of time this is an excellent way to provide on-the-job training to potential project managers.

Performance Evaluation and Career Planning

Evaluation of a project manager's performance is often more difficult than evaluating other managers. This is because so many factors affect the project over which the project manager has little direct (legal) authority and control. A highly successful project may or may not be the direct result of the project manager's efforts, just as an unsuccessful project may have had the best project manager in the organization in charge of it. At this stage in the evolution of the project management approach, no formalized or systematic method of evaluating project manager performance has been published.

Another area of potential difficulty is the follow-on assignments of project managers, and the affect on their careers of a two or three year project manager assignment. Highly successful project managers may be in an even more difficult position since top-level positions commensurate with their abilities are less frequently in need of filling. Top management attention must be given to this problem area if the best qualified persons are to be attracted to the project manager assignment.

Two factors provide possible solutions to this problem. First, the number of projects and their recognition are growing, hence the demand for project managers is increasing. Flexibility in assignment of project managers between divisions and areas, assuming similar kinds of projects and no substantial language problems, can also be of assistance in this regard since one division having a capable, unassigned project manager can allow transfer to another in need of such a manager.

Second, the consolidation of project management functions within the organization, usually in the form of a project management office

(PMO) can provide assistance in the overlapping of project assignments, the development of project manager skills, and the continuity of future assignments.

Recognition of project management as a possible career assignment and provision for planned professional growth in this area will further assist in attracting the needed capabilities. The similarities between the project manager job and higher level positions in general management have led to the realization that project experience is valuable in the development of general management skills.

Project Management Specialists

There is a continually growing need for project management specialists who provide the planning, risk analysis, estimating, scheduling, accounting and cost control, configuration control, reporting, and other specialized staff support services needed for large, complex programs and projects. These specialists are a primary source for new project managers.

4.12 CONCLUSION

Understanding and proper use of the integrative roles in project management are vital to successfully managing complex projects in large organizations. If any of these key integrative roles are left vacant or improperly defined, severe conflicts and significant loss of effectiveness will be encountered. Even the most advanced project management information systems will not compensate for mistakes in defining and assigning qualified people to these integrative roles.

CEO DEMANDS: INTEGRATIVE PROJECT MANAGEMENT ROLES

The achieve effective project management the CEO must demand that:

1. All of these integrative project management roles are clearly understood and properly assigned to qualified people.
2. The general manager understands and fulfills that office's project management responsibilities.

(continued)

---

3. A project sponsor be appointed for every major project and given appropriate indoctrination to carry out this role effectively.

4. An experienced manager of project management be appointed reporting to a senior executive of the organization.

5. An appropriate home (such as a Project Management Office, as discussed in Chapter 8) be established within the organization for the project management discipline.

6. All multiproject and program managers be given the training needed to ensure their effective performance.

7. Each project manager respects the functional lines of authority when giving project direction to team members.

8. Functional managers and project leaders respect the project lines of authority as exercised by the project managers.

5

« »

Integrative and Predictive Project Planning and Control

Systems, tools, and methods for integrative and predictive project planning and control are at the heart of the project management discipline.

Integrative means that all phases of the project and all the elements of information mentioned later are logically linked. *Predictive* means that the system forecasts what will happen in the future based on the current plans and estimates, with the actual physical progress and reported expenditures constantly updating the schedule and cost forecasts and comparing these with the authorized baseline budgets and schedules. The goal is to predict undesirable results in sufficient time to allow corrective actions to be taken to assure that the undesirable results do not become the reality.

5.1 REQUIREMENT FOR INTEGRATIVE AND PREDICTIVE PLANNING AND CONTROL

The second key concept of the project management discipline requires that:

- Every project be planned and controlled on an integrated basis.
- Including all contributing functional areas or organizations.

- Through all of each project's life-cycle phases: conception, definition, design, development/manufacture/construction, installation/initial use/operation, and close-out.

- Including all the elements of information (schedule, resources, cost, technical, risk) pertinent to the situation, together with (1) resource allocation and management reports; and/or (2) earned value techniques (Fleming and Koppelman, 2000) with cost and schedule variance reports where appropriate.

- Using Web-enabled project management software systems and procedures.

- Linking all projects within programs and project portfolios so that the pertinent information can be summarized for senior executives to provide appropriate strategic direction on all projects.

The Need for One Integrated Project Management Information System

Most organizations are faced with the need to plan and execute many projects simultaneously using common resource pools, creating the need to use one common project planning and control information system for all projects. Effective application of the powerful computer-supported project planning and control systems available today requires using one integrated system (usually consisting of project-oriented subsystems that are properly linked) for each and every project within the organization to:

- Systematically define and control the project's objectives and scope.

- Evaluate and proactively manage individual project risks together with the aggregate project portfolio risks.

- Define and control the specification, quality, configuration, and quantity—scope—of intermediate and final products (or deliverables) of the project.

- Systematically define and control the project scope and the work to be carried out using the project/work breakdown structure (P/WBS) approach.

- Estimate the labor, material, and other costs associated with (1) each project's deliverable products and related work elements and (2) each summary element in the P/WBS.

- Plan and control the sequence and timing of the project deliverables and related work elements using a top-level project master schedule plus an appropriate hierarchy of more detailed, integrated schedules.

- Authorize and control the expenditure of funds, work hours, and other resources required to execute the project.

- Provide the information—regarding both (1) actual progress and expenditures and (2) forecasts in the future—required by project managers, department managers, functional task leaders, and work package leaders on a timely and reasonably accurate basis.

- Continually evaluate progress and predict and mitigate problems with scope, quality, cost, schedule, and risk, using earned value project management methods where appropriate.

- Report to management and customers on the current status and future outlook for project scope, quality, cost, and schedule completion, including postcompletion reports.

There are times when customer demands or other factors such as joint venture needs may require that a specific project planning and control system be used for a particular project that is different from the corporate system. In such cases, the different system must be capable of linking with and providing summary information to the corporate system so that all project information, and particularly the time-related resource data, can be viewed on an integrated basis for the total organization.

5.2 PROJECT MANAGEMENT INFORMATION SYSTEMS

There are many ways to define and depict a project management system. Cleland (2001, p. 12) has defined an overall project management system consisting of seven subsystems:

1. Facilitative organizational subsystem.
2. Project control subsystem.
3. Project management information subsystem.
4. Techniques and methodologies subsystem.
5. Cultural ambiance subsystem.
6. Planning subsystem.
7. Human subsystem.

Tuman (1988, pp. 652–691) presents detailed descriptions and analyses of project management information and control systems from several perspectives, reflecting his long experience in developing and implementing computer-based systems for project planning and control. He defines a "project management and control system" of broad scope, as shown in Table 5.1, including both technical and risk information and control systems, in addition to a project information and control system.

Table 5.1   Definition of a Project Management Information and
Control System

Technical Information and Control System	Project Information and Control System	Risk Information and Control System
Engineering Management Module Procurement Management Module Construction/ Production Management Module Test Management Module Configuration Management Module	Project/Work Breakdown Structure Module Planning and Scheduling Module Cost Management Module —Cost estimating —Cost estimating support —Craft and crew —Unit material —Unit labor hours —Source document —Cost control —Cost projection Accounting module Data entry module Online query module	Planning Assurance (Risk Assessment) Module Quality Assurance Module Reliability Module Maintainability Module Safety Assurance Module

Source: John Tuman Jr., "Development and Implementation of Project Management Systems," Chapter 27, *Project Management Handbook,* (2nd ed.). Ed. David I. Cleland and William R. King (New York: Van Nostrand Reinhold, 1988), p. 673. Used with permission.

However you define such information systems, they all consist of:

- *Documents* (containers of information).
- *Procedures, processes, and software systems* for preparation, maintenance, preservation, transmittal, and utilization of the documents that are used for creating, planning, evaluating, and executing projects within a given organization.

Table 5.2 presents a summary of the documents typically used for project planning, authorizing, controlling, and reporting. These documents are described and discussed in detail later in Chapters 10, 12, and 14. Procedures must exist for the preparation and use of each of these documents, as specified in the detailed project management process for each category of projects. Computer software systems incorporating essentially all of these documents and procedures have proliferated within the past 10 years and have made it possible to use one integrated information system for managing all projects within the organization.

Table 5.2   Summary of Typical Documents for Project Planning, Authorizing, Controlling, and Reporting

Planning (See Chapter 10)	Authorizing (See Chapter 12)	Controlling (See Chapter 12)	Reporting (See Chapter 14)
Project Summary Plan	Master Contract Release	Management Reserve Transaction Register	Monthly Progress Reports:
Project/Work Breakdown Structure (P/WBS)	Project Release	Cost Expenditure Reports	—Narrative
Task Responsibility Matrix	Subcontracts and Purchase Orders	Updated planning and authorizing documents, comparing actuals with budgets and schedules:	—Project Master Schedule
Project Master Schedule	Task Work Orders	—Project Master Schedule	—Cost Performance Reports
Integrated Project Network Plan		—Milestone Charts	—Risk Tracking Reports
Project Interface and Milestone Event List		—Other	Management Reviews of Critical Projects:
Project Budget		Cost Performance Reports	—Major Project Identification Data
Project Funding Plan		Schedule Variance Reports	—Summary Status Reports
Project Chart of Accounts		Earned Value and Cost Variance Reports	—Above Reports as required
Task Statements of Work		Technical Perf. Measurement Reports	
Task Schedules		Risk and Issue Tracking Reports	
Task Budgets		Milestone Slip Charts	
Detailed Network Plans		Trend Analysis Charts	
Technical Performance Planned Value Profiles and Milestones		Task Estimates to Complete (ETC) and Estimates at Completion (EAC)	
		Action Item Lists from Project Review Meetings	

Level of Detail in Project Planning, Authorizing, Controlling, and Reporting Documents

Determining how much detail is needed and practical has always been a fundamental problem in achieving effective project management. Available automated systems apparently can handle an unlimited amount of detail, but the people involved in estimating, reporting, and evaluating the information have limits on the time they have available for planning and control purposes and in their ability to integrate and digest large amounts of data. A related problem of equal significance has always been how to effectively integrate project management systems and information with all the other business information and systems in the organization.

Two basic concepts provide invaluable assistance in resolving these two related problems:

1. *Systematic, hierarchical breakdown* of the project using the project/work breakdown structure concept to define the work packages (or tasks) that form the basic elements of project planning and control, and to provide a logical structure for summarizing information for evaluation, control, and reporting purposes.

2. The systematic use of the *project interface management* concept to identify the points of interaction between project plans and schedules and other established planning and control systems in the organization.

These concepts, coupled with the power of today's automated systems, enable organizations to work at the appropriate, economically and practically feasible level of detail. Chapters 5, 8, 10, and 13 discuss these topics in more detail.

5.3   COMPUTER-SUPPORTED PROJECT MANAGEMENT INFORMATION SYSTEMS (PMIS)

Since the coming of the computer age and concurrent with the introduction in the 1950s of planning methods such as PERT/CPM/PDM network planning and scheduling, computer software applications for project planning, scheduling, and control have been vital tools for project management. For many years there was a tendency in the project management field to equate a PMIS with these computer software packages, and even to equate such packages with project management as a discipline. Today, most practitioners recognize that there is much more to project management than software systems.

Computers and software packages are essential elements of today's PMIS. Automation of the large amounts of complex, interrelated information required to manage a large project or to manage multiprojects in a dynamic, high-technology environment, has made possible the development and effective use of integrated project management information systems. Only in recent years with the advent of Web-enabled systems have we been able to realize the full automation of all project management documents in one integrated, computer-supported system.

Electronic Creation, Storage, Processing, and Retrieval of PMIS Documents and Information

All of the documents listed in Table 5.2 can be created, stored, processed, and retrieved in digital format using today's project management software applications operating on desktop, notebook, or hand-held computers and Wed-enabled communication systems. *How* the information and documents are used by project managers, and the persons holding the other key integrative project management roles, is specified in the detailed project management process of the organization.

Web-Enabled Project Management

Timmons (2000) states, with some justification, that "Our future success (as project managers) will be determined by how well we are able to apply the power of the Internet."

Developing and implementing a fully integrated, Web-enabled PMIS within a given organization is a complex project in itself. Timmons describes a logical approach to evolving such a system, points out some of the pitfalls in trying to fit one commercially available system into a complex organization, and describes how such a Web-enabled system was developed in one organization. His design "was developed around three fundamental requirements: form data posting, data linking, and process authorization." Form data posting stores all information, excluding images, in databases. This means developing electronic forms that convert paper data into electronic databases, enabling the information to be exchanged on an ordinary Web browser.

Data linking is made possible by an open database standard that allows linking between different software manufacturers. This eliminates double data entry and improves the accuracy of data through data validation checks.

Process authorization controls access to databases, provides the process flow of data into and out of the project databases, and provides reliable configuration control on critical project data through electronic signatures.

Among the many advantages and efficiencies of Web-enabled project management, Timmons describes streamlining the design process, enhancing reporting requirements, 24-hour availability of the Web-enabled document repository, improved project baseline control, having a virtual project turnover list (completion punch list), and simplifying storage and handling of vendor information (drawings, maintenance records, test records, manuals, etc.).

Distributed Project Management (DPM) Software

Web-enabled project management software is becoming known as distributed project management and is a very large and rapidly growing market:

> A wide variety of industries require the use of collaboration tools. In addition to IT-related organizations, users of collaboration tools come from a variety of non-IT companies such as those in architecture, engineering, aerospace, defense, energy, health care, pharmaceutical, manufacturing, telecommunications and construction industries.
>
> A study conducted by Datatech, a Massachusetts-based market research and technology assessment firm, found that vendors who can deliver technologies for project collaboration will have the competitive advantage. The market for these specialized tools is projected to surpass $3 billion by 2004. Likewise, California-based research and management consulting firm Collaborative Strategies LLC reported that distributed project management (DPM) revenues are expected to reach $1.5 billion by 2003. While the U.S. is the early adopter of these tools, Europe and Asia are now demonstrating that they also have a clear need for project collaboration tools.
>
> Definite trends are now emerging in the DPM marketplace. There is a strong movement away from complex, desktop-based applications to easy-to-use, browser-based systems even though there is an increasing shift from simple, local projects to distributed, more complex projects. (Patterson, 2002, p. 2)

Project Management Software Applications

The most comprehensive listing now available of project management software applications, the PMI® *Project Management Software Survey* (PMI, 1999), identifies the software categories that are shown in Table 5.3 and relates them to the appropriate PMBOK® Guide knowledge areas. Each of these categories is discussed briefly in the following sections.

PM Software Suites

These software suites, which are collections of compatible software modules each having specific capabilities within most of the software categories listed next, have been developed within different areas of

Table 5.3   Software Categories and Related Knowledge Areas

Software Category ·	PMBOK® Guide Knowledge Areas
Suites (36)	All
Process/Scope Management (19)	Integration Management
Schedule Management (43)	Time Management
Cost Management (27)	Cost Management
Resource Management (27)	Human Resources Management
Risk Management and Assessment (15)	Risk Management
Communications Management (17) Subcategories: Graphics add-ons (21) Timesheets (25) Web publishers/organizers (15)	Communications Management

Source: Summarized from *Proceedings of the PMI 1999 Seminars & Symposium,* Philadelphia, PA, October 10–16, 1999. Newtown Square, PA: Project Management Institute, p. 3. The number of software application products surveyed in each category is shown in parentheses, as listed in Appendix B of the PMI Survey. The categories are not all mutually exclusive.

application. The construction and military/aerospace application areas are the most common sources for these suites. In spite of these origins, most of the suites listed are applicable to many industries and areas of application.

For most of the suite products, the modules that comprise them can be evaluated separately, but the great advantage of using a suite is the fact that all the modules are integrated, enabling easy interchange of information between them. These products are suitable for the full range of small to large organizations and simple to large, complex projects. "Engineering, research and development, government, software, medical, electronics, aerospace, larger professional services and consulting companies, large-scale IT departments, telecommunications: all can benefit from the implementation of a project management suite. Some suites target specific kinds of business users" (PMI, 1999, p. 15).

Key Features

- All project life-cycle phases can be included.
- All projects in the enterprise are handled, with several types of summarization (P/WBS, organization, chart of accounts, other) provided at user-defined levels.
- Information is provided to support strategic decisions.
- Can be linked to other management information systems.

Process/Scope Management Software

Process-oriented software integrate the project management process with the work processes of the contributing functional organizations. These products can be applied to the project management process and methodology and can integrate other supporting methodologies, such as a product development or a software development process. "Process management support can include simply documenting the methodology and related reference material, or can be as comprehensive as including risk assessment, business opportunities justification, return on investment analysis, issues logging, communications, estimating, and continuous improvement to the methododology" (PMI, 1999, p. 83).

Key Features
- Provide process flowcharting.
- Accommodate supporting software and reference materials.
- Guidance to the user through the organization's process methodology.
- Automated linkages with other project management software.

Schedule Management Software

Products in this category, which form the heart of most project management applications, enable program and project planning, scheduling, monitoring, and control for single projects, programs, multiprojects, and all projects within a portfolio or an enterprise. "Scheduling is a requirement for all projects, across all application areas and industries, so this category of products is both widely used and almost universally applicable to most business/or project processes" (PMI, 1999, p. 121).

Key Features
- Ability to plan and sequence activities using CPM/PDM/PERT or Gantt chart methods.
- Produce project master schedules based on the project/work breakdown structure (P/WBS), with subordinate detailed schedules at several levels.
- Critical path calculation.
- Resource allocation and leveling of varying degrees of accuracy and sophistication.
- Schedule status and forecasts based on progress to date, with controllable baselines.

- Schedule reports, including Gantt charts and network logic diagrams.
- Some products can handle critical chain with buffers or resource critical path calculations (Chapter 10 and the Appendix).

Cost Management Software

Cost management software applications range from simple tools that are linked with the cost tracking capabilities of scheduling tools to sophisticated programs to manage all cost elements across the entire life cycle of the project—from conceptual estimates to the final summarization and analysis of the cost at completion.

Key Features
- Proposal pricing based on labor categories, rates with escalation, and estimated quantities.
- Budget management with baseline control.
- Forecasting, including rate escalation.
- Performance measurement, including earned value.
- Variance analysis (schedule and cost.)

Resource Management Software

A resource management system matches available human and other resources to resource requirements and communicates with the managers and planners where and when deficiencies and overages exist or are predicted.

The 27 resource management software products listed in the 1999 PMI Survey do not include any enterprise resource planning (ERP) applications, which enable all resources, both project and nonproject, to be managed on an integrated basis. ERP applications are designed to integrate all business functions into one system and are applied to any or all aspects of an enterprise: finance, marketing, engineering, manufacturing, field operations, project management, and others. PeopleSoft, Oracle, and SAP offer the three most widely used ERP applications, with each having its strengths and weaknesses. Project management software can be integrated into any of these ERP applications. Some of the project management software suites and some resource management systems listed in the 1999 PMI survey claim to handle enterprise-wide resources on their own. Whether or not these can also handle significant nonproject resources may be worthy of investigation.

Communications Management Software

These tools enable the accumulation and efficient dissemination of all pertinent project information to affeted managers and team members.

Key Features

- Progress reporting: physical, schedule, and cost.
- Automation and communication of project documents.
- Web-enabled communication between all project team members.
- Bulletin boards, message triggers, and other team notification devices.

Timesheets (Communications Management Subcategory)

Capturing the work hours expended on specific project tasks is crucial to good project control. Timesheet tools facilitate this by enabling team members to electronically record and report their expended hours. These tools range from very simple to very sophisticated.

Key Features

- Electronic to-do lists for project team members.
- Audit trail for changes to timesheets.
- Interfaces with other project management software packages to automate updates to the project schedule.
- Interfaces with financial systems.
- Customizable views and reports for project team members and managers.

Graphics Add-Ons (Communications Management Subcategory)

This category of tools takes data generated in other software packages and presents it in customizable graphical formats. Traditional project management graphics like Gantt charts, network logic diagrams, breakdown structures, and PERT charts are examples of project management graphic outputs. Examples are given in several chapters in Part II.

Key Features

- Ability to extract data from project management software and other data sources.
- User capability to filter, sort, and select the information and specify various formats customized to specific user needs.

Web Publishers and Organizers (Communications Management Subcategory)

Web organizers is a category of products that accepts a variety of project-related documents and assembles them into a Web site, complete with hyperlinks, creating an online project workbook or placing the entire project management process on the Web, as previously discussed.

Key Features

- Ability to publish reports that are viewable with common Web browsers.
- Creation of electronic project workbooks.
- Publishing project documents and linking via hyperlinks for Web posting.
- Establishing Web-enabled project management processes.

5.4 SELECTION AND IMPLEMENTATION OF PROJECT MANAGEMENT SOFTWARE APPLICATIONS

The project management software market is large, rapidly evolving, and highly competitive. Selection of the best available software suite or packages from among the many competing products to support the various aspects of project management for a specific organization is a complex and demanding project in itself.

Definition of a PM Software Selection, Adaptation, and Implementation Project

Unless an organization is simply in need of a rudimentary scheduling application for use on one simple project, the selection, adaptation, and implementation of a modern project management software suite or set of applications is a challenging, complex project that must be created, planned, and executed using the best project management practices and tools. The basic outline of such a project is presented here as a starter-kit to assist any organization to achieve the objective of upgrading their project planning and control processes, tools, and procedures.

Typically a PM software selection, adaptation, and implementation project will have the four phases shown in the first level of the project/work breakdown structure in Table 5.4. Some of the major elements of each phase are described to provide a better understanding of the complexities involved.

Table 5.4   Preliminary Definition of a Pm Software Selection, Adaptation, and Implementation Project

1. Project Conception (Life-Cycle Phase 1)
   a. Statement of the strategic objectives of the organization that the new project management software application will support.
   b. Description of the future state of project management within the organization that is envisioned within which the new PM software application will operate.
   c. Identification of the logical stages of the development of the PM discipline within the organization, possibly correlated to the stages in a particular project management maturity model (discussed in Chapter 3), with an indication of where the new software to be implemented fits into these stages.
   d. Establish target milestone dates and order of magnitude estimates of the investment required to achieve the project objectives (money and key human resources).
   e. Assign a Project Sponsor and a Project Manager and promulgate an appropriate project charter.
2. Project Definition (Life-Cycle Phase 2):
   a. Statement of project objectives: technical, schedule, and cost.
   b. Systematic definition of the project: elaboration of this project/work breakdown structure (P/WBS), to include:
      i.   Specification of requirements for the new software system (project portfolios; project categories; number of projects; number of resources; business and project processes and documents to be interlinked; existing databases, protocols, hardware and software platforms and servers; other).
      ii.   Documentation of existing and future or reengineered project management processes.
      iii.   Screening of available software to produce a short list for final evaluation.
      iv.   Requests for proposals from short list vendors and evaluation of proposals to select final competitors.
      v.   Test applications of finalists and evaluation of results.
      vi.   Design of modifications to existing systems and procedures required to integrate selected system/applications with business and project processes and documents during the implementation phase, especially if the objective is a Web-enabled project management information system.
      vii.   Recommended system to be acquired and modification work to be accomplished for implementation.
      viii. Detailed plan for the implementation phase, including training as required at all levels.
      ix.   Project master schedule for the implementation phase using the P/WBS structure.
      x.   Cost and resource estimates based on the P/WBS and the project master schedule.
      xi.   Proposal to management for approval of the implementation.

(continued)

Table 5.4 *(Continued)*

3. Project Implementation (Life-Cycle Phase 3):
    a. Project start-up team planning sessions to produce:
        i.   Task/responsibility matrix specifying responsibilities at each level of the P/WBS for the implementation phase.
        ii. Detailed hierarchical schedules based on the P/WBS and project master schedule using CPM/PDM or critical chain network plans.
        iii. Commitment by all project team members to the plans and schedules.
    b. Execution of the defined tasks as scheduled.
    c. Periodic project review meetings to identify problems and issues and assure their prompt resolution.
    d. Reporting to senior executives on progress, problems and to resolve issues as required.
4. Project Closeout (Life-Cycle Phase 4):
    a. Terminate all project work and sign off on all deliverables.
    b. Document the project plans, procedures, experiences and results, including verification of how well the project objectives were achieved, lessons learned, and recommendations for follow-on or future project management improvement projects.
    c. Sign-off of project completion by the project sponsor and project manager.

Time Duration of a Software Selection, Adaptation, and Implementation Project

Depending on the organization's size and complexity and its degree of maturity in project management, the selection, adaptation, and implementation of major improvements in its project management software will require six to twelve months (or more in some cases) to achieve. It may be desirable to implement such major improvements in several stages, either by operating or geographic division, by project portfolio, by project category, or in some other logical fashion.

Factors to Be Considered by Purchasers of Project Management Software Applications

There are many factors to consider when selecting a project management software package as indicated in Table 5.5. A number of these important factors are not directly related to the actual functions or operation of the package. Users have learned through bitter experience that there is a rather high mortality rate among software vendors, and the sudden disappearance of a vendor after considerable effort has been expended to implement and train people in the use of their package is disconcerting and expensive. This means that user support is not available and that the

Table 5.5   Typical Factors Considered by Purchasers of Project Management Software Packages

1. Vendor Reliability and Reputation

Length of time in business	Geographic areas providing sales and
Reputation	support
Size of organization	International areas supported
Focused on project management	Client or reference list
Number of products	Training provided
Financial strength/reliability	Consulting provided

2. Product

General product information	User interface (menu, graphics, mouse)
Synergy with other products	Import/export data to other systems
Project definition data	Calendars: number, use, date formats
Work breakdown structure	Outline format
Scheduling features	Database architecture
Activity definition data	Monitoring data
Resource data	Cost data
Reporting (C/SCSC, other)	Graphic outputs

3. Documentation

Online and multiple-level help	Tutorial
commands	Online tutorial
Additional training materials	Quick reference card
Error correction procedures	
clearly documented	

4. User Support

User support dedicated telephone	24-hour hot line
Toll-free (800) telephone line	Training classes
Workshops for special topics	Consulting to users
Notification to users of upgrades	User groups
Newsletters	Electronic mail
Web site support	

5. Contract Issues

Package functions	Package efficiency
Site licensing	Delivery dates
Modifications to package	Installation and acceptance
Education and training	Support commitment
Upgrade and enhancement policies	Warranty, maintenance agreements
Vendor liability	Price and terms
Vendor bankruptcy (escrow)	Licensee defaults payment
Licensee bankruptcy	Proprietary interest
Confidential data	

Source: Ellodee A. Cloninger, *Project Management Software Buyer's Guidelines* (Cupertino, CA: Pmnet, 1988). Used with permission.

package will not be improved and updated to take advantage of the rapid progress in computer and communications technology.

Each of the product factors listed in Table 5.6 must be further detailed to compare the numerous competing packages objectively. As examples, two of the factors listed in Table 5.5 have been expanded in Table 5.6. It is only at this level of detail that a purchaser can determine if the product will potentially meet the specified user requirements.

Table 5.6   Examples of Typical Detailed Factors to Consider When Selecting a Project Management Software Package

1. Resource Data

Number of resources per project	Number of resources per activity
Resources applied across activity:	Resource constrained schedules
—Uniformly	Resource levelling:
—Unevenly	—Automatic
System notification of resource constraining the schedule	—Across multiple projects
Resource interrupts permitted	Priorities assigned to resources:
Interactive graphic resource profiles	—Early or late dates
Resource reports across multiprojects	—Float/slack values
Change resource units during project	—Other
Multiple billing rates per resource	Resource unit change reflected in schedule change
Absolute resource limits allowed	

2. Cost Data

Types of cost data supported:	Cost fields supported:
—Actual costs	—Fixed
—Committed costs	—Variable
—Original estimates	—User defined
—Revised estimate/how many	Cost summaries supported:
—Target costs	—Activity
Resource costing by:	—Resource
—Total project	—Time unit
—Activity	—Project/work breakdown structure
—Time period	—Across multiprojects
—Prorated over time	—Organization structure
—Work breakdown structure	User defined multiple cost escalation rates
User override system calculated escalations	Cost constraint schedules

Source: Ellodee A. Cloninger, *Project Management Software Buyer's Guidelines* (Cupertino, CA: Pmnet, 1988). Used with permission.

Sources of Assistance in PM Software Selection

It is virtually impossible for the average user of these systems to keep abreast of the continual improvement of the many new software packages available in this field. A number of computer-oriented magazines publish the results of their surveys and ratings of these packages, and several software rating companies offer specialized reports of their proprietary tests. The journals, proceedings, and other publications of various professional associations devoted to or connected with the project management field publish evaluations, findings, and user experience related to project management software applications. An Internet search on "project management" with produce hundreds of hits including the many software developers and vendors of project management applications. The international, national, and regional meetings of the project management professional associations held in many countries almost always have related software vendor, consultant, and trainer exhibitions and demonstrations. Most of the PM software vendors have periodic user conferences that are open to prospective buyers.

5.5   PROJECT PLANNING AND CONTROL AND PMIS

Several important factors related to project planning and control and project management information systems are discussed in the following section.

Systems Do Not Manage or Execute Projects: People Do

The best, most advanced, most comprehensive project management information system (PMIS) will not manage or execute a project: People do that. The general manager, project portfolio steering group, project sponsor, project manager, functional project leaders, and other key team members are the only means of managing projects. People are the only resource that executes projects. Chapters 10 through 14 describe in detail widely accepted practices and processes for planning, risk analysis and mitigation, scheduling, budgeting, authorizing, monitoring, evaluating, and controlling complex projects. For simple projects, most of this information can be carried in one person's head, but for complex high-technology projects, it must be documented using the forms and procedures described.

A good PMIS is a valuable tool that can greatly assist these people in managing their projects. The project management triad—the integrative roles, integrative and predictive planning and control systems, and project teamwork—must be well balanced and mutually supportive to be effective. People must read, absorb, understand, and take action on the information that the system presents to them. In fact, it is these people who create and enter the information into the system in the first place. These points, which may seem obvious, are restated here to help avoid a common trap: Many managers still believe that all they need to introduce or improve project management in their organization is the latest and greatest project management computer software package. They are disappointed and angry when six months after the package has been purchased and installed their projects are still out of control.

Improve the Overall Project Management System, Then Automate the Result

Improvements in an organization's project management capabilities must move forward on three fronts: the integrative roles, project teamwork, and integrated planning and control. As discussed in Chapter 3, documenting and improving the organization's overall project management process is perhaps the most fertile field for improvement efforts in most organizations today. Automating a disjointed, inefficient, archaic process with the best project management package will produce only marginal benefits.

Project Planning Templates and Project Libraries

Many aspects of project planning lend themselves to development of templates or standardized modules that can be stored in hard copy or electronic libraries for future use. Although each project, by definition, is unique and has not been carried out precisely in the same manner before, many if not most of the tasks that make up the project are repetitious. The results of each task may be slightly different, and the duration and resources required may change somewhat, but the basic steps—the process—followed in each task are often identical to a previous task.

Systematic project definition, using the project/work breakdown structure approach, enables recognition and definition of many standardized modules. Key milestone and interface events are frequently identical from one project to another, even though the time between such events may vary considerably. At the task/work package level, the action network plans are at least 80 percent identical in the logical flow of work for similar tasks, even though the duration of some activities in the network plan may vary from project to project. Patterns of resource usage at the task level are often remarkably similar from one project to another.

Rather than ask each new project manager and project team to start with a clean sheet of paper (or blank computer screen) on each new project, it is more efficient to provide the team with a library of planning templates—linked to the appropriate life-cycle phase or subphase—from which they can select, adapt, and integrate to form the plan for their new project.

In past years, network planning templates had to be printed in hard copy, perhaps using transparent adhesive film, which could then be pasted together and marked up manually to form an overall plan. Today, these templates are stored electronically in computer files. They can be called up on the computer screen and projected on a large screen in the team planning theater described in Chapter 11, modified by the team members in joint session, and linked to form an integrated plan. The team members can be given hard copies to review in detail, or they can return to their individual offices and call up the project planning file on their desktop computers to further refine the plan and proceed to the next lower level of detail in the schedule hierarchy. Alternatively, they can carry the files with them on a disc, insert it into their own computer, and proceed with their planning work.

The best experience and most efficient work flow, based on many prior projects and inputs from seasoned veterans, can thus be handed to the less experienced project managers and team members for use in creating their project plans.

In this approach, there is always a danger of having too much standardization and depending too much on established routines, which would stifle creativity and improvement. The project teams must use these templates as guides only, and constantly look for ways to better them. When such improvements are made, they can then be made part of the planning template library, and all others in the organization will then immediately have the benefit of the improvements. These electronic files can easily be transmitted anywhere in the organization or the world via the Internet and Intranets.

CEO DEMANDS: INTEGRATIVE AND PREDICTIVE PROJECT PLANNING AND CONTROL (PP&C)

To achieve effective integrated and predictive project planning and control the CEO must demand that:

1. Every project is planned and controlled within the guidelines specified in the corporate project management process documentation.

(continued)

2. All project planning and control systems and procedures are integrated so that all project information is current and consistent throughout the organization.

3. Only one summarizing project planning and control system is used throughout the organization.

4. The corporate project management process includes a detailed description of the corporate project planning and control system.

5. All information modules shown in Table 5.3 are included in the corporate project management process and the overall corporate information and control system.

6. All project planning, authorizing, controlling, and reporting documents (with specifically approved exceptions) be produced by supporting computer software systems.

7. The project management planning and control system is Web-enabled and uses the full capability of the Internet.

8. The concepts of the P/WBS and project interface management be applied to achieve an effective, sustainable level of detail in project documentation.

6

‹ ›

Project Team and
Key Human Aspects of
Project Management

Recognition that projects are planned and executed through the integrated efforts of a diverse group of people—namely, the project team—and then getting those people to actually function as a team is a fundamental concept underlying effective project management. Together with the identification of the integrative roles discussed in Chapter 4, and the integrative and predictive planning and control systems discussed in Chapter 5 and later chapters, the principles of the project team and teamwork form the triad of concepts that differentiates project management from other types or forms of management. While teamwork is not unique to project management, it is a fundamental requirement for effective management of projects.

In this chapter, the conditions for effective project teamwork are discussed, and a few of the key human aspects of special importance in project management are presented. There are many important topics in the area of interpersonal relations and the management of human resources (communications, negotiations, personal time management, decision making and problem solving, motivation, supervisory skills, leadership, etc.) that are not included here because a number of excellent books are available on these subjects.

6.1 THE PROJECT TEAM CONCEPT

A project is comprised of a number of diverse tasks. Therefore, different people—each having the required expertise and experience—are needed to perform each task. In the broadest sense, all persons contributing to a project are members of the project team. On larger projects where several hundred or even several thousand people are working, we must identify the _key_ project team members. These key team members will include the project manager (the team leader), the functional project leaders, and the lead project support people. More specific identification of the key project team members is given in Chapter 9.

The term _project team members_ is used here generically, and includes people within the project's parent organization as well as people in outside organizations, such as consultants, contractors, vendors, and suppliers. If a project is large enough to be broken in subprojects, then the team concept applies equally to those subprojects. The overall project team would include the subproject manager (or functional project leader) as a team member. In many projects, the client or customer is an active contributor and therefore is included as a member of the team. When possible, inclusion on the project team of representatives of other outside organizations that contribute in some way to the project can be very beneficial. Such organizations include financial institutions, regulatory or oversight agencies, and labor unions.

To have an effective project team, as distinct from simply a group of people working on loosely related tasks, several conditions are necessary:

- Identification of the project team members and definition of the role and responsibilities of each.
- Clearly stated and understood project objectives.
- An achievable project plan and schedule.
- Reasonable rules (procedures regarding information flow, communication, team meetings, and the like).
- Leadership by the project manager.

If one or more of these conditions is not present, it will be difficult to achieve effective teamwork.

6.2 EFFECTIVE TEAMWORK

To have an effective team, the team players must be identified. Project managers often fail to do this, or they may only identify their team members on an "as-needed" basis when a new task comes up that cannot be performed by someone already on the team. In some cases, the project manager may know the team members, but will fail to inform the other members, so only the project manager knows who is on the team.

A useful practice in identifying who is on the project team is to start by identifying the *project stakeholders,* or all those persons who have a stake (a vested interest, responsibility, decision power) in the project and its results. Briner, Giddings, and Hastings (1990) have suggested mapping the principal stakeholders and the project team, as shown in Figure 6.1 (pp. 41–46).

After completing the mapping exercise, a listing of all project team members is compiled and distributed to the entire team. This list should include each team member's full name, address (regular and electronic mail), voice and facsimile telephone numbers, and any other pertinent communication information. Frequently, this list will include home telephone numbers. For those project teams that have established escalation procedures (for resolving issues, conflicts, or other problems), the team member's immediate supervisor with office and home telephone numbers are also listed.

The general duties and responsibilities of each team member will normally be documented by the organization's human resource practices, following the pattern shown in the examples in Chapter 9. However, for effective project teamwork, it is imperative to define the responsibilities of each team member for each task to be carried out on their specific project. The best tool available for this purpose is the task/responsibility matrix illustrated in Chapter 10. This must be based on the project/work breakdown structure, also described in Chapter 10.

Clearly Stated and Understood Project Objectives

The basic project objectives will usually be known prior to identifying the project team members. However, a team effort is required to clarify, expand on, and quantify these initial project objectives to produce statements of objectives that all members of the team understand, accept, and are committed to. Hastings, Bixby, and Chaudhry-Lawson (1987) point out that teams must be aware that there are multiple and often conflicting sets of expectations about their performance on the project, including expectations from outside the project, the team, and each individual team member. These authors suggest thinking about good performance and successful achievement along two dimensions—the hard/soft dimension and the acceptable/excellent dimension. The hard/soft dimension refers to two different kinds of *criteria* of performance, and the acceptable/excellent dimension refers to two different *standards* of performance.

The Hard/Soft Dimension

The hard/soft dimension concerns the tangible and intangible aspects of performance. Hard criteria tend to be measurable, the most frequent being

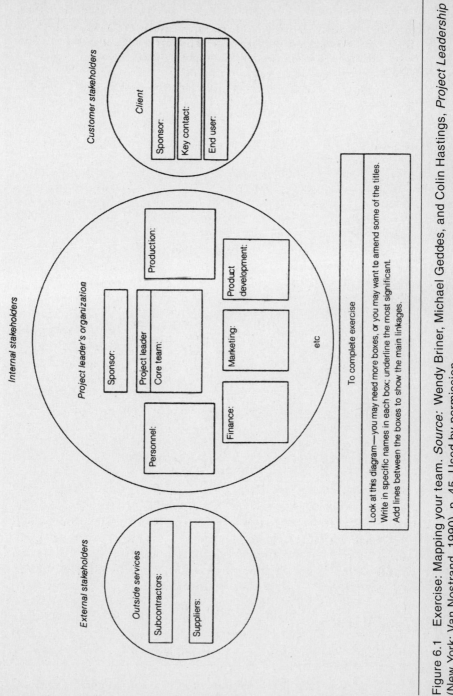

Internal stakeholders

External stakeholders

Customer stakeholders

Project leader's organization

Sponsor:

Project leader
Core team:

Personnel:

Production:

Finance:

Marketing:

Product
development:

etc

Outside services

Subcontractors:

Suppliers:

Client

Sponsor:

Key contact:

End user:

To complete exercise

Look at this diagram—you may need more boxes, or you may want to amend some of the titles.
Write in specific names in each box; underline the most significant.
Add lines between the boxes to show the main linkages.

Figure 6.1   Exercise: Mapping your team. *Source:* Wendy Briner, Michael Geddes, and Colin Hastings, *Project Leadership* (New York: Van Nostrand, 1990), p. 45. Used by permission.

to do with time, cost, resources, and technical standards. Soft criteria on the other hand are more subjective and difficult to measure. Yet, they are clearly used frequently in evaluating performance. They are more about "how" the task was accomplished, the attitudes, skills, and behavior demonstrated by the team and its members.

In setting success criteria ordinary teams tend to concentrate on *hard* criteria only and ask questions such as, "How many, how much and when?" Superteams do all this too (and mostly more punctiliously) but add another dimension. They also draw out clients' and sponsors' more subtle expectations, those to do with ways of working and the relationships with the client, to attitudes adopted on such things as quality, reliability and attention to detail. These are all factors that are crucial to a client's ultimate satisfaction. Equally these soft criteria are explored, clarified and agreed with the sponsor, and service departments.

The Acceptable/Excellent Dimension

The acceptable/excellent dimension on the other hand concerns standards of performance. And it is around this dimension that the whole Superteam idea was originally crystallized. In a world where the best is no longer good enough, the frontiers of performance are always being stretched. "The best can always be bettered" could almost be the Superteam motto. We find many teams who think that their performance is good, but who in fact are underperforming. They may be averagely good when compared with those other teams they see. Their performance is acceptable but in no way outstanding. . . . Superteams strive to be different, and achieve just a little bit more than the competition. They are constantly looking for ways to do things better, constantly testing their assumptions about what is achievable and searching for ways to overcome any problems that lie in the path (Hastings et al., 1987, pp. 35–37).

An Achievable Project Plan and Schedule

Effective teamwork depends heavily on having a project plan and schedule that reflects the way the team members will actually do the work. The team must understand and be committed to the plan and schedule, which must be reasonably achievable. Chapter 10 presents the basic project planning and scheduling tools that have been developed over the past several decades, and Chapter 11 describes more recently developed methods for setting the stage for effective project teamwork.

Reasonable Rules

Trying to achieve good teamwork on a complex project without having established reasonable rules, procedures and practices for how the project will be planned, the work authorized, progress reported and evaluated, conflicts resolved, and so on, is like collecting the best athletes from six different sports and turning them loose on an open, unmarked field with instructions to "play the game as hard as you can."

Each organization must develop its own set of project procedures covering the topics of importance within its environment. On large projects, such procedures are usually tailored to the specific needs of that project and issued to all team members in the form of a project procedures handbook, manual, or some similar document. The project procedures usually rely on established corporate practices and procedures wherever possible, and avoid duplication or conflict with such practices. Many of the tools, methods, and practices described in this book will be tailored and incorporated into the project procedures.

Leadership by the Project Manager

Extensive literature exists on the subject of leadership, and it is not the intent here to treat this complex and important subject in great detail. The key point to be made is that the project manager is expected to be the *leader* of the project. Successful project managers have used many different styles and methods of leadership, depending on their own personalities, experience, interpersonal skills, and technical competence on the one hand, and the characteristics of the project and its environment on the other. Owens concluded the following regarding project leadership and related behavioral topics:

> *Leadership behavior.* Project managers cannot rely on one particular leadership style to influence other people's behavior. Different situations call for different approaches, and leaders must be sensitive to the unique features of circumstances and personalities.
>
> *Motivational techniques.* An awareness of unfulfilled needs residing in the team is required to successfully appraise motivational requirements and adjust a job's design to meet those needs.
>
> *Interpersonal and organizational communications.* Conflict situations occur regularly. A problem-solving or confrontation approach, using informal group sessions, can be a useful resolution strategy.
>
> *Decision-making and team-building skills.* Participative decision making meets the needs of individual team members and contributes toward effective decisions and team unity (Owens, 1982, p. 11).

In their discussion of the project leader as integrator, Briner et al. (1990, pp. 18–30) identify 14 integrative processes that are important to the leader of a project. These are illustrated in Figure 6.2 and more fully explained in their book, *Project Leadership*.

The following sections of this chapter describe useful ideas for project managers to improve their leadership skills.

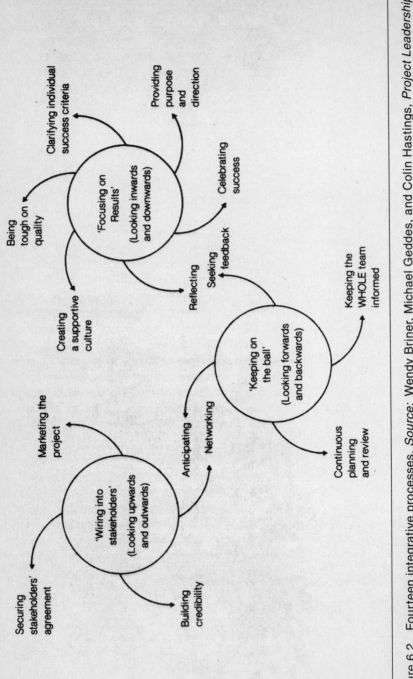

Figure 6.2 Fourteen integrative processes. *Source:* Wendy Briner, Michael Geddes, and Colin Hastings, *Project Leadership* (New York: Van Nostrand, 1990), p. 19. Used by permission.

6.3 CONFLICTS AND THEIR RESOLUTION

The results of a research project by Thamhain and Wilemon (1975) involving 100 project managers identified seven sources of potential conflict:

1. *Project priorities.* The views of project participants often differ over the sequence of activities and tasks that should be undertaken to achieve successful project completion. Conflict over priorities may occur not only between the project team and other support groups but also within the project team.

2. *Administrative procedures.* A number of managerial and administrative-orientated conflicts may develop over how the project will be managed; that is, the definition of the project manager's reporting relationships, definition of responsibilities, interface relationships, project scope, operational requirements, plan of execution, negotiated work agreements with other groups, and procedures for administrative support.

3. *Technical opinions and performance trade-offs.* In technology-oriented projects, disagreements may arise over technical issues, performance specifications, technical trade-offs, and the means to achieve technical performance.

4. *People resources.* Conflicts may arise around the staffing of the project team with personnel from other functional and staff support areas or may arise from the desire to use another department's personnel for project support even though the personnel remain under the authority of their functional or staff superiors.

5. *Cost.* Frequently conflict may develop over cost estimates from support areas regarding various project work breakdown packages. For example, the funds allocated by a project manager to a functional support group might be perceived as insufficient for the support requested.

6. *Schedules.* Disagreements may tend to center around the timing, sequencing, and scheduling of project-related tasks.

7. *Personality conflict.* Disagreements may tend to center on interpersonal differences rather than on "technical" issues. Conflicts often are "ego-centered."

Conflict over schedules is reported to be strong throughout the project life cycle while the other sources of conflict change perceptibly as the project matures. Conflict over project priorities ranked second to schedules throughout the life cycle, human resources ranked third, disagreements over technical opinions and tradeoffs fourth, and administrative procedures fifth. Personality conflicts ranked low in intensity by the project managers, although it is sometimes difficult to determine if a particular conflict is one over technical issues or personality, for example. Cost, although very important as a basic performance measurement factor, ranked lowest as a conflict source. Many of the other conflicts have an impact on project schedule and cost, of course.

Conflict Handling Modes

The most and least important modes of conflict resolution, as reported by Thamhain and Wilemon (1975), are:

1. *Confrontation problem solving.* Facing the conflict directly which involves a problem-solving approach whereby parties work through their disagreements.

2. *Compromising.* Bargaining and searching for solutions that bring some degree of satisfaction to the parties in a dispute. Characterized by a "give-and-take" attitude.

3. *Smoothing.* De-emphasizing or avoiding areas of difference and emphasizing areas of agreement.

4. *Forcing.* Exerting one's viewpoint at the potential expense of another. Often characterized by competitiveness and a win/lose situation.

5. *Withdrawal.* Retreating or withdrawing from an actual or potential disagreement.

While confrontation was the most favored mode for dealing with superiors, compromise was more favored in handling disagreements with functional support departments.

Responsibility Conflicts

Conflict over administrative procedures often results from overlapping responsibilities between project and functional managers. The functional project leader receives direction from two persons, the project manager and the functional superior. This dual responsibility can lead to ambiguities and to increased conflict if the charter of the project manager is not properly defined and understood.

Conversely, responsibility conflicts are minimized if all parties have a clear understanding of the role and responsibilities of the project manager. In an oversimplified manner, the division of responsibilities may be described as:

- _The project manager_ provides direction regarding _what_ the project tasks are, _when_ they should start and finish to meet the overall project goals, and _how much money_ is _available_ to perform the work.

- _The functional manager_ provides direction regarding _who_ will perform the tasks, _how_ the technical work will be accomplished, and _how much money_ is _required_ to perform the work.

It is impossible to differentiate these responsibilities sharply. In each case, negotiation between the project and functional managers is usually necessary. There will still be numerous occasions where honest differences can only be resolved by higher authority, but the objective is to call on such authority only when absolutely necessary. The concept of the project manager as an interface manager as described in Chapter 13 has proven to be a useful way to minimize such conflicts.

Conflict in Project Management Is Inevitable

Conflict of the various types described is inevitable in planning and controlling projects. It is important for project managers to be aware of the potential sources of conflict and to be alert to when they might occur over the life cycle of the project. This knowledge can help the project manager avoid much of the detrimental effects of conflict and to get the most beneficial results from the conflict and the process of resolving it. Beneficial results from conflict include development of new information that enables better decisions. In dealing with conflict the project manager needs to know the advantages and disadvantages of the various methods for conflict resolution so that she can use the most effective method for that particular situation.

6.4   FRAMEWORK FOR PROJECT TEAM DEVELOPMENT

Mower and Wilemon (1986) have developed a useful framework for team development. The ideas that emanate from that framework are called _actions for team building,_ and state:

> Team development is a process similar to individual development. Just as people mature through certain phases, teams go through noticeable phases. Teams mature in terms of task progress and in terms of interpersonal relations. At each phase of development certain problems can occur. Team managers can stave off such problems through team building. In this way team progress is not slowed. (pp. 297–298)

Mower and Wilemon's framework (Table 6.1) describes four phases of task development and four phases of interpersonal relations development. In

Table 6.1   A Framework for Team Development

Team Development Tasks	Personal Issues Facing Team Members	Examples of Team Building Actions for Each Development Phase
Phase I		
Climate Setting/ Initiating What's our mission? How will we get started?	*Inclusion* How will I fit in? What will the other team members be like?	Clarifying the team's mission "Signing on" and including members Establishing a positive climate Building team identity
Phase II		
Goal Setting/ Work Planning What specific goals need to be developed? What roles need to be performed? What team procedures do we need?	*Power and Conflict* Will my contribution count? How can I influence the team? How can I maintain my identity and also be a "team player"?	Identifying goals Assigning and negotiating roles Identifying needed team procedures Determining how the team will relate to the "external world," e.g., management, the sponsor, functional groups Balancing team and individual recognition Managing conflict
Phase III		
Implementing How do we keep up momentum and team morale? How do we maintain performance standards? How do we stay on track?	*Personal Performance within a "Larger System"* What standards will I try to meet: mine? the team's? the organization's? How do I keep up my energy and interest? How do I relate to the team manager?	Assessing the impact of team norms on performance Assessing on-going performance Encouraging lagging performers Keeping team progress visible Reaffirming team-leader trust
Phase IV		
Evaluating Team Results/Following Up Did we meet our performance expectations? How do we sell team results? What are our next steps?	*Dealing with Success/ Failure and Transition* How has my contribution been evaluated? What have I learned? How satisfied am I? How do I let go of the team?	Reviewing team progress Sharing experiences and feelings Consolidating the learning Recognizing individual contributors Celebrating Providing closure

Source: Judith Mower and David Wilemon, "A Framework for Developing High-Performing Technical Teams," *Engineering Team Management.* David I. Cleland and Harold Kerzner, Van Nostrand, Reinhold, New York, 1986, p. 300. Used by permission.

addition, typical examples of team-building actions used in each phase are briefly identified. This framework also applies, in microcosm, to planning and running team meetings.

In summary, the ability to create and lead a project team that is focused on well-understood objectives with a sound project plan, using appropriate operating procedures and integrative planning and control methods, lies at the heart of effective project management.

6.5 BUILDING COMMITMENT IN PROJECT TEAMS*

The Importance of Commitment in the Matrix

Since the project manager role usually must be carried out within a functional organization structure (for the total project at the owner or sponsor level, or pieces of the project at the contractor, subcontractor, supplier, or other contributing organization level), the resulting matrix creates a number of difficulties. These include confusion regarding responsibilities and authority, conflicts between functional and project goals and priorities, and related problems (Elmes and Wilemon, 1988, pp. 54–63).

One of the greatest challenges, or sources of difficulty, for the project manager in the matrix situation relates to commitment: First, how to get the commitments from the functional contributors that are necessary to achieve project objectives; and second, how to assure that these commitments, once made, are in fact fulfilled (Lawrence and Lorsch, 1967, pp. 142–151). This is the human management part of the task—getting behavior to reflect project goals, priorities, and interdependencies.

The project manager's job can be viewed as comprising two parts:

1. *Planning and Control.* Setting project goals and objectives; developing integrated plans, schedules and budgets; achieving the best allocation of available resources; authorizing and controlling the work; monitoring progress, replanning, identifying variances, taking or causing corrective actions.

2. *Leadership.* Influencing others and developing a sense of commitment in all persons contributing to or involved in the project.

*This section has been adapted from Rossy, Gerald R., and Russell D. Archibald, "Building Commitment in Project Teams," *Project Management Journal, XXIII,* 2 (June 1992). The authors wish to thank Dr. Frank Wagner for his contribution to the initial development of some of the concepts presented in this section.

Project plans and schedules are important prerequisites for gaining commitments on projects. Functional managers and project leaders have to know what tasks they are committing to and when the resources required for these tasks will be required, before they can make a serious personal commitment to the project manager. Progress must be monitored, plans and schedules revised, and any scope or schedule changes communicated in order to assure that the functional contributors honor their commitments. Any changes in past performance and future plans must be communicated to those whose commitments are affected by these changes. These topics are discussed extensively in the project management literature, but their importance with regard to commitment has not been widely recognized.

Two levels of commitment on projects can be identified: *organizational,* primarily indicated by the commitment of money, people, and other resources to a task or project; and *personal,* indicated by an individual's sense of dedication to assigned responsibilities, tasks or projects. Our discussion applies to both of these levels, but we will focus primarily on the personal level of commitment. (Personal aspects of commitment are also involved in organizational commitments, since these are made by persons acting for the organization rather than for themselves as individuals.)

Leadership and Commitment

While much has been written about leadership and its importance in management, little information has been published about the role of commitment in the leader's ability to lead, and its logical counterpart in followers (Buchanan, 1974, 1985; Mowdray et al., 1982; Salaneik, 1977). Exacting commitment from oneself and from others are opposite sides of the same coin; together they provide the necessary energy to bring together the resources and motivation of a project team.

Before commitment can be developed in others, the project manager must provide vision, direction, and support to the project team members. *Providing vision* consists of defining and communicating direction, goals, and values in a way that is clear and understandable to all members of the project team (Kouzes and Posner, 1988, p. 108). This vision is usually communicated at the corporate level through the strategic planning process, policy manuals, and mission statements although it can just as easily be communicated through the "language of the (organization's) surrounding culture" (Elmes and Wilemon, 1988, p. 54). At the operational level, however, projects are the building blocks for implementing corporate vision. Creation and selection of projects to be funded, or choosing which requests for proposals for new projects to respond to, unambiguously communicate the vision that top managers have for the organization. At the project level, it is equally important to provide vision through clearly stated objectives and through communicating how the project supports the higher level objectives and strategies of the organization.

Developing commitment also requires giving individuals the *direction* and *support* needed to carry out their responsibilities. This second set of needs is satisfied through job descriptions, annual and quarterly objectives (MBOs), budgets, and so on, for the structured, functional organization. At the project level, individuals are given direction and support through the basic planning and control tools and procedures: Statements of project objectives and scope, the project/work breakdown structure, the project master plan and schedule, detailed task plans and schedules, integrated evaluation and control procedures, the task/responsibility matrix, and the like.

All of these topics are discussed in other chapters and, while they are necessary to successfully manage a project, they are not sufficient. There must also exist a strong *sense of commitment* on the part of those who will do the work and accomplish the goals. Our focus here is on the means for obtaining commitments and assuring that those commitments are fulfilled.

While commitment is critical to any endeavor, whether individual or group, little information is available about what leads to commitment and even less about how to manage it. In the following sections, we will examine what is required to get the commitment of others and how the project manager can be a critical factor in managing that commitment.

Understanding Commitment

Most management research has focused on "organizational commitment"—identifying the determinants of organizational loyalty and their relationship to turnover of personnel. With a few exceptions, the relationship between commitment and organizational performance has essentially been ignored, especially with respect to how it applies within the culture of project management and matrix environments. We will examine what commitment is and how it can be directed to improve project management effectiveness.

In discussing the process through which an individual becomes committed to organizational beliefs, Sathe observes that "he or she internalizes them, that is, when the person comes to hold them as personal beliefs or values" (Sathe, 1985, p. 12). For our purposes, individual commitment is defined as consisting of two separate facets: (1) having a clear set of beliefs, values, and goals; and (2) behaving in a manner that is consistent with those beliefs and goals. Commitment is knowing where you want to go and being persistent in your efforts to get there. Project managers must be able to demonstrate a high level of commitment in their own behavior and to instill an equal degree of commitment in those with whom they work. Winograd and Flores (1986) describe an effective organization as one that has a strongly woven web or network of commitments that are made, observed, and honored, and that the manager's role is to create, coordinate, and enforce those commitments. Members of a project team cannot be expected to have strong commitment to the project unless (1) the objectives are clear and understood, (2) a plan and schedule exists to which the team members can personally commit, and (3) the project manager displays strong commitment within their areas of responsibility.

Development of commitment takes place throughout the life cycle of a project. It can be thought of as a process of socialization and group development through which the project members develop and reinforce specific values and norms. This socialization can be accelerated through the use of "start-up workshops" to more quickly obtain the buy-in of project team members and clients. (See Chapter 12.)

Key Behaviors for Managing Commitment

Understanding the importance of commitment and what it means is not sufficient to elicit commitment from others. As with any other aspect of project leadership, managing commitment requires specific skills that individuals may or may not already have in varying degrees. Even those individuals with well-developed skills often have what might be termed "unconscious competence." They are successful but are not fully recognizant of what it is that makes them able to gain commitment from others. To maximize their effectiveness, project managers must become more "consciously competent" about how they can best manage commitment.

Two general types of behaviors, in combination, are needed to promote commitment—*supporting* behaviors and *innovating* behaviors. Supporting behaviors are those that lead to and build overall commitment. Innovating behaviors are those that create opportunities and the desire to exceed initial performance expectations and goals through improvements. Each of these two classes of behavior can be further divided into more specific skills. A balance among these behaviors is needed to obtain commitment from others.

Supporting Behaviors

Four key supporting behaviors build project management commitment:

1. Focusing on what is most important.
2. Demonstrating through example.
3. Rewarding contribution and results.
4. Managing disrespect.

Innovating Behaviors

Commitment is helpful only up to a certain point. There are times when commitment can be dysfunctional. That time arrives when an individual's inflexibility prevents him or her from recognizing or searching for a better way to accomplish goals. Any commitment must be balanced with a willingness to change when necessary. In project situations, tradeoffs are often required between project scope, quality, performance, cost, and schedule, especially when unexpected and unplanned events occur. A team member who remains totally committed to the original plans, regardless of changing circumstances, is not effective. Because of the need to frequently respond to changes, the project manager and project team members need to understand the higher level vision, objectives, and strategies which the project is intended to support, in order to respond most effectively to those changes. This can also be described as management innovation.

We have identified four behaviors to be important in managing commitment to innovation. They are:

1. Searching for improvements.
2. Challenging expectations.
3. Creating an open environment.
4. Encouraging risk-taking.

Where to Apply Commitment Building Behaviors

Up to this point we have only discussed *how* a project leader must act—what behaviors he or she must exhibit day in and day out to ensure that the project team achieves results on schedule and under budget. There is a second important part to the equation, *where* these behaviors should be applied—the targets of the eight commitment behaviors discussed above.

There are six key areas in which project leaders should be practicing commitment building behaviors. Each of these areas must be continually *supported* and when necessary, *improved*. They are:

1. Organizational values.
2. The organization and higher management.
3. The project clients and sponsors.
4. The project goals and tasks.
5. The project team and its members.
6. Themselves as project managers.

Summary and Conclusions

To be successful, project leaders must develop commitment in an environment with a variety of conflicting demands and factors. That commitment is demonstrated by a balanced combination of what we have described as *supporting* and *innovating* behaviors. The keys to obtaining commitment from others are simple in concept but require constant attention and reinforcement. They are:

1. Providing others with a positive role model for all aspects of commitment to others (that is, leading by example).
2. Encouraging continuous feedback from everyone on performance, progress, and opportunities for improvement.
3. Giving adequate attention to both supporting current plans and striving for improvements.
4. Maintaining a balance among priorities.

Project managers who gain the commitment of their project team members, and actively manage that commitment throughout the planning and execution of their projects, will have a higher probability of achieving their project objectives.

CEO DEMANDS: PROJECT TEAMS

Regarding project teams, the CEO must demand that:

1. The importance of the project team concept be conveyed to all contributors to every project in the organization.
2. Every project team member understands:
   a. The project objectives.
   b. The project plan and schedule.
   c. The rules to be followed in the project management life-cycle process, including issue and conflict escalation procedures.
3. Every project manager receives adequate leadership, conflict resolution, and commitment building training.

7

‹ ›

Organizing the Project Management Function and Office

Creating the proper organizational setting for project management must be accomplished in the absence of well-known principles such as those that apply when organizing a traditional, functionally oriented structure. No single organizational pattern has yet emerged to answer the following organizational questions:

Organizing to Manage Individual Projects

- How will the project manager and other integrative responsibilities (discussed in Chapter 4) be assigned and interrelated?

- To whom should project managers report? At what level, and within which part of the organization?

- Who should be assigned as full-time project office members reporting directly to a given project manager, and who should contribute as project participants while remaining in their functional departments?

- How are specialist staff skills in project planning and control, contract administration, finance, legal, and so on, best provided to project managers and teams?

Management of Multiple Projects

- Who is responsible for development and operation of multiproject, integrated project planning and control systems?

- Who should hold what specific responsibilities for multiproject management and to whom should they report?

Overall Project Management Function for the Enterprise

- Where will the manager of project management be located organizationally?
- How will this important position relate to the project portfolio steering group, the sponsors assigned to major projects, and the various program and project managers?
- Should there be established a project management office (PMO) and/or center of project management excellence at the corporate or lower level to provide a home for the project management function and for the manager of project management?

In this chapter, the underlying factors influencing the answers to these questions are discussed and where possible some basic guidelines are set forth. Illustrations are provided of various organizational arrangements used by a number of different companies.

7.1   ORGANIZATIONAL ALTERNATIVES FOR PROJECT MANAGEMENT

Three basic alternative forms of organization have been used for the planning and execution of projects: (1) purely functional, (2) function/project matrix, and (3) purely project (that is, a functional organization devoted solely to one project). Each of these has its strengths and weaknesses. Each can be made to work, with varying degrees of effectiveness, depending upon the characteristics of the basic organization (size, degree of rigidity, nature of the business, culture, and habits) and of the projects (number, size, complexity, degree of uniqueness, duration, and other factors discussed in Chapter 2).

Companies and agencies typically evolve their approach to managing their projects through some combination of these basic forms. Initially, most organizations are structured along the classic functional pyramid lines, with separate departments for marketing, engineering, financial, manufacturing or other operations, and staff specialists for legal, treasury, human resources, administration, and so on. Product lines, geography, technologies, and customers are often also represented in the pyramidal structure. As projects within the functional organization become more numerous, larger, and more complex, and as schedule and/or cost performance becomes more critical, the managers introduce changes which lead them either to a functional/project matrix solution or to establish essentially stand-alone, "projectized" organizations.

Often, a series of failures in the purely functional organization (as discussed in Chapter 3) forces the senior managers to look for a better way. It is rarely possible to establish a completely separate organization for each and every project due to the cost of duplicating all the needed specialized skills and facilities. The result is that most organizations find themselves in a function/project matrix of some kind.

The Functional/Project Matrix Organization

Operating in a functional/project matrix organization is well known to be rife with difficulties. It is not an easy task to introduce the role of the project manager into a long-established, highly bureaucratic functional structure, and then to achieve the proper balance of responsibility and authority between functional and project managers. The crux of the problem is that at some level people within the functional departments must receive direction from two sources: functional and project. They view this as "having two bosses," and that is thought to be a violation of good management practice. Without the proper understanding of the difference between functional direction on one hand and project direction on the other, this situation will produce substantial, undesirable, and costly conflict.

Chapter 4 describes the several important integrative roles in project management, including the functional and project manager roles. The differences between project and functional direction are defined there. These undesirable conflicts can be minimized if all concerned have a sound understanding of these roles and conduct themselves accordingly. The responsibilities and authority of these roles are further discussed in Chapters 8 and 9. As described in Chapter 13, project managers who conduct themselves as interface managers will be involved with minimum conflict with all project contributors.

There is a broad range of organizational possibilities in designing a matrix organization. Figure 7.1 illustrates the matrix continuum from weak to strong between a fully functional and fully separate project organization. Many organizations can trace their continuing maturity in project management along this continuum.

The Project Taskforce

Frequently organizations find it useful to physically locate a large part of the project team in one place to enhance communication, control, and teamwork. Large engineering/construction companies often use this

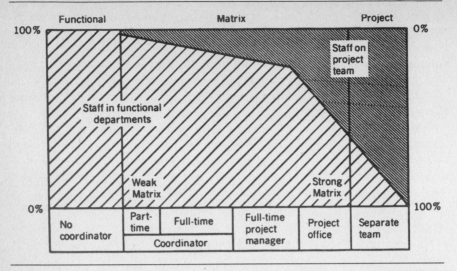

Figure 7.1   Organizational Continuum 1. *Source:* Robert, Youker, "Organizational Alternatives for Project Management," *Project Management Quarterly,* 8, no. 1 (March 1975). Used by permission.

approach. Some may view this as a "projectized" organization, but many times it is still a matrix, since the functional contributors are not always transferred formally (especially for performance reviews and pay increases) from their home departments to the project department. However the physical proximity of most if not all team members overcomes some of the problems of a matrix situation and usually improves the team efficiency.

7.2   REPORTING RELATIONSHIPS OF PROJECT MANAGERS

After a major project has been identified and the decision made to assign a project manager, the next decisions regarding the level in the organization and the specific part of the organization in which she will be placed are crucial to the manager's effectiveness.

Reporting Location of a Project Manager

The project manager must report to the line executive or manager who will actually resolve essentially all of the conflicts within and between the projects to be managed. Thus, a project manager could properly report to the manager of a department, division, product line, or to the general manager or managing director of a company. For very large projects involving several companies, he would probably report to the managing director of the "lead house" that has prime contractual responsibility.

The size, scope, and nature of the project are key factors in determining where the project manager should report. The number of projects within the organization and the existence or absence of a project management office or other formalized multiproject responsibility will also influence the decision. The executive rank, seniority, experience, and personality of the project manager will also have a direct effect on the final decision regarding the reporting location.

Project managers typically feel that their job would be easier if they reported to the highest executive in the organization. Experience indicates that this is not always the case. A reporting level that is too high can be as ineffective as one that is too low, for different reasons. If the reporting level is too high, the result can be serious and unneeded conflict with senior line managers, impeded communication with functional managers contributing to the project, or unresponsiveness to the project manager caused by the separation of several levels of organization, causing him to resort to using the power of his reporting position, further increasing conflict and retarding communication. If too low, as for instance reporting to a department (or lower) manager when four other departments are contributing significantly to the project, the result can be inability of the project manager to get needed cooperation from the other departments, or inability to evaluate critically and objectively the contribution of the department to which he is assigned. In either case, the project will suffer because the project manager is not located at the level commensurate with the needs of the project.

7.3   PROJECT MANAGEMENT OFFICE

One measure of the maturity of an organization in project management is the recognition that it must establish a home for the project management function—the project management office (PMO), or some similar title—at an appropriate level and reporting to an appropriate senior executive.

The term *project office* is sometimes used for this project management office. It is recommended that the project office title be used only to refer to a specific, individual project (or program) office, that is, the office of one project (or program) manager, as described in Chapters 8 and 9. The project management office has distinctly broader and different responsibilities than an individual project/program office.

An additional possible organizational entity must be recognized that impacts the project management capabilities of an organization. That is what can be termed generically a *multiproject operations planning and control* function that provides planning, scheduling, and control for a large number of smaller projects, as defined in Chapter 2. None of these smaller projects can justify the assignment of a full-time project manager or the full application of systematic project management planning and control. However, in the aggregate, these projects can comprise a significant portion of the organization's overall business. This function is discussed in some detail in Chapter 8. Conceivably, this function could be included within the responsibilities of a PMO that are described next.

Alternative Charters for the Project Management Office

Current project management literature describes a wide range of alternative charters for PMOs at various levels in an organization. A PMO can be designed to meet the needs of a total enterprise or corporation, a business unit, an operating division, a project portfolio, or a multiproject program.

The organizational scope and services to be performed for the organization by the PMO can vary widely as indicated by the following possible alternatives:

Range of Organizational Scope
- Corporate/enterprise-wide.
- Business unit/operating division.
- Product line.
- Project portfolio.
- Multiproject program.
- Individual projects (replacing or overlapping with the individual project office).

Range of Responsibilities
- Design, develop, implement, operate, and continually improve the enterprise-wide project management system.
- Design, develop or acquire, implement, operate and continually improve (through appropriate management research and development) the organization's project management processes, systems and tools:
  —The project portfolio management process.
  —The project life-cycle management process (PLCMS) for each category of projects in the organization.

—Project management computer software applications in support of the PLMCS for each project category and the enterprise-wide project management system.

- Acquire, disseminate, and apply project management knowledge (the PM Center of Excellence):

—Identify best project management and related practices within the organization's industrial or other sector.

—Capture, document, archive, retrieve and promulgate the organization's project management experiences, good and bad, within the organization for use with continual improvement efforts.

—Disseminate this information throughout the organization in practical, useful ways to all affected persons.

—Assure that the available information and knowledge is actually being applied appropriately within the organization.

- Provide project management training and indoctrination:

—Design and deliver, in close cooperation with and through the appropriate training departments, the manager and specialist training and indoctrination needed to properly implement and use the organization's project management processes, systems, and tools.

—Evaluate and recommend the use of external training resources in project management as appropriate.

- Provide project management consulting and mentoring:

—Conduct project risk assessments as requested using the most appropriate risk analysis and management approach for the situation.

—Provide proposal assistance as required to assure that the project management aspects of proposals are adequately covered.

—Provide facilitator/consulting assistance for project start-up planning workshops (see Chapter 12).

—Conduct project performance audits of active projects as requested to identify opportunities for improvement and recommend corrective actions.

—Provide on-the-job mentoring, training, and consultation to program and project managers and to project specialists as required in all aspects of project management, including the operation and use of project management software applications.

- Develop and supply project managers and project management specialists:

—Develop and oversee the administration of career paths in project management for project managers and project planning and control specialists.

—Establish through the appropriate human resources departments effective performance and salary review procedures for project and program managers and project management specialists.

—Establish assignments within the PMO that provide useful experience to project management specialists and unassigned or potential project managers in preparation for their assignment to positions with greater responsibilities.

• Provide direct support to individual projects:

—Provide administrative support to active project managers.

—Provide specialist support to active project managers in risk management, project planning, resource estimating, project control, reporting, variance analysis, issue tracking, change control, contract administration, and other areas as required.

—Establish and operate a project control center with appropriate graphic displays and audio/visual aids and equipment for use in conducting project review meetings with each project team.

It is not recommended that an organization attempt to establish a PMO overnight with all of these potential responsibilities. Rather a logical evolutionary plan must be established that builds on the existing situation and in a series of steps or phases extends the PMO responsibilities as its success is demonstrated through its performance to date.

Implementation and Evolution of the PMO

The development of an effective project management office is normally an evolutionary process in most organizations. Block (1998) presents a useful discussion of the range of services that can be provided by such offices at different organizational levels together with a plan for their implementation.

Knutson (1999) identifies three basic variations in the role of the project management office together with their primary responsibilities:

1. The PMO in a staff role:
   a. Keeper of the methodology.
   b. Mentoring/coaching.
   c. Librarian.

   d. Source of history.

   e. Prescreening of phase review reports.

2. The PMO in an enterprise-administrative role; the above plus:

   a. Multiproject reporter.

   b. Priority-setting coordinator.

   c. Resource tracker.

   d. Administrator.

   e. Monitor.

   f. Change controller.

3. The PMO in a line role; all of the above plus:

   a. Manager of projects.

   b. Leader.

Implementation of a PMO in an Information Technology (IT) Organization

Stratton (2001) describes how the PMO concept was used at two levels, the corporate (national) level and the program level, to implement "key operations engineering (OE) disciplines, which enable the perennially short-handed IT departments to function and scale to meet the demands of today's fast-paced business environment." He describes the responsibilities of the PMO at each of these levels and explains how the PMOs focus on basic processes that are simple and easy to use and prescribe how to accomplish tasks and roles on programs and projects. Their national level PMO is called the *3P PMO Process,* referring to *Process > Proposal > Project,* with a number of phases within each of these. Each phase is defined in detail with its required deliverables. They track all programs and projects through this 3P PMO Process and its subsidiary phases, and use qualified metrics at the national level to determine the profit margin on each program and project. Stratton (2001) also presents detailed illustrations of the program scorecards used to track and report on the programs and projects and their deliverables.

Benefits of a Project Management Office

Block (1998) lists the benefits of a PMO that matures into a full-service provider of project management as:

Global recognition.
Profitability improvement.

Productive project teams.

Organizational improvement.

Culture shift to project management.

Staff professionalism in project management.

Predictable, reusable PM tools and techniques.

As a result, "The hidden benefit of the project [management] office is the gradual assimilation of project management into the entire organization" (Block, 1998). Indeed, this is the ultimate goal for creating the PMO organization.

Problems and Pitfalls with PMOs

Not every attempt at establishing a PMO has been successful over the years. Many PMOs have been established, flourished for a time, and then have disappeared. The fundamental issue is one of centralization versus decentralization, coupled with the temptation that many practitioners have to build an empire.

The issue of how much centralization can be addressed by looking at the range of responsibilities of a PMO that were listed earlier. Some of these, having to do with the overall processes, methods, systems, and tools for the total organization, clearly should be centralized. Others, primarily those dealing with planning and control of individual programs and projects and the reporting relationships of the several program and project managers, are not so clear-cut.

One principle that is important to recognize is that the project planning and control support services provided to a major project manager should be directly controlled by that manager. Especially on larger projects that required full-time support specialists, these persons should report directly to the project (or program) manager. Attempts to centralize those support services and simply dish out the information to the various project managers usually are not very successful, for several reasons. The detailed knowledge of the schedule, budget, expenditures, and related forecasts are the life blood of the project and vital to every project manager. Having this information produced entirely by an independent centralized staff that knows the problems it reveals even before the project manager is aware of them is not acceptable to an experienced project manager. The result will often be that he will develop his own set of plans and schedules that he will use to manage the project, thus creating much duplication of effort and confusion in the various management reports that are being circulated.

The question of whether some or all project managers should report to the manager of project management in the PMO is also a difficult one. If all major project managers so report this results in the manager of project management becoming an extremely powerful position—and therefore a likely target to be "cut down to size" by political rivals in the organization. Depending on the reporting level of the PMO and its organizational scope, it may be much more effective to have the individual project managers report to various line executives. The manager of project management can still exert her staff authority in the project management discipline over all of the project managers, but would not have day-to-day line authority over all projects.

If the person given the job of manager of project management sees the assignment as an opportunity to build a PMO empire, and tries to capitalize on the interest in project management in that way, without considering all of the longer term ramifications and respecting the position and authority of the involved program and projects managers, then the PMO will probably not last very long.

Example of a Failed PMO

McMahon and Busse (2001) provide a useful and interesting description of the rise and fall of a project management office in the information system (IS) area. Some of the problems they describe that led to the fall of the PMO are:

- Staffing the PMO with PM experts with little knowledge of IS.
- Reluctance of the IS manager to spread the word about the benefits of PM and the PMO outside the IS department.
- The IS applications manager had several reservations about PM and the PMO concept, leading to dissension and mistrust in the leadership team, staff conflict, and some staff turnover.
- The Y2K effort was a primary driving force in setting up the PMO and when it was over the impetus for moving toward an enterprise-wide PMO was removed. After Y2K there was pressure to use the budget dollars on other initiatives.
- The PMO manager left the organization followed by the departure of the corporate champion for the PMO concept.
- A new IS director took over with a new set of initiatives, and this was the final blow for this PMO, which was disbanded.

McMahon and Busse list these recommendations for assuring the success of a PMO implementation:

- *Place it at the top.* It is critical that the PMO be placed at the highest operational level or reporting to a steering committee at the highest operational level.

- *Build deep roots.* The importance of building coalitions, enterprise level placement of the PMO, and recurring staff education all contribute to building deep organizational roots that cannot be pulled out by a change in personnel, no matter the level.

- *Communicate.* Establish a communication plan to the entire organization regarding the benefits of a PMO.

- *Demonstrate value added.* Implement easy-to-read reports distributed to the entire enterprise via company intranet or e-mail that describe successes and demonstrate the benefits of learning from failures.

- *Lessons learned sessions.* On completion of each project hold a lessons learned session open to all levels of participants, and build a knowledge management repository.

- *Build project manager professionalism.* Treat the project manager role as a professional one, develop formal staff training, encourage professional affiliations and certification.

These authors list a number of other actions that will continue to build professionalism in project managers and the project specialist staff.

7.4   STAFFING PROJECTS: THE PROJECT OFFICE AND PROJECT TEAM

Alternative Staffing Methods

The three basic alternatives (ordinarily used in combination) in staffing a project are:

1. Assign people directly to the individual project office, under the control of the project manager.
2. Assign tasks required for the project to specific functional departments or specialized staffs.
3. Contract for project tasks with outside organizations.

The project manager typically desires to have all the people contributing to his project assigned full-time to the project organization or office that he directly manages. In most situations, this is undesirable, if not impossible, because:

- Skills required by the project vary considerably as the project matures through each of its life-cycle phases.
- Building up a large, permanently assigned project office for each project inevitably causes duplication of certain skills (often those in short supply), carrying of people who are not needed on a full-time basis or for a long period, and causing personnel difficulties in reassignment.
- The project manager may tend to be diverted from his primary task and become the project engineer, for example, as well as having to become concerned with the supervision, administration, and personnel problems of a large office rather than concentrating on managing all aspects of the project itself.
- Professionally trained people often prefer to work within a group devoted to their professional area, with permanent management having qualifications in the same field, rather than to be isolated from their specialty peers by being assigned to and physically located with a project staff.
- Projects are subject to sudden shifts in priority or even to cancellation, and full-time members of a project office are thus exposed to potentially serious threats to their job security; this often causes reluctance on the part of some people to accept a project assignment requiring transfer to a project office.

All of these factors favor keeping the full-time project office staff as small as possible and depending on established functional departments and specialized staffs to the greatest extent possible for performance of the various tasks necessary to complete the project. This approach places greater emphasis on the planning and control procedures used on the project.

On the other hand, there are valid reasons for assigning particular persons with various specialties to the project office. These specialties usually include:

- Systems analysis and engineering (or equivalent technical discipline), and product quality and configuration control if the product requires such an effort.
- Project planning, scheduling, control, and administrative support.

Experience of many companies indicates that at least these specialties must be under the direct control of the project manager if he is to be able to carry out his assigned responsibilities effectively. Setting up a large project office staff by transferring people to it from the functional departments may be done to achieve better control of the work, in the absence of effective planning and control procedures or systems.

Organization of Project Participants

The team of project participants includes all persons to whom specific project tasks have been assigned, including those directly under the project manager in the project office, in functional departments, on specialized staffs, or in outside organizations.

Figure 7.2 illustrates a generalized organization for an industrial project showing all participants and indicating the persons and functions desirable to have in the project office (under the direct authority of the project manager), and those participants almost always indirectly related to the project manager. The persons and facilities that may vary in their reporting relationship, depending on the situation, are also indicated.

Some or all members of the product design group are justified in being assigned to the project office if:

- Continuous, close communication is required with other members of the project office.
- They are needed for extended periods of time (e.g., six months or more).
- There is otherwise a low confidence that they will be able to spend the agreed upon time and effort on the project. In other words, inadequate control of work assignment exists.

Extreme care is required to select only those persons who are definitely justified in being assigned to the project office before such transfers are made. A practical alternative is to identify those engineers and other specialists within the functional departments who are to perform the assigned project tasks, and physically group these people together, either within the functional department or within the project office. In this case, the people are not formally transferred to the project office but maintain their permanent relationships to their functional departments.

The manufacturing project coordinator should probably remain within the functional manufacturing organization because of the need for close coordination and contact with the manufacturing people.

The field project manager will probably retain a permanent relationship with the field organization, such as the installation or other field operations department, and report to the project manager on an indirect basis, especially if the project is relatively short or if the field project manager is involved with several projects at once. When this phase of the

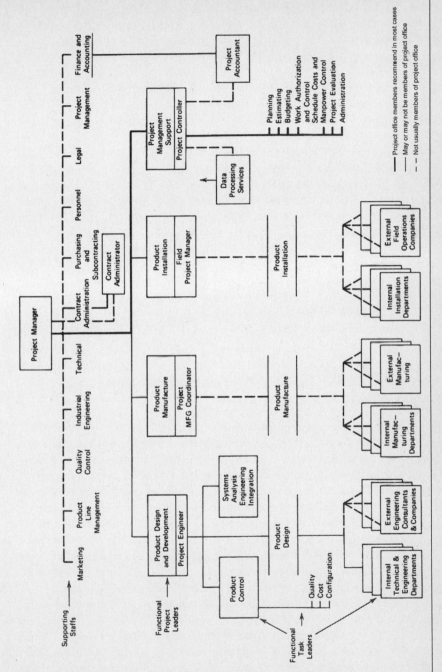

Figure 7.2 Generalized organization of the project team.

159

project covers an extended period (six months or more), it is recommended that the field project manager be assigned to the project office.

Effect of Staffing Method on the Project Manager's Authority

If all required people are placed directly under the project manager her role is quite similar to that of a multifunctional division manager. For the reasons discussed earlier, this rarely occurs except in very large, high priority projects.

In practice, much (and in many cases, most) of the work is performed for a project by people in various functional departments or outside the parent organization of the project. These people do not report organizationally to the project manager, but he must still integrate their efforts to achieve the project objectives. The result is the matrix situation discussed earlier and in Chapter 4, where task leaders are receiving direction from both a functional boss and a project boss. The authority of the project manager in this project/functional situation is changed considerably from that which he has on a fully autonomous project.

Under these conditions, effective project management requires that the project manager act as an "interface manager" and that adequate project support services be provided to the project manager to establish control of the project through integrated planning, scheduling, and evaluation.

Relationships between Project and Functional Managers: Interface Management

It is difficult to convey a good understanding of the project manager role to functional managers whose experience has been wholly within traditional, functional organizations. The project manager's responsibilities are integrative and relate to the interaction between the various contributing functions for his specific project. These responsibilities overlay those of the functional managers but do not change the basic accountability of each functional manager for his portion of the project.

If the general manager to whom all the functional managers report were to retain the project manager role himself, then the functional manager would readily understand and accept his role as project manager. But when responsibility for the project is assigned to someone other than the general manager, the functional managers may have difficulty accepting the idea.

The concept of the project manager as an *interface manager* is useful to clarify her relationships with functional managers and others outside her direct control. Within this concept, the project manager's prime responsibilities are to:

- Identify the various interfaces between functional departments and other elements of the project.
- Develop plans and schedules that incorporate these interface points.
- Communicate the current and future status of all interfaces to all affected functional contributors.
- Monitor progress in all areas and periodically evaluate the project to identify problems and initiate appropriate corrective action.

Interface management is described more fully in Chapter 13. Project managers who practice interface management find they do not need to invade the prerogatives of the functional managers, and their relations noticeably improve. By being helpful to the functional managers in this manner, her role will be welcomed enthusiastically.

7.5 PRODUCT AND PROJECT SUPPORT SERVICES

In addition to the people and facilities required to design, manufacture, and install (or otherwise put into use or operation) the product to be created, specialized project management support services are needed to assist the project manager in carrying out her responsibilities. As described in Chapter 4, these responsibilities include achieving the technical (product) objectives within the established limits of time and cost. The specialized support services relate to both the *product* and *project* planning and control functions described in more detail in Chapter 10. Figure 7.3 shows one example of the organization of the product support services for a major electronic project under contract.

Product Support Services

The services of greatest importance to the product, and which may be provided by assigned members of the project office, are:

Technical Management
- Direct the product design and development work.

Systems Analysis, Engineering, and Integration
- Analyze and specify product performance requirements and criteria.
- Evaluate and integrate detailed designs by all project participants.
- Design and specify the system tests and product functional tests, and evaluate test results.
- Carry out design review practices.

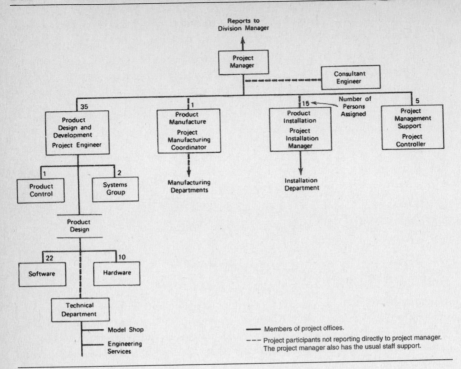

Figure 7.3   Example of organization for a major electronic project under customer contract.

Product Control

- Establish detailed performance objectives and assure achievement in product quality, reliability, and maintainability.
- Document a baseline system and product configuration, and control and document any changes to that configuration.
- Establish detailed estimates of product cost and revise these as design changes or other revised information become available.

Project Management Support Services

These include specialized functions related to the following:

- *Contract administration,* as described in detail in Chapter 9, usually performed by a contract administrator assigned to the project but usually not considered a member of the project office under the direct control of the project manager.

- *Project accounting*, performed by a member of the accounting department designated for the project, and usually reporting indirectly to the project controller (or equivalent).

- *Specialized project management support services,* usually performed by members of the project office under the direction of a project controller (or similar title). These are discussed in the following chapters.

The number of people required to carry out the management support functions will vary, depending on the size and complexity of the project, from one person (the project manager), perhaps with a secretary, to 10, 15, or more on very large projects. In general, it is desirable to hold the project office to a minimum number of people (see Chapter 9).

Centralized versus Decentralized Project Management Support Services

In situations involving a number of relatively small projects, it is not possible to provide a project manager and supporting project staff for each. In this case, a centralized project management support group is required to provide the planning and control services for whoever is responsible for the projects, whether this is a line manager, a project manager, or a multiproject manager.

As previously discussed, experience indicates that a centralized group is less effective in support of those major projects that could justify one or more full-time people performing support functions. Because these functions deal with vital information regarding the current health and ultimate success of the project, a project manager on a large effort often will not entrust the information to an outside group. If these services are offered or imposed from outside the project then the project manager will generally shield the outsiders from key information and ignore their efforts of assistance. This often results in developing internal methods for performing these functions, which may be less effective and more costly than if qualified specialists were placed within the project office.

Central Planning for Multiprojects

In most large companies, major projects exist together with numerous smaller projects. Thus, there is frequently a need for a centralized project support staff to plan and control the smaller projects, as well as for equivalent specialists assigned to the various major project offices. The central staff can be used as a training ground for persons to be assigned to major project offices and to coordinate development of improved methods, procedures, and systems, including multiproject planning, resource allocation, and control systems.

The concept of a full-blown operations planning and control function, supported by a computer-based operations planning and control system, is presented in Chapter 8. Where such a function exists, it can provide very effective planning and control support to the various project managers.

Figure 7.4 shows an example of this type of multiproject management support in a large telecommunications company.

Relationships between the Individual Project Office, Central Planning and Control, and Information Processing Services

Effective use of advanced project management software applications requires skilled information processing support services. As discussed in

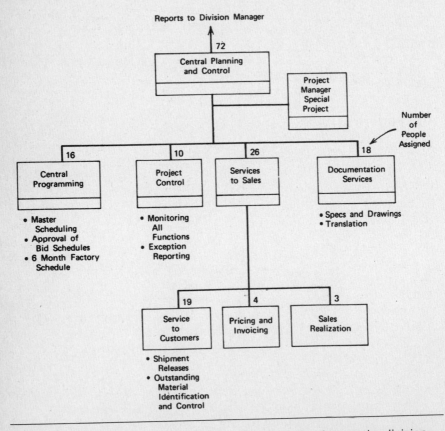

Figure 7.4   Example of central planning and control for a major division.

Chapter 5, these services must be made available as directly as possible to the project managers or project controllers within the project offices. Figure 7.5 illustrates the recommended relationships.

7.6 CHARTING ORGANIZATIONAL RELATIONSHIPS AND RESPONSIBILITIES

Because the project manager responsibilities and relationships do not conform to traditional organizational theory and practice, it is difficult to illustrate these relationships accurately using the familiar organizational charting methods. Organizations have prepared different kinds of charts in attempting to portray the project management situation graphically, to enable analysis and improved understanding.

Various alternative organizational arrangements have been and continue to be developed and used for the project management function. As previously discussed, most of these result in what is usually termed a *matrix* organization, wherein the project manager's relationships are overlaid on the basic organizational structure, forming a matrix of reporting, direction-giving, and coordinating lines of communication and linkage. The most common forms of the resulting organization are shown in Figures 7.6 through 7.9.

Responsibility Matrix

Traditional organization charts and position descriptions are necessary and valuable, but they do not show how the organization really works. Another approach that comes closer to this goal has evolved and is generally referred to as linear responsibility charting to produce a responsibility matrix. To be most effective, the members of a work group should actively participate in developing such a chart to describe their roles and relationships. Such development resolves differences and improves communications so that the organization works more effectively. The responsibility matrix is useful for analyzing and portraying any organization, but it is particularly effective in relating project responsibilities to the existing organization. This important tool is described in more detail in Chapter 10.

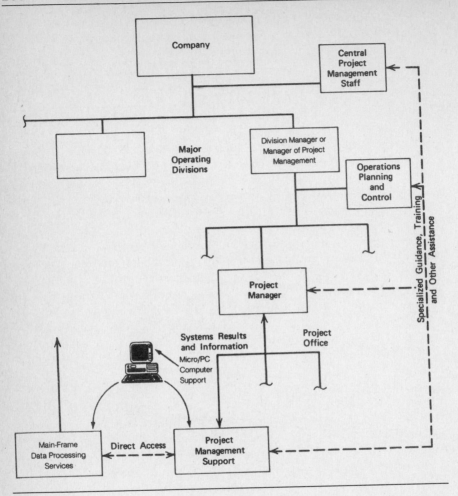

Figure 7.5   Recommended relationships between central staff, operations planning and control, project office, and data processing services.

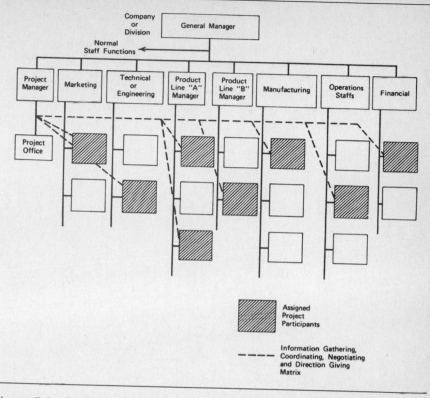

Figure 7.6   Generalized organization chart with project responsibility delegated to full-time project manager. The matrix relationships include direction giving information to carry out decisions of the project manager, in addition ot the communicating and coordinating functions.

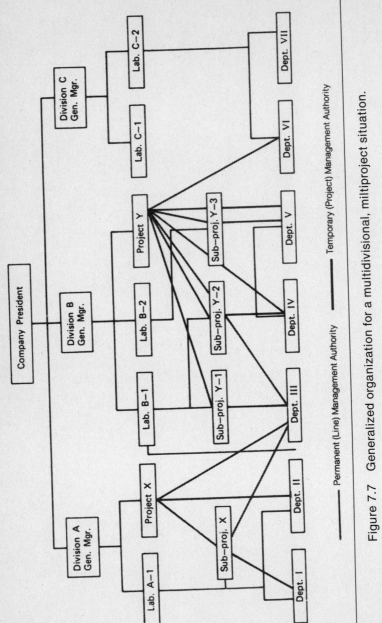

Figure 7.7 Generalized organization for a multidivisional, miltiproject situation.

——— Permanent (Line) Management Authority   ——— Temporary (Project) Management Authority

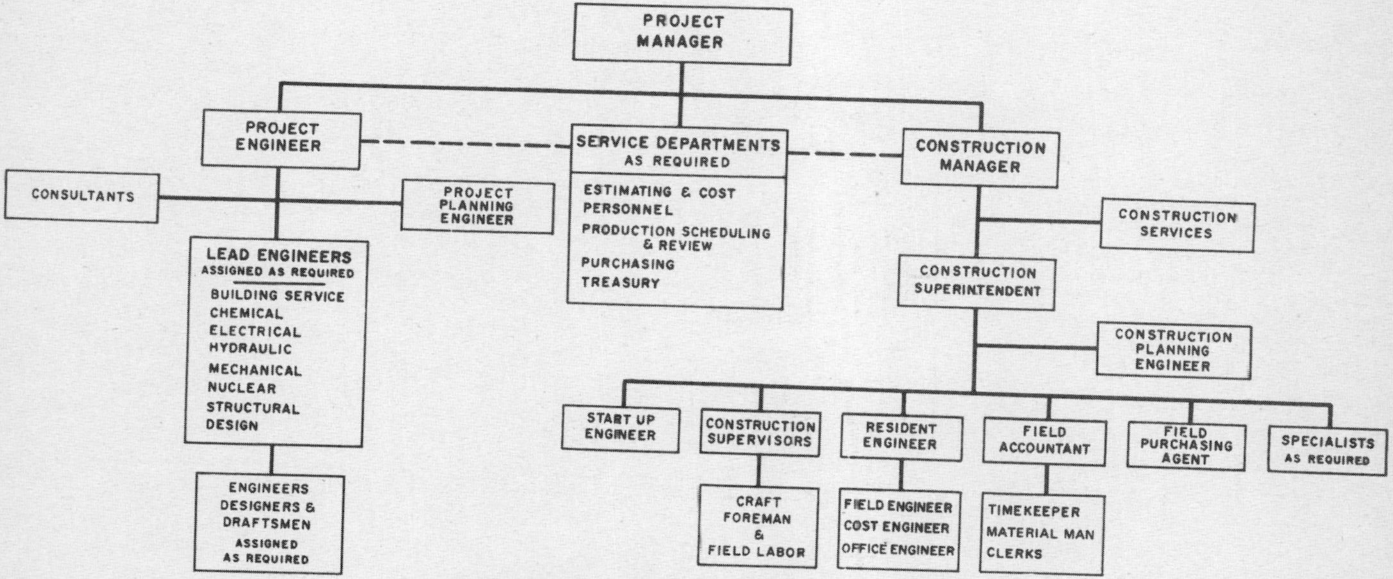

Figure 7.8 Typical organization chart for a large engineering-construction company.

CONSULTANTS

PROJECT MANAGER

PROJECT ENGINEER

CONSTRUCTION MANAGER

PROJECT PLANNING ENGINEER

SERVICE DEPARTMENTS
AS REQUIRED

ESTIMATING & COST
PERSONNEL
PRODUCTION SCHEDULING
& REVIEW
PURCHASING
TREASURY

CONSTRUCTION SERVICES

CONSTRUCTION SUPERINTENDENT

CONSTRUCTION PLANNING ENGINEER

LEAD ENGINEERS
ASSIGNED AS REQUIRED

BUILDING SERVICE
CHEMICAL
ELECTRICAL
HYDRAULIC
MECHANICAL
NUCLEAR
STRUCTURAL
DESIGN

ENGINEERS
DESIGNERS &
DRAFTSMEN
ASSIGNED
AS REQUIRED

START UP ENGINEER

CONSTRUCTION SUPERVISORS

CRAFT FOREMAN
&
FIELD LABOR

RESIDENT ENGINEER

FIELD ENGINEER
COST ENGINEER
OFFICE ENGINEER

FIELD ACCOUNTANT

TIMEKEEPER
MATERIAL MAN
CLERKS

FIELD PURCHASING AGENT

SPECIALISTS
AS REQUIRED

WHENEVER PERSONNEL ARE ASSIGNED TO A PROJECT THEY RETAIN A FUNCTIONAL
RESPONSIBILITY FOR THE ADEQUACY AND INTEGRITY OF ANY ASSIGNED DIVISION
OF THE WORK, TO PERFORM IT IN ACCORDANCE WITH ESTABLISHED POLICY AND
PROCEDURE AS SET BY THE APPROPRIATE HEADQUARTERS CORPORATE DEPARTMENTAL
AUTHORITY. FOR THE PERIOD OF SUCH ASSIGNMENT, HOWEVER, AND WHETHER
ASSIGNED ON A FULL-TIME OR PART-TIME BASIS, THEY ARE ADMINISTRATIVELY
RESPONSIBLE TO ACCOMPLISH THE ASSIGNED DIVISION OF THE WORK IN ACCORDANCE
WITH THESE ESTABLISHED FUNCTIONAL STANDARDS UNDER THE SUPERVISION
AND DIRECTION OF THE RESPONSIBLE HEAD OF THE PROJECT.

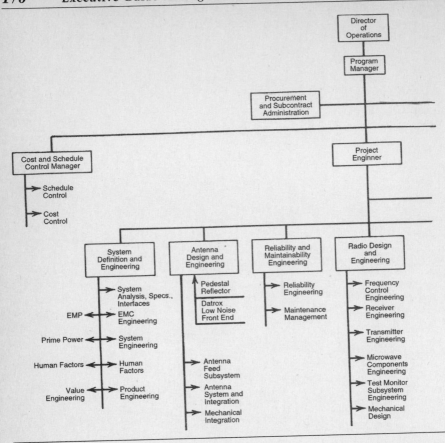

Figure 7.9   Program organization chart. This chart is typical of those submitted to a customer to emphasize the strength of the company's program/project management approach. However, in most cases, few of the people represented on the chart actually report to the program or project manager. The lines on such a chart must be clearly understood to represent project-related direction only, with team members reporting on a "hard-line" basis to their functional managers.

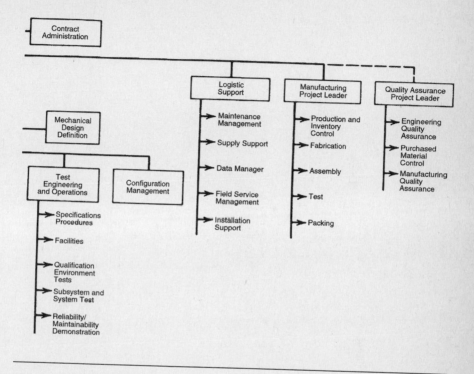

Figure 7.9   *(Continued)*

CEO Demands: Organizing the PMO and the PM Function

To obtain the full benefits of project management for the entire organization the CEO must demand that:

1. Full-time program and project managers be appointed for each major program and project, as defined in Chapter 2, each reporting to the most appropriate senior executive.

2. Multiproject managers be appointed for those minor projects that do not justify full-time project managers, with appropriate planning and control support provided as required in the form of a multiproject operations planning and control function (as described in Chapter 8).

3. An experienced manager of project management be appointed reporting to a senior executive.

4. An appropriate home for the project management function be established in the form of a PMO under the direction of the manager of project management.

5. The responsibilities of the PMO be defined in several stages of evolution and implemented according to plan commensurate with the organization's capacity to absorb the resulting changes.

8

‹ ›

Managing Project Portfolios, Programs, and Multiple Projects

It is rare to find a project in any organization today that exists by itself without interaction with other projects. The reality is that projects must be managed as interrelated efforts at four levels in large organizations: project portfolio, multiproject program, multiple small/minor projects, and the individual major project levels.

The first three levels are discussed in this chapter. The processes, systems, procedures, and tools for managing individual major projects are discussed in Part II of the book, Chapters 9 through 15. These levels are not mutually exclusive: a major project can be within a program and a portfolio, for example, and if so it would require management at all three of these levels. A small project can be managed as one of a group as well as part of a project portfolio.

Multiproject Environment

The multiproject environment that exists in most large organizations imposes complications at each of these project levels and at each level of the functional organization. The basic problems result from competition between and within projects for resources and for management attention. Since no organization possesses completely unlimited resources, it is not possible simultaneously to plan and execute all the projects that can be conceived. In addition to resource constraints, many projects depend on the results and products from other projects.

At appropriate levels in the organization, the multiproject requirements and priorities must be brought together to assure that all projects are completed to realize the maximum benefits for the entire organization.

The need for some means to integrate these multiproject requirements is frequently not fully recognized. The result is that a number of projects are individually managed from different parts of an organization with a great deal of effort being exerted by the various project managers to win available skills or other resources. A very strong project manager may thus be successful on one project but the company may suffer severely from the delays that result in other projects.

Multiproject Objectives

The higher order objectives of multiproject management, in comparison to managing a single project, include:

- Completing all projects to best achieve the overall strategic goals of the organization.
- Determining both long-term and short-range priorities between projects to enable appropriate decisions regarding allocation of limited resources.
- Identifying and understanding the comparative risks involved in each project, deciding which are acceptable to the organization, and managing the accepted risks proactively.
- Acquiring and maintaining an adequate supply of resources to support all projects, including people, facilities, material, and money; but at the same time assuring that these resources are gainfully and efficiently employed in approved, productive work required to complete the approved projects.
- Integrating these multiproject requirements with other ongoing activities and operations not directly related to projects (such as production of off-the-shelf products).
- Developing and using organizational patterns and management processes and systems to satisfy the ever-changing project needs, and to provide organizational stability, professional development, and administrative efficiency for persons managing and supporting various projects.

8.1   MANAGING PROJECT PORTFOLIOS

The development and application of the project portfolio management process must be planned as a management project. The most appropriate approach is to assign the manager of project management, assuming there is one, as the project manager. Persons who are obvious candidates to be members of the project portfolio steering group should be included on the project team with appropriate responsibilities. Other members of the team will be drawn from the project management office (PMO) staff and probably will also include experienced internal or external consultants in strategic and project management.

The project objective is to design, develop, and implement the project portfolio management process for the specified parts of the organization. The project scope defines exactly which parts of the organization are to be included in the implementation. During the initial implementation of the process, the senior members of the project team are transformed into the project portfolio steering group. This group is established formally when the process design has been approved and its implementation is authorized.

The project portfolio management process described in Chapter 1 consists of the following twelve basic steps. Comments on each step indicate how the process is developed and applied.

1. *Define the* project portfolios *required within the organization.* This would normally be done as a part of the organization's strategic planning and management process. The defined portfolios would reflect the organization's growth strategies, reporting structure, geographic markets, product lines, and other significant factors.

2. *Define the* project categories *within each portfolio based on uniform criteria for the entire organization.* The list of project categories for the organization is prepared by the project team reflecting the factors discussed in Chapter 2 (Section 2.4).

3. *Identify and group all current and proposed projects within appropriate categories and programs.* Preparing the inventory of projects discussed in Chapter 1 (Section 1.4) is a necessary prerequisite for this step. Grouping the currently approved projects by the team into their appropriate categories will generally be straightforward. Creating and selecting new projects is further discussed in a following section.

4. *Validate all projects with the organization's strategic objectives.* The implementation project team with the project portfolio steering group compares the objectives and scope of each project within a portfolio and ascertains that these are directly linked to one or more of the organization's strategic objectives. If not, higher level managers must decide if the project will be cancelled or retained in the portfolio after suitable modification.

5. *Prioritize projects within programs and portfolios.* The implementation project team designs and recommends the methods and procedures for prioritizing projects and programs within each portfolio. Further

discussion of project prioritization methods is presented in a following section. The project portfolio steering group then applies these methods and establishes the current project priorities, with supporting assistance from the PMO staff.

6. *Develop the project portfolio master schedule.* The implementation team designs and develops the format for this master schedule and enters summary information for each project and program within each portfolio reflecting the currently approved project priorities. This can take the form of a large, graphic, time-scaled display showing the beginning and end of each project or program together with a few major milestones for each. This should also display any logical dependencies between projects or programs in each portfolio, and any such dependencies between projects in different portfolios. This display can be automated and Web-enabled using available project management software.

7. *Establish and maintain the key resources databank.* A significant element of the design of the project portfolio management process will be the selection of which key resources are to be included in this databank. The number of such resources should be kept small, at least initially. As experience is gained in the practicalities of maintaining and using such a databank, additional resources can be added to it.

8. *Allocate available key resources to programs and projects within portfolios.* This step requires development of fairly detailed plans and schedules for each active program and project within each portfolio. These initial project plans will include estimates of what key resources are required over time to plan and execute each project as scheduled. As resources are allocated, the project schedules will obviously be affected. When the projects are reprioritized (Step 5), these resource allocations are revised and the projects are then rescheduled.

9. *Compare financial needs (primarily cash flow) with availability.* This also requires fairly detailed plans and schedules for each program and project with cost estimates linked to schedules. Planning templates (see Chapter 10) for newly conceived projects can be used until more detailed plans for them are available.

10. *Decide how to respond to shortfalls in money or other key resources and approve the list of funded projects and their priorities.* The steering group makes these decisions regarding allocation of funds. It then oversees the repetition of Steps 5 through 10 until available money and other key resources have been allocated on an optimum basis.

11. *Plan, authorize, and manage each program and project using the organization's project management process and supporting systems and tools for*

each project category. The manager of project management and the supporting staff assigned to the PMO provide direction and assistance as required and reflecting the PMO charter (as discussed in Chapter 8) to carry out this step.

12. *Periodically reprioritize, reallocate resources to, and reschedule all programs and projects as required within each portfolio.* Repeat Steps 1 through 12 as required on a monthly or quarterly basis. Reflect changes in strategies, products, markets, competition, and technologies, as well as progress made to date (or the lack thereof) on each project. Add newly proposed and approved projects. As further discussed later in this chapter, the project portfolio steering group gives strategic direction to each project sponsor who interprets that direction and communicates it to the affected project manager(s).

Responsibilities of the Project Portfolio Steering Group

The project portfolio steering group responsibilities include:

- Approving the design of the project portfolio management process during its initial implementation, and any significant subsequent changes to it.
- Active participation in the operation of the project portfolio management process:
  —Integrating and validating the organization's strategic objectives with the programs and projects within the project portfolios over which the group has cognizance.
  —Establishing and integrating the relative priorities of projects within each portfolio at appropriate preestablished intervals and when required by major events or changes in the projects or their environments.
  —Approving new projects for inclusion in the assigned portfolios and reprioritizing all portfolio projects when such new projects are added.
  —Communicating the current project priorities to their sponsors and through the sponsors to the program and project managers, as well as to the functional management structure of the organization.
- Recommending to the CEO and other cognizant senior managers the acquisition of additional financial and other resources when required to plan and execute the projects needed to achieve the strategic objectives of the organization on a timely basis.

- Identifying opportunities for improvement and recommending improvements in the project portfolio management process and the other project management processes, systems and tools.

In large, complex organizations, there will usually be more than one project portfolio to be managed, and these may overlap and compete for available corporate resources and management attention. The CEO, general manager, or other senior executive or multiportfolio steering group may be required to resolve interportfolio conflicts—unless one portfolio steering group holds responsibility for all portfolios.

Relationships between the Project Portfolio Steering Group, Project Sponsors, the Project Management Office, and Project/Program Managers

The *project portfolio steering group* provides strategic direction for all programs and projects within the portfolios under its cognizance. The currently approved portfolio master schedule reflects the key resource allocations and project priorities that have been established by the steering group. This master schedule includes the currently agreed target dates for key milestones in each program and project. This information is transmitted to the project sponsors and the manager of project management.

The *project sponsors* assigned to major programs and projects inform the manager of project management, the cognizant program and project managers, and also the affected functional managers, of any changes to the resource allocations and priorities for their projects. The sponsors also communicate to those managers any other information (both internal and external to the organization) of a political, economic, technological or other pertinent nature that may have an effect—good or bad—on their programs or projects.

The *manager of project management* communicates the resource allocation, priority and milestone information contained in the portfolio master schedule to the managers of all programs and projects for which a sponsor has not been designated. Depending on the manager of project management's charter he may carry out the responsibilities of the sponsor for all such projects.

The *program and project managers,* both of individual major programs and projects and of multiple smaller projects, receive their strategic direction from either their project sponsors or the manager of project management. The manager of project management will provide operational support and professional project management guidance to the program and project managers if this is within the scope of his charter. Each program and project manager must reflect any resource, priority, schedule, or other strategic changes to their program or project in their plans, estimates and schedules, and quickly provide an assessment of the impact of such changes to their project sponsor and/or the manager of project management.

The project sponsors and the manager of project management immediately transmit these impacts to the project portfolio steering committee for inclusion in the next iteration of the project portfolio planning process.

8.2 PROJECT SELECTION

The complexities and processes involved in new project selection vary considerably depending on the category of projects in question. The four high-technology categories identified in Chapter 2 as the primary focus of this book are:

1. Communication systems.
2. Information systems.
3. Product and service development.
4. Research and development.

Project selection within each of these categories is discussed next. Although each project category requires a somewhat different approach the selection process is focused in all of them on the three main goals of portfolio management, according to Cooper, Edgert, and Kleinschmidt (2001) in their reporting the results of their industry studies:

1. *Maximizing the value of the portfolio against an objective,* such as profitability, return on investment, or likelihood of success (see Chapter 3, pp. 29–72).

2. *Balance in the portfolio:* The most popular balancing dimensions used were risk versus reward, ease versus attractiveness, and breakdown by project type, market and product line (see Chapter 4, pp. 73–104).

3. *Link to strategy:* Strategic fit and resource allocation that reflects the business's strategy were the key issues here (see Chapter 5, pp. 105–144).

"Of the three, no one goal seemed to dominate; moreover, no one portfolio model or approach seemed capable of achieving all three goals" (Cooper et al., 1999, p. 29).

Dye and Pennypacker (1999) have compiled a very useful compendium of articles that discuss and present a wide range of industrial experience and practices relating to portfolio management in general and project selection and prioritization in particular. These articles focus primarily on the information system, new product, and R&D project categories.

Selecting New Communication Systems Projects

Selection of projects in this category will be made both by the buyers and the sellers of new communication systems. Only in rare cases will a supplier of these systems execute such a project for its own end use.

Selection by buyers of communication systems projects.   For the buyer of a new communication system the decision to proceed with such a project is motivated by its growth strategies. Senior management must determine what the communication needs of the organization are now and will be at some point in the future, and allocate the required financial resources to meet those needs. The requirement for allocation of its internal key resources (such as communications and information technology specialists) to the planning and execution of the new project is also a consideration in the selection process. Buyers of communications systems are found in every industrial and governmental sector worldwide.

The most difficult part of the selection process for the buyer will generally be choosing between two or more competing proposals from the suppliers of such systems. The basic criteria for that choice include price, system features and performance, supplier reputation and previous experience, the technology involved and its compatibility with existing communications systems, delivery date, and performance and maintenance warranties. These criteria are the primary basis for the buyer's risk analysis on such new projects.

Selection by sellers of communication systems projects.   The sellers or suppliers of such systems will use a rather different selection process. Since such projects are at least a major part (perhaps the entirety) of their primary business they are constantly looking for and encouraging potential buyers to issue requests for proposals (RFPs) of these projects, or better yet to sign a contract for them without competing proposals being submitted. When an RFP is received, the seller will examine it carefully to determine if they have the capabilities needed to respond with a proposal that will completely fill the stated need on schedule and at the same time be profitable for them.

The selection of new projects for which to submit proposals is the critical point in the seller's decision process. Their risk analysis must include not only the planning for and execution of the project itself, should their proposal be accepted, but the risk that perhaps several such proposals will be accepted by several buyers and the supplier will not have the resources needed to deliver all of them at the time that they have proposed. This could occur since the supplier must submit more proposals than will be accepted because no supplier can expect a 100 percent acceptance rate for their proposals. Successful suppliers of these projects have learned the hard way that effective project management must begin during the proposal stage. In other words, they apply the total project life-cycle management system (PLCMS) described in Chapter 3 (Section 3.6) during preparation of their proposal.

Once a contract has been signed, there will be one project, and both the buyer and seller must collaborate in its planning and execution since for most projects in this category both will make significant contributions to the project. However, the supplier usually has the lead responsibility for managing such a project.

Selecting Information Systems Projects

In most organizations, there is a greater demand for information systems projects than can be met with available funding and specialized resources. The many users of the information systems within the organization continually submit requests for such new projects. The selection process must choose which of the many possible projects should be added to the portfolio and approved for funding and execution. Essentially all projects in this category are for improvement of internal business processes and performance or to offer new services to outside customers, although many such projects will use the services of outside software developers under contract for their planning and execution. New information systems projects that are intended to produce hardware and/or software products for sale to other users are considered to be in the category of new products and services, discussed later.

Miller (1997, p. 56) identifies four areas in which criteria have typically been established to help organizations choose between information technology projects:

1. *Customer:* Commitment in terms of need.
2. *Strategy:* Alignment with company goals and objectives:
   —Profitability: Measuring the IT project's cost savings.
   —Process improvement: Ability to improve business processes in a timely manner.
   —Employee satisfaction.
3. *Technology:* Ability to meet technical requirements:
   —Core competency: Organizational capability to perform the project.

—Cost competitiveness: Ability to provide a competitive solution.

—Integration: With existing technology.

4. *Delivery:* Ability to successfully deliver the project on schedule, within budget and meeting the quality specifications.

Bridges (1999) recommends establishing twelve to fifteen criteria based on these items to support IT decision making.

Selecting New Product and Service Projects

As with information systems projects, "There are far more new product ideas or projects conceived than resources to commercialize them. Moreover the great majority of these projects are unfit for commercialization. In an ideal new product process, management would be able to identify the probably new product winners in advance, and be able to allocate the firm's development resources to these projects. As a result, failure rates would be low, misallocated resources would be kept to a minimum, and the return would be maximized" (Cooper, 1985, p. 34).

Cooper (1985) lists the four models to initial screening of new product projects as benefit measurement, economic, portfolio selection, and market research models (p. 36).

The extensive industry research conducted by Cooper identified eight "factors or underlying dimensions" that were found to impact on new product outcomes:

1. Product superiority, quality, and uniqueness.
2. Overall product/company resource compatibility.
3. Market need, growth, and size.
4. Economic advantage of product to end user.
5. Newness to the firm (negative).
6. Technological resource compatibility.
7. Market competitiveness (negative).
8. Product scope.

A practical seven-step approach for organizations to develop their own new product screening model is given by Cooper (1985, p. 40). An example of a commercially available computer-based scoring model is NewProd™ 3000 (a registered trademark of R. G. Cooper and Associates Consultants, Inc; see www.prod-dev.com), which is "based on the profiles and outcomes of hundreds of past new product projects. It serves as both a diagnostic tool and a predictive model. It is premised on the fact that the profile of a new product project is a reasonable predictor of success" (p. 67). The profile characteristics used are shown in the list of eight factors.

Selecting New Research and Development Projects

This category includes a broad range of projects from exploratory, undirected research to very specific new or improved product, service, or process development. The obvious new product and service projects generally should be placed in that project category, discussed earlier.

Methods for screening and selecting research and development (R&D) projects will reflect the R&D phase that a particular idea or embryo project is in. Lambert (1993, pp. 388–389) identifies three major R&D phases:

1. Phase I research phase is exploring, or basic.
2. Phase II research phase is feasibility, or application.
3. Phase III—the development phase—can best be described as refinement, or optimization.

The product or result of Phase I is most often a research report or document, not a physical product. The typical product of Phase II is a prototype or laboratory scale test plus documentation. At some point in Phase III, the project becomes a new product or service development project and then must be moved to that category and managed accordingly.

Project selection occurs at the start of each of these phases. Hosley (1993, p. 386) recommends: "Compile as large list of possible projects that capitalizes on the company's strengths, together with an estimate of potential sales, required investment, and probably success." The next step is to "Prioritize items from the list so that the gap (between where the company is now and where it wants to be in ten years) is filled year-by-year." Since most R&D projects will mature into new product or service projects the methods used for selecting the latter can also be applied to selecting R&D projects.

General Rules for Selecting Projects

Frame (1999, p. 180) provides five general rules for project selection that, if followed, will lead to better choices:

1. Be explicit about what is important in choosing projects.
2. Identify explicit procedures for choosing projects, then stick to them.
3. Be prepared to rigorously challenge all assertions.

4. Prepare a project selection team whose members represent a broad array of stakeholders.

5. Involve key project personnel in the selection process.

Some Problems with Portfolio Management Models

The project portfolio management process is dynamic and deals with constantly changing, uncertain information. Cooper et al. (1999, p. 30) state that "Portfolio models suffer from imaginary precision. A universal weakness is that virtually every portfolio model we studied *implied a degree of precision far beyond people's ability to provide reliable data;* that is, the model's sophistication far exceeded the quality of the input data." Also, "Many portfolio models yield information overload" (p. 33). Care is obviously needed to keep the process as simple as possible while still achieving its objectives. As with product or process design it is far easier to produce a very complicated, impressive looking or sounding process that is ultimately unworkable than it is to produce an elegantly simple result that does the job.

8.3   ESTABLISHING AND CONTROLLING PROJECT PRIORITIES

When several projects are competing for limited resources, the need for a method of determining and communicating the relative priority of each project is easily recognized. However, developing a practical method to satisfy that need has proved to be a difficult job.

The Need for Project Prioritization

Effective planning of each project and forecasting of its resource needs will assist in predicting potential conflicts with other projects if all are similarly planned. Decisions can then be made whether to supply additional resources or to delay or otherwise replan one or more projects. Some measure of project priority is needed to make such decisions. Predicting such potential conflicts is the only way to enable effective management action that can avoid the actual conflict in a crisis atmosphere. Unfortunately, such planning is often impractical in the early conceptual phases of most projects, primarily because of the time and cost involved in preparing such detailed plans. The dilemma is that executives are reluctant to invest too much in the early phases when they know that a large percentage of projects in these phases will be killed. But without an adequate investment in planning during these early phases, truly informed decisions cannot be made.

Even in the most thoroughly planned projects unforeseen problems or needs can cause short-term conflicts. When these occur, the person allocating a limited resource to one or the other project must have accurate knowledge of their current relative priorities.

In the absence of an effective prioritizing method, decisions are made daily at the first-line management and supervisory levels regarding relative project priorities. It is conceivable that contradictory decisions are made on different parts of the same two projects, with the result that both projects suffer delay in the end.

In addition, it is often difficult to translate priorities established by management into appropriate action at, for example, the level where material is requisitioned. In spite of such difficulties, the need for current project priorities to penetrate to the lowest level of the organization is essential if management decisions are to be carried out effectively.

Factors Influencing Project Priorities

While the relative importance of these factors vary depending on the organization and the type of project involved, the following list includes most of the factors that affect project priorities (not necessarily in order of importance):

Completion or delivery date, and its proximity.

Penalty risks.

Customer importance.

Competitive risks.

Technical risks.

Regulatory agency risks.

Health and product liability risks.

Management sponsor.

Return on investment.

Magnitude of costs, investment, and/or profit, and related risks.

Impact on other projects.

Impact on other affiliated organizations.

Impact on a particular product line.

Political and visibility risks.

Such factors must be translated into some form of a model in order to be useful to management, as discussed in the next section.

Prioritization Models

Models for project prioritization range from simple to complex. There are two basic classifications: projects that are funded, and those that are on hold and not funded. A more useful approach is to create a three-tier list:

1. *Priority projects:* Those that take precedence over all others.
2. *Normal projects:* Those that are funded and active but do not bear the priority label.
3. *Back-burner projects:* Those that are on hold, waiting for funding or resources to become available.

Buss (1999, p. 188) describes the use of four priority grids with a common vertical axis of all four grids showing the level of investment (low, medium, high) and the horizontal axis of each separate grid showing a range of low, medium, and high for:

Financial benefits.

Intangible benefits.

Technical benefits.

Fit with business objectives.

All projects are placed in their respective positions on each of the four grids, and then a consensus is reached regarding their relative overall priority ranking.

At the complex end of the scale are prioritization models with quantified criteria weighting risk and return mathematical approaches. These often depend on subjectively prepared numbers to produce deceptively accurate looking results. For new product prioritization, the references provided earlier under project selection also deal extensively with new product prioritization models.

Lower Level Priority Rules to Resolve Interproject Schedule and Resource Conflicts

Only about 15 percent of the activities in any one project are truly critical to meeting its completion date. Thus, from a multiproject point of view, the overall project priorities discussed in the preceding sections should only be applied when conflicts occur between the truly critical activities of two or more projects.

For this approach to be used, it is necessary to plan and schedule each project in such a way that the critical 15 percent of the activities can be identified. The network planning discipline with resource information, as discussed in Chapter 10, is the most effective method of doing this in a consistent manner. When two or more projects are planned in this way, information is provided that allows application of various lower level priority rules as shown in Table 8.1. Other similar priority rules may be developed and used.

8.4   MANAGING MULTIPROJECT PROGRAMS

As previously discussed, programs are defined as being comprised of two or more projects. Classic program management comes from large U.S. Department of Defense weapon systems efforts and NASA aerospace endeavors. Typically, these require a program manager at a high level of the governmental agency sponsoring the effort, with project managers identified within each of the private contractors that are carrying out the design, development, fabrication, assembly, test, and other required operations for the portion of the program for which they have executed contracts with the government. In some cases, these contracts are so large that they are actually multiproject programs with a number of subcontractors executing the projects.

In other economic and industrial sectors organizations have found it useful to group related projects within a program. Such projects might be related to a particular product line, operating division, or geographic area. Projects within a program are usually closely related in some way, in addition to using common resources. Such interrelationships include logical dependencies like a test result or product from one project that is

Table 8.1   Rules for Resolving Conflicts between Projects without Resorting to Overall Project Priorities*

Conflict between Activities in Different Projects	Priority Given to:
Critical (from a schedule or resource viewpoint)	Project with highest overall current priority.
Critical versus noncritical	Critical activity (regardless of overall project priority).
Noncritical versus noncritical	Activity with least slack or shortest critical chain buffer (allowable delay); if equal slack, shortest, or longest activity; if same duration, use current project priority. Alternatively, give priority to activity using largest number of critical resources.

* Slack or float calculations must reflect resource constraints.

required before a task or activity within another project can be started or completed. Programs could conceivably be considered as being synonymous with small portfolios.

Program versus Project Managers

The similarities and differences between the program and project manager roles have been discussed in Chapter 4 (Section 4.7).

Programs may not have a well-defined life cycle of their own since they are comprised of two or more projects that each have their own life cycles. Programs usually have longer durations than projects and may continue for indefinite periods of time as projects are completed and new projects added. As a result, the program manager assignment will typically be more permanent or longer in duration than that of a project manager. That may make it more difficult to maintain the continuity of responsibility in one program manager, and this in turn places more importance on establishing and maintaining adequate files and records for the program so that a newly assigned program manager will inherit the complete information needed for successfully completing the program.

8.5   MANAGING MULTIPLE PROJECTS

This book is directed primarily to situations involving a number of major projects as they are defined in Chapter 2. However, of equal importance in many organizations are the project management needs in the situation where a large number of relatively small projects exist. This is typical of many high technology companies that design, manufacture, and install complex products or systems.

To illustrate this point, consider the situation where one or more contracts with customers cover a large number of specific central office telephone exchanges or central telephone switches (PBXs) and related communication systems on a user's premises. Each of these contracts is in reality a project, requiring hardware engineering work, software modification, procurement, manufacturing, assembly, customer training, installation, and test. These overlapping projects flow through marketing, hardware and software engineering, one or more factories, and only emerge as clearly distinct projects during installation, where typically the installation department manages a number of geographically separate sites. In such situations, it is not possible or even desirable to appoint a project manager for each PBX with responsibility through engineering, manufacturing, and installation. In some cases, a project manager is appointed for a group of related exchanges for a single customer, or for a very large, complex PBX and system. The general practice is to appoint a supervisor for each exchange only during the installation phase, reporting to the installation department.

Even though project managers may not be appointed to every project in this situation, management of the projects on an integrated basis is still of vital importance to meeting the contract cut-over dates. Since a typical telephone switching equipment division is predominantly devoted to the execution of these somewhat repetitive (but never identical) projects, the division general manager typically retains the overall project management responsibilities. This places even greater emphasis on the need for organization, methods, and systems that enable truly integrated planning and control of all projects through all their life-cycle phases. This situation is very similar to a manufacturing "job shop" where each order flowing through the shop is for a similar but not identical product. Job shop scheduling software applications have existed for many years, and the approach discussed here for multiple small projects is simply an extension of that concept to include the functions of marketing, engineering, procurement, manufacturing, and installation.

Centralized planning and control offices have been established in some companies to provide the needed marketing-engineering-manufacturing-installation planning and master scheduling where this multiple small project situation exists. The planning manager, overseen by the division general manager, coordinates these plans and master schedules, and does the appropriate follow-up to assure compliance. These offices are useful in training and developing individuals with the special skills required for project management support personnel on major projects. Table 8.2 summarizes the key differences between these two commonly encountered situations.

PERT/CPM/PDM Network-Based Project Management Systems

Significant benefits are realized from the proper use of network-based systems in both the multiple major and multiple small project situations, including:

- Improved planning and scheduling of activities and forecasting of resource requirements.
- Identification of repetitive planning patterns that can be followed in a number of projects, thereby simplifying the planning process.
- Ability to reschedule activities to reflect interproject dependencies and resource limitations following known priority rules.
- Ability to use the computer effectively to produce timely, valid information for multiproject management purposes.

Table 8.2   Key Differences between Multiple Major and Small Projects

	Multiple Major Projects	Multiple Small Projects
Project manager role	Assigned to a manager who does not have a functional responsibility.	Retained within the line organization with integrated staff assistance in planning and coordination. Possibly several projects are assigned to a project (or program) manager or project coordinator.
Project team	Key team members may report to the project manager or may only be physically located together or may stay in their functional organizations.	Project work always assigned to functional departments; in field phase full-time team is assigned to each project.
Integrated planning and control	Each project planned and controlled on an integrated basis; multiproject conflicts resolved above project manager level. Different systems often used on different projects.	All projects must be planned and controlled on an integrated basis within one multiproject operations planning and control system; conflicts resolved by multiproject and/or functional managers.

The concept of multiproject operations planning and control is discussed further in Section 8.7.

Interdependencies between and within Projects

Projects and activities within projects can be interrelated in three basic ways:

1. *Result-of-action:* The results produced by completion of an activity in one project or task must be available before an activity in another project or task can begin.

2. *Common-unit-of-resource:* An engineer, for example, must complete an activity in one project or task before she can begin another activity in another project or task.

3. *Rate-of-use-of-common-resources:* Two or more projects or tasks are using one resource pool, such as a group of pipefitters; when the rate of use of the resource by the projects exceeds the supply, the projects or tasks become interdependent on each other through the limited resource pool.

The first two interdependencies can be represented by interface events as discussed in Part II, and especially in Chapter 13. The third interdependency is treated in more detail in the following section and in Part II.

8.6   RESOURCE MANAGEMENT FOR PROJECTS

A common cause of project delays resulting in penalties and other undesirable effects is the overcommitment of the organization to contracts or projects with respect to available resources. Cost overruns can also occur when the limitations of available resources are not considered at the time of project commitment and during project execution. Resource management therefore becomes important to project managers, to those responsible for multiproject situations, and to functional managers contributing to projects. It involves:

- Estimating and forecasting the resource requirements by functional task for each project and summarized for all projects. This requires linking project action plans and schedules with resource estimates and actual expenditures.
- Acquiring, providing, and allocating the needed resources in a timely and efficient manner.
- Planning the work for accomplishment within the constraints of limited resources.
- Controlling the use of resources to accomplish the work according to the project plan.

An important difference has been observed in human resource management on one or a few large projects compared with multiple smaller projects. On a large project, the required resources usually will be obtained somehow, either through hiring additional people on a permanent or temporary basis, or by using contractors, consultants, or "body shops." On multiple smaller projects, the available, always limited resources usually must be carefully allocated to support all the projects and it is often more difficult to augment the resource pools with outsiders.

Resources to Be Managed

A variety of resources must be managed, including time, money, people, facilities, equipment, and material. Time is a fundamental resource that cannot be managed like the others. Time flows at a constant rate and time that is not used can never be recovered. It cannot be stored or accumulated for later use. Time is the element that interrelates all other resources with the project plan.

The other resources listed earlier are forecasted, provided, and controlled in accordance with established procedures in all organizations for the management of departments, divisions, and other organizational elements. However, procedures and tools for performing these resource management tasks on a project basis are frequently inadequate.

Procedures and Tools for Project Resource Management

Effective procedures for estimating, forecasting, allocating, and controlling the resources on one or many projects are described in Part II. On major projects and in multiproject situations, computer-supported systems are frequently the only practical way to handle the dynamic need to replan, reschedule, and reallocate resources considering the large volume of detailed information involved. Chapter 5 describes the capabilities, selection, and implementation of such tools, including enterprise resource planning (ERP) software aplications.

Resource Constrained Project Planning, Scheduling, and Control

The relatively new concepts of the critical chain and the resource critical path are discussed in Chapter 10, Section 10.17. These methods focus heavily on linking resources to plans and schedules (see Appendix).

8.7   MULTIPROJECT OPERATIONS PLANNING AND CONTROL

Situations involving multiple projects, large or small, frequently require the establishment of an operations planning and control function. This may be set up within a division, a product line, or for an entire company. Operations planning and control integrates and controls, on a master plan level and for all contracts and/or projects, the functions of marketing, engineering, procurement, manufacturing, and installation, usually within a specific product line or division. Such a function within a particular organization can provide significant benefits to the organization's project management capabilities and to the project management office, resulting in improved:

- Project planning and control support to each multiproject manager, with reduction in planning and control staff in each project office. (The risks of overcentralizing such support for major projects have been discussed earlier.)

- Ability to resolve conflicts between projects and to control relative priorities of projects, expecially for multiple smaller projects.
- Uniformity of project planning and control practices, enabling higher management to review all projects on a more consistent basis.
- Forecasting of resource requirements for all projects.

Nature of the Problem

The need exists for top management to have confidence that planning is directed toward optimum corporate and project performance. It must have adequate feedback on actual compared to forecasted achievement for functional, corporate, and customer performance goals to be able to evaluate the consequences of specific cost trade-offs and specific alternative business strategies, quickly and quantitatively.

Central planning functions tend to stop short of filling those management needs, because they usually lack the capability to:

- Monitor functional planning continuously at a manageable level of detail.
- Evaluate the corporate impact of forecasted functional achievement accurately and routinely.
- Carry out quantitative analyzes, within a reasonable time, of the consequences of alternative business strategies.
- Replan, on time, matching available resources with contract requirements.
- Issue top level schedules reflecting a balanced, coordinated load between engineering, manufacturing, and installation or field operations.

What is needed is a planning capability in a position to evaluate functional plans and their impact on corporate and project performance objectives, with tools powerful enough to evaluate the effect of discrete contract-oriented decisions on project performance, and so placed in the organizational structure to be able to offer solutions to problems transcending functional organizational boundaries.

Solution: Operations Planning and Control

The solution to this need is to establish an operations planning and control function with supporting system. The function would have the following charter:

- Optimization of corporate and project performance goals by coordination of planning activities in the marketing, engineering, manufacturing, and installation functions through generation of corporate master schedules.

- Coordination of functional planning by means of continuous workload versus capacity evaluation, recognizing functional dependencies in project execution, with a planning horizon extending as far as firm, proposed, and forecasted project activities will allow.
- Continuous evaluation of functional capabilities relative to requirements to (1) allow forecasting of performance against corporate and project goals and (2) highlight areas of deviation where management action is required to resolve cases of potential capacity shortage or surplus.
- Development and maintenance of supporting systems for simulation purposes: to evaluate the likely consequences of alternative business strategies in order to offer possible solutions to senior management.

Potential Benefits

The potential benefits of the operations planning and control function are:

- Improving cross-functional communications with a positive effect on functional performance.
- Improving overall contract and project performance.
- Improving corporate performance by improved resource planning and utilization.

Examples of specific benefits include:

- Reduction of project cycle time.
- Increased direct labor efficiency.
- Increased utilization of tools, test equipment, and other facilities.
- Reduction of gross inventory.
- Reduced exposure to contract penalties.

The final effect of all these benefits is to enable the company to handle more projects, and produce more sales revenue and net income without increasing total personnel and capital investment.

Operations Planning and Control Overview

Operations planning and control reflects the application of currently accepted management concepts combined with network-based systems. It is the result of viewing the problem outlined above from a management perspective, which recognizes that the proper organizational structure is requisite to the implementation of a planning and control system, and that an organization with inadequate systems and procedures will be ineffective. To solve the problem addressed by operations planning and control, both organizational considerations and systems development must be welded together.

Organizational Considerations

The operations planning and control function must report at a level that ensures complete objectivity and impartiality. The exact placement of the function in a given organization will depend on the company product line structure and its size. It is clear that the function must report at a director level with responsibility for overall corporate planning, or to the division or product line manager responsible for engineering, manufacturing, and installation.

In those companies with more than one product line, where normal product cycle time exceeds one year, and contributions from two or more functions are required to execute the project, then a separate operations planning and control organization should exist within each product line, and overall coordination should be supplied by a similar function reporting to a corporate level manager.

Operations planning and control performs a distinctly different corporate role from that usually associated with the management of large projects. Project managers are responsible for large one-of-a-kind projects. If they use a network-based system for controlling the project, it will be structured to reflect a great amount of detail and will generally not be related to other large projects. Operations planning and control on the other hand deals with contracts that reflect a high degree of similarity and are generally smaller than those found under the control of a project manager. The operations planning and control manager can, however, make a valuable contribution to project management by reserving capacity assigned to the project when preparing the master schedule; by providing an effective interface with the functions; and by providing most or all of the project planning and control information required for the major projects.

Supporting Systems

To perform the operations planning and control organization function, systems support will be required for operations scheduling and evaluation, planning evaluation, and resource allocation.

Organization and System Interface

The concept of operations planning and control and the interface between the involved organizational functions and the supporting systems are illustrated in Figure 8.1. The operations planning and control function plans, schedules, monitors, reports, and controls, *at the master schedule level,* all orders and contracts (projects) through all contributing functions.

The set of bridging networks integrates the functional plans and schedules for all projects. The networks are also linked to the supporting functional systems by the downward flow of master scheduling information, and the upward flow of progress and status information. This means that the bridging networks must incorporate milestone or interface events common to both the operations planning and control systems and the functional systems. These milestone/interface events must meet the needs of both types of systems.

Experience indicates that the two elements of operations planning and control—the organizational function and the system—must be developed and introduced concurrently. One element without the other simply will not work. Additionally, if one element is implemented prematurely less than desirable results will be produced.

Standard and Unique Milestones

Boznak (1987) describes a system for multiproject planning and control based on a four-phased project process (design, procure, build/test, and deliver/support) with a set of standardized milestone events that are scheduled and controlled by the project manager, and a set of project-unique milestones scheduled and controlled by the functional project leader or manager. The project manager controlled milestones in Boznak's approach are standardized, coordinative, business-level, and summary in nature.

The functional project leader controlled milestones are project unique, coordinative, functional-level, and detailed in nature.

This multiproject system produces several types and levels of reports, including customer satisfaction report; multiyear master plan, containing all projects; detail reports of various kinds; management action reports, listing all milestones not on schedule; and monthly performance summary, showing schedule compliance by project and functional organization.

There are a number of ways to plan, schedule, track, and control multiple projects within an organization. The key to success is to have a coherent, integrated, consistent system for doing this, and to make sure that everyone is using the same system.

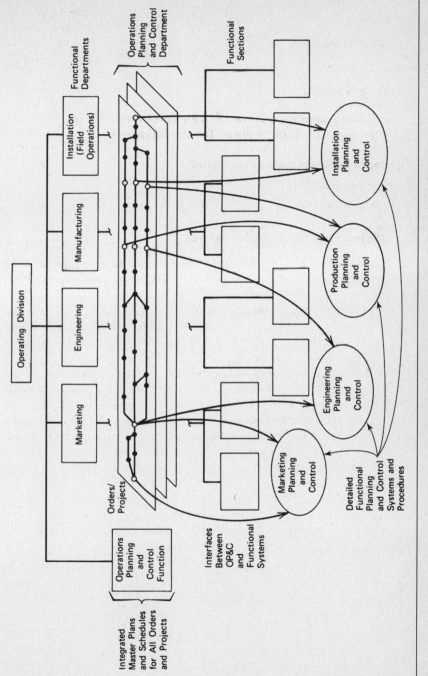

Figure 8.1 General illustration of operations planning and control concept.

CEO DEMANDS: PROJECT PORTFOLIO, PROGRAM, AND MULTIPROJECT MANAGEMENT

Regarding project portfolios and multiproject management the CEO must demand that:

1. A well-defined project portfolio management process be implemented on each defined project portfolio.

2. A project portfolio steering group be assigned the responsibilities described here to achieve effective operation of the portfolio management process for each portfolio in the organization.

3. Resources be managed in multiproject situations using available multiproject resource estimating and allocating methods and software applications.

4. Multiproject and multicontract operations planning and control systems be implemented within appropriate operating divisions of the organization.

PART

II

‹ ›

Managing Specific Projects

Chapters 9 through 14 contain specific, detailed information for guidance and use in establishing practices and procedures for specific projects. Since it is not practical to provide examples related to every type of project of interest to all readers, the emphasis in Part II is on major commercial and product development projects in manufacturing companies. However, the material can readily be adapted to other types of projects in other environments.

For simplicity, the word *project* will be used throughout Part II, although in most instances *program* can be used interchangeably. These terms were defined in Chapter 2.

9

‹ ›

Organizing the Project
Office and Project Team

The approach described in this and the following chapters is based
on typical major project situations involving the design, manufacture, assembly, and testing of complex hardware and software systems.
This presumes the following conditions:

- The project (or program) warrants a full-time project manager.
- The project office is held to minimum size, with maximum use of
  functional contributors in existing departments.

This chapter summarizes the functions of the project office and the
project team under these conditions, describes the duties of key persons
involved in the project, and discusses their relationships.

As discussed in Chapter 8, the situation frequently occurs wherein one
project manager is responsible for several projects or, when multiple small
projects exist, the division or other general manager retains the project
manager responsibility himself. In still other situations, a manager of projects is appointed. In such cases, a centralized Operations Planning and
Control function is usually required, as described in Section 8.7.

9.1 FUNCTIONS OF THE PROJECT OFFICE
AND PROJECT TEAM

The *project office* supports the project manager in carrying out his or her
responsibilities. Thus, the project manager's basic charter, organizational

relationships, and the nature of the project itself will influence the makeup of the project office. The presence or absence of other projects and of a project management office or a central planning office will also affect the organization of the project office.

The *project team* includes all functional contributors to the project, as well as the members of the project office. The general functions to be carried out during completion of the overall project by members of the project team are:

- Management.
- Product design and development.
- Product manufacture.
- Purchasing and subcontracting.
- Product installation, testing, and field support.

The relationships of these functions to the project manager are shown in the generalized project organization chart in Figure 7.2. Each of these functions is discussed in the following paragraphs.

Management

The management functions are those functions necessary to enable the project manager to fulfill basic responsibilities: Overall direction and coordination of the project through all its phases to achieve the desired results within established budget and schedule. These functions are summarized in Chapter 7 and discussed in detail in the remainder of the book.

Product Design and Development

The basic purpose of this general function is to produce adequate documentation (and often a prototype product or system) so that the product may be manufactured in the quantity required within the desired cost and schedule. These functions may be defined as:

- Systems analysis, engineering, and integration.
- Product design.
- Product control (quality, cost, configuration).

Systems analysis, engineering, and *integration* functions include: system studies; functional analysis and functional design of the system or product; and coordination and integration of detailed designs, including functional and mechanical interfaces between major subsystems or components of the product.

Product design functions include the detailed engineering design and development functions needed to translate the functional systems design into specifications, drawings, and other documents which can be used to manufacture, assemble, install, and test the product. This may also include the manufacture and test of a prototype or first article system or product, using either model shop or factory facilities on a subcontract basis.

Product control functions include: product quality control, using established staff specialists and procedures; product cost control, including value engineering practices; product configuration control including design freeze practices (to establish the "baseline" design), engineering change control practices, and documentation control practices.

The term *product* refers to *all* results of the project: hardware, software, documentation, training or other services, facilities, and so on. A new organizational entity can also be a result of the project.

The project office in a specific situation may perform none, a few, or all of these product design and development functions, depending on many factors. Generally, a larger share of these functions will be assigned to the project office (together with adequate staff) when the product is new or unusual to the responsible unit, or when there is little confidence that the work will be carried out efficiently and on schedule within established engineering departments. When several engineering departments, for example, from different product lines or different companies, are contributing to the product design and development, the functions of systems analysis, engineering and integration, and of product control, should be assigned to the project office. Figure 7.3 illustrates a project with a large technical staff assigned to the project office for an electronic telephone switching system contract.

Except in the situation described above, these functions are usually performed by project team members within existing engineering departments, under the active coordination of the project manager.

Product Manufacture

This general function is to purchase materials and components, fabricate, assemble, test, and deliver the equipment required to complete the project. These functions are carried out by the established manufacturing departments within the project's parent company or by outside companies on a subcontract or purchase order basis.

The project manager, however, must coordinate and integrate the manufacturing functions with product design and development on one hand and field operations (if any) on the other. The lack of proper integration between functions is the most common cause of project failure.

In order to achieve this integration, it is necessary to appoint a project manufacturing coordinator or equivalent who will, in effect, act as a project manager for product manufacture. This person is a key project team member, and may be assigned full time to one major project or may be able to handle two or more projects at one time, if the projects are small.

It is recommended that the project manufacturing coordinator remain within the appropriate manufacturing department. When two or more divisions or companies perform a large part of the product manufacture, each must designate a project manufacturing coordinator, with one designated as the lead division for manufacture. If it is not possible to designate a lead division, then the coordination effort must be accomplished by the project office.

Purchasing and Subcontracting

This function is sometimes included with the product manufacture area, but it is normally important enough to warrant full functional responsibility.

A separate project purchasing and subcontracting coordinator with status equivalent to that of the manufacturing coordinator should be appointed to handle all purchasing and subcontracting matters for the project manager. This person should be a part of the purchasing department to maintain day-to-day contact with all persons carrying out the procurement functions.

Product Installation, Testing, and Field Support

Many projects require field installation and testing, and some include continuing field support for a period of time. In these cases, a field project manager (or equivalent) is required.

When field operations are a part of the project, this phase is usually clearly recognized as being of a project nature and requiring one person to be in charge. This field project manager is almost always a member of an established installation department (or equivalent) if such a department exists within the responsible company. Since engineering and manufacturing operations frequently overlap the installation phase, the overall project manager's role continues to be of critical importance to success while field operations are in progress. However, in the relationship between the project manager and the field project manager, the project manager retains the overall responsibility for the coordination of the entire project.

Assignment of Persons to the Project Office

As a general rule, it is recommended that the number of persons assigned to a project office under the supervision of the project manager be kept as small as possible. This will emphasize the responsibility of each functional (line) department or staff for their contribution to the project and retain to the maximum degree the benefits of specialized functional departments. It will also increase flexibility of functional staffing of the project, avoid unnecessary payroll costs to the project, and minimize reassignment problems when particular tasks are completed. This will enable the project manager to devote maximum effort to the project itself, rather than supervisory duties related to a large staff.

With adequate project planning and control procedures, a qualified project staff can maintain the desired control of the project. In the absence of adequate planning and control procedures to integrate the functional contributions, it is usually necessary to build up a larger staff with as many functional contributors as possible directly under the project manager in order to achieve control. This is an expensive and frequently awkward approach, and it aggravates the relationships between the project manager and contributing functional managers.

The persons who should be assigned (transferred) permanently to the project office are those who:

- Deal with the management aspects of the project.
- Are needed on a full-time basis for a period of at least six months.
- Must be in frequent close contact with the project manager or other members of the project office in the performance of their duties.
- Cannot otherwise be controlled effectively, because of organizational or geographic considerations.

The recommended assignment location of each of the key people on the project team follows:

Project manager. The project manager is always considered the manager of the project office (which could be a one-person office).

Project engineer. The project engineer may be assigned to the project office in charge of product design and development where the product is new to the company or where several divisions are involved, as discussed earlier. Otherwise, the project engineer should remain within the lead engineering department.

Contract administrator. The contract administrator should remain a member of the contract administration staff, except on very large programs extending over a considerable period of time, but may be located physically in the project office while remaining with his or her parent organization.

Project controller.   The project controller should always be assigned to the project office, except where not needed full time or where a centralized planning and control function adequately serves the project manager.

Project accountant.   The project accountant should remain a member of the accounting department, except on very large programs extending over a considerable period of time. Like the contract administrator, she may physically be located in the project office while remaining with her parent organization.

Manufacturing coordinator.   The manufacturing coordinator should remain a member of the manufacturing organization, preferably on the staff of the manufacturing manager or within production control. When more than one division is to contribute substantially to product manufacture, it may be necessary to assign this person to the project office to enable effective coordination of all contributors.

Purchasing and subcontracting coordinator.   This coordinator should remain a member of the purchasing department in most cases.

Field project manager.   The field project manager should remain a member of the installation or field operations department, if one exists, except under unusual circumstances that would require him to be assigned to the project office.

Project Team Concept

As discussed in Chapter 6, whether a person is assigned to the project office or remains in a functional department or staff, all persons holding identifiable responsibilities for direct contributions to the project are considered to be members of the project team. Creating awareness of membership in the project team is a primary task of the project manager, and development of a good project team spirit has proven to be a powerful means for accomplishing difficult objectives under tight time schedules. Outside contributors (vendors, contractors, consultants, architects, etc.) are also members of the project team, as are contributing customer representatives.

The Project Organization Chart

Figure 7.8 shows a typical representation of a project team in the format of a classic organizational chart. This type of representation can be confusing if not properly understood, but it can also be useful to identify the key project team members and show their relationships to each other and to the project manager for project purposes. This recognizes that such a chart does not imply permanent superior-subordinate relationships portrayed in the company organization charts.

9.2   PROJECT MANAGER DUTIES

Within the general statement of the project manager responsibilities given in Chapter 4, the following description of project manager duties is presented as a guide for development of specific duties on a particular project. Some of the duties listed may not be practical, feasible, or pertinent in certain cases, but wherever possible it is recommended that all items mentioned be included in the project manager's duties and responsibilities, with appropriate internal documentation and dissemination to all concerned managers.

Project Start-Up

- Identify key project team members and define their responsibilities.
- Rapidly and efficiently plan and start up the project (see Chapter 11).
- Assure that all equipment, documents, and services are properly delivered to the customer for acceptance and use within the contractual schedule and costs.
- Convey to all concerned departments (both internal and external) a full understanding of the customer requirements of the project.
- Participate with and lead responsible managers and key team members in developing overall project objectives, strategies, budgets, and schedules.
- Plan for all necessary project tasks to satisfy customer and management requirements, and assure that they are properly and realistically scheduled, budgeted, provided for, monitored, and reported.
- Identify promptly all deficiencies and deviations from plan.
- Assure that actions are initiated to correct deficiencies and deviations, and monitor execution of such actions.
- Assure that payment is received in accordance with contractual terms.
- Maintain cognizance over all project contacts with the customer and assure that proper team members participate in such contacts.

- Arbitrate and resolve conflicts and differences between functional departments on specific project tasks or activities.
- Maintain day-to-day liaison with all functional contributors to provide communication required to assure realization of their commitments.
- Make or force required decisions at successively higher organizational levels to achieve project objectives, following agreed escalation procedures.
- Maintain communications with higher management regarding problem areas and project status.

Customer Relations

In close cooperation with the customer relations or marketing department:

- Receive from the customer all necessary technical, cost, and scheduling information required for accomplishment of the project.
- Establish good working relationships with the customer on all levels: management, contracts, legal, accounts payable, system engineering, design engineering, field sites, and operations.
- Arrange and attend all meetings with customer (contractual, planning, engineering, operations).
- Receive and answer all technical and operational questions from the customer, with appropriate assistance from functional departments.

Contract Administration

- Identify any potential areas of exposure in existing or potential contracts and initiate appropriate action to alert higher management and eliminate such exposure.
- Prepare and send, or approve prior to sending by others, all correspondence on contractual matters.
- Coordinate the activities of the project contract administrator in regard to project matters.
- Prepare for and participate in contract negotiations.
- Identify all open contractual commitments.
- Advise engineering, manufacturing, and field operations of contractual commitments and variations allowed.

- Prepare historical or position papers on any contractual or technical aspect of the program, for use in contract negotiations or litigation.

Project Planning, Control, Reporting, Evaluation, and Direction

- Perform, or supervise the performance of, all project planning, controlling, reporting, evaluation and direction functions as described in following chapters, as appropriate to the scope of each project.
- Conduct frequent, regular project evaluation and review meetings with key project team members to identify current and future problems and initiate actions for their resolution.
- Prepare and submit weekly or monthly progress reports to higher management, and to the customer if required.
- Supervise the project controller and his staff.

Marketing

Maintain close liaison with marketing and utilize customer contacts to acquire all possible marketing intelligence for future business.

Engineering

- Ensure that engineering fulfills its responsibilities for delivering, on schedule and within product cost estimates, drawings, and specifications usable by manufacturing and field operations, meeting the customer specifications.
- In cooperation with the engineering, drafting, and publications departments, define and establish schedules and budgets for all engineering and related tasks. After agreement, release funding allowables and monitor progress on each task in relation to the overall project.
- Act as the interface with the customer for these departments (with their assistance as required).
- Assure the control of product quality, configuration, and cost.
- Approve technical publications prior to release to the customer.
- Coordinate engineering support related to the project for manufacturing, installation, legal, and other departments.
- Participate (or delegate participation) as a voting member in the Engineering Change Control Board on matters affecting the project.

Manufacturing

- Ensure that manufacturing fulfills its responsibilities for on-schedule delivery of all required equipment, meeting the engineering specifications within estimated manufacturing costs.
- Define contractual commitments to production control.
- Develop schedules to meet contractual commitments in the most economical fashion.
- Establish and release manufacturing and other resource and funding allowables.
- Approve and monitor production control schedules.
- Establish project priorities.
- Approve, prior to implementation, any product changes initiated by manufacturing.
- Approve packing and shipping instructions based on type of transportation to be used and schedule for delivery.

Purchasing and Subcontracting

- Ensure that purchasing and subcontracting fulfills their responsibilities to obtain delivery of materials, equipment, documents, and services on schedule and within estimated cost for the project.
- Approve make-or-buy decisions for the project.
- Define contractual commitments to purchasing and subcontracting.
- Establish and release procurement funding allowables.
- Approve and monitor major purchase orders and subcontracts.
- Specify planning, scheduling, and reporting requirements for major purchase orders and subcontracts.

Installation, Construction, Testing, and Other Field Operations

- Ensure that installation and field operations fulfill their responsibilities for on-schedule delivery to the customer of materials, equipment, and documents within the cost estimates for the project.
- Define contractual commitments to installation and field operations.
- In cooperation with installation and field operations, define and establish schedules and budgets for all field work. After agreement, release funding allowables and monitor progress on each task in relation to the overall project.

- Coordinate all problems of performance and schedule with engineering, manufacturing, and purchasing and subcontracting.
- Except for customer contacts related to daily operating matters, act as the customer interface for installation and field operations departments.

Financial

In addition to the financial planning and control functions described in later chapters:

- Assist in the collection of accounts receivable.
- Approve prices of all change orders and proposals to the customer.

Project Closeout (See Chapter 14)

- Ensure that all required steps are taken to present adequately all project deliverable items to the customer for acceptance and that project activities are closed out in an efficient and economical manner.
- Assure that the acceptance plan and schedule comply with the customer contractual requirements.
- Assist the legal, contract administration, and marketing or commercial departments in preparation of a closeout plan and required closeout data.
- Obtain and approve closeout plans from each involved functional department.
- Monitor closeout activities, including disposition of surplus materials.
- Notify finance and functional departments of the completion of activities and of the project.
- Monitor payment from the customer until all collections have been made.

9.3 FUNCTIONAL PROJECT LEADER DUTIES

The functional project leaders direct, lead, and integrate the activities of the project team members (all persons contributing to the project) within their specific function. This manager may be a senior functional manager, but it is usually recommended that this role be delegated to a subordinate who can devote the required amount of time to the project leader job. If the assignment is for a large project requiring a full-time functional project leader, it obviously cannot be a person who also has responsibility for managing the functional department. Frequently, the assignment is given to a person who is also directly responsible for carrying out one or more specific tasks within the functional department in question, causing potential conflicts due to the project leader's favoring the tasks for which they are responsible. This is a dilemma that is not easy to solve; some organizations have given the project leader role for more than one project (none of which requires a full-time assignment) to the same person.

The specific duties of the functional project leader will vary considerably, depending on the nature of the particular function that person represents. The project leader is really a mini-project manager, and many of the project manager's duties described above can be translated to the functional project leader, with appropriate limitations on the scope of activity. A well-established functional project leader role is that of the project engineer, whose duties are described in some detail in the following section. These duties, and those of the other team members following, can also be used as a guide to defining other functional project leaders' duties, again with appropriate translation to fit the specific function.

9.4   PROJECT ENGINEER DUTIES

The project engineer is responsible for the technical integrity of the project and for cost and schedule performance of all engineering phases of the project. Specifically, the responsibilities of the project engineer are:

- Ensure that the customer performance requirements are fully understood and that the company is technically capable of meeting these requirements.
- Define these requirements to the smallest subsystem to the functional areas so that they can properly schedule, cost, and perform the work to be accomplished.
- Ensure that the engineering tasks so defined are accomplished within the engineering schedules and allowables (manpower, materials, funds) of the contract.
- Provide technical direction as necessary to accomplish the project objectives.
- Conduct design review meetings at regular intervals to assure that all technical objectives will be achieved.
- Act as technical advisor to the project manager and other functional departments, as requested by the project manager.

In exercising the foregoing responsibilities, the project engineer is supported by the various engineering departments through the designated engineering project leaders.

Proposal Preparation and Negotiation

During the proposal phase, the project engineer will do the following:

- Coordinate and plan the preparation of the technical proposal.
- Review and evaluate the statement of work and other technical data.
- Establish an engineering proposal team or teams.
- Within the bounds of the overall proposal schedule, establish the engineering proposal schedule.
- Reduce customer engineering requirements to tasks and subtasks.
- Define in writing the requirements necessary from engineering to other functional areas, including preliminary specifications for make or buy, or subcontract items.
- Coordinate and/or prepare a schedule for all engineering functions, including handoff to and receipt from manufacturing.
- Review and approve all engineering subtask and task costs, schedules, and narrative inputs.
- Coordinate and/or prepare overall engineering cost.
- Participate in preliminary make-or-buy decisions.
- Participate in overall cost and schedule review.
- Participate, as required, in negotiation of contract.
- Bring problems between the project engineer and engineering functional managers and project leaders to appropriate engineering directors for resolution.

Project Planning and Initiation

The project engineer is responsible for the preparation of plans and schedules for all engineering tasks within the overall project plan established by the project manager. In planning the engineering tasks, he or she will compare the engineering proposal against the received contract. Where the received contract requirements dictate a change in cost, schedule, or technical complexity for solution, he will obtain approval from the director of engineering and the project manager to make the necessary modifications in engineering estimates of the proposal. During this phase, the project engineer will:

- Update the proposal task and subtask descriptions to conform with the contract, and within the engineering allowables prepare additional tasks and subtasks as required to provide a complete engineering implementation plan for the project.
- Prepare a master engineering schedule in accordance with the contractual requirements.
- Prepare, or have prepared, detailed task and subtask definitions and specifications. Agree on allowables, major milestones, and evaluation points in tasks with the task leaders and their functional managers.
- Through the functional engineering managers or project leaders, assign responsibility for task and subtask performance, and authorize the initiation of work against identified commitments based on cost and milestone schedules, with approval of the project manager.
- Using contract specifications as the base line, prepare, or have prepared, specifications for subcontract items.
- Participate and provide support from appropriate engineering functions in final make-or-buy decisions and source selection.
- Prepare, or have prepared, hardware and system integration and acceptance test plan. Review the test plan with Quality Assurance and advise them as to the required participation of other departments.

Project Performance and Control

The project engineer is responsible for the engineering progress of the project and compliance with contract requirements, cost allowables, and schedule commitments. Within these limits, the project engineer, if necessary, may make design changes and task requirement changes in accordance with the project concept and assume the responsibility for the change in concert with the functional engineering project leaders and with the knowledge of the project manager. No changes may be made that affect other functional departments without the knowledge of that department, documentation to the project manager, and the inclusion of the appropriate charge-back of any variance caused by change. The project engineer maintains day-to-day liaison with the project manager for two-way information exchange. Specific responsibilities of the project engineer are to

- Prepare and maintain a file of all project specifications related to the technical integrity and performance.
- Prepare and maintain updated records of the engineering expenditures and milestones and conduct regular reviews to insure engineering performance as required.

- Initiate and prepare new engineering costs-to-complete reports as required.

- Establish work priorities within the engineering function where conflict exists; arbitrate differences and interface problems within the engineering function, and request through functional managers changes in personnel assignments if deemed necessary.

- Plan and conduct design review meetings and design audits as required, and participate in technical reviews with customer.

- Prepare project status reports as required related to engineering.

- With the project manager and other functional departments, participate in evaluation and formulation of alternative plans as required by schedule delays or customer change requests.

- Assure support to purchasing and subcontracting, manufacturing, field operations, and support activities by providing liaison and technical assistance within allowables authorized by the project manager.

- Modify and reallocate tasks and subtasks, open and close cost accounts, and change allowable allocations within the limits of the approved engineering allowables, with the concurrence of the functional managers involved. Provide details to the project manager of all such actions prior to change.

- As requested by the project manager, support legal and contracts administration by providing technical information.

- Review and approve technical aspects of reports for dissemination to the customer.

- Authorize within the approved allowables the procurement of material and/or services as required for the implementation of the engineering functional responsibility.

- Adjudicate technical problems and make technical decisions within scope of contractual requirements. Cost and schedule decisions affecting contractual requirements or interfaces with other functions are to be approved by the appropriate engineering function manager with the cognizance of the director of engineering (or his delegate) and the project manager.

- Approve all engineering designs released for procurement and/or fabrication for customer deliverable items.

- Bring problems arising between the project engineer and engineering functional managers to the engineering director for resolution.

- Bring problems arising between the project engineer and functions outside engineering to the project manager for resolution, with the cognizance of the director of engineering and the director of the other functions.

9.5   CONTRACT ADMINISTRATOR DUTIES

Contract administration is a specialized management function indispensable to effective management of those projects carried out under contract with customers. This function has many legal implications and serves to protect the company from unforeseen risks prior to contract approval and during execution of the project. Well-qualified, properly organized contract administration support to a project manager is vital to the continuing success of companies responsible for major sales contracts.

Contract administration is represented both on the project manager's team and on the general manager's staff. A director of contract administration has the authority to audit project contract files and to impose status reporting requirements that will disclose operational and contractual problems relating to specific projects. The director of contract administration is also available to provide expertise in the resolution of contract problems beyond the capability of the contract administrator assigned to a given project.

The project contract administrator is responsible for day-to-day administration of (1) the contract(s) that authorize performance of the project and (2) all subcontracts with outside firms for equipment, material, and services to fulfill project requirements.

Proposal Preparation

- When participation of an outside subcontractor is required, assure that firm quotations are obtained based on terms and conditions compatible with those imposed by the customer.
- Review with the legal and financial departments all of the legal and commercial terms and conditions imposed by the customer.
- Review the proposal prior to submittal to assure that all risks and potential exposures are fully recognized.

Contract Negotiation

- Lead all contract negotiations for the project manager.
- Record detailed minutes of the proceedings.
- Assure that all discussions or agreements reached during negotiations are confirmed in writing with the understanding that they will be incorporated into the contract during the contract definition phase.
- Assure that the negotiating limits established by the Proposal Review Board (or equivalent) are not exceeded.

Contract Definition

- Expedite the preparation, management review, and execution of the contract, as follows:

  —Clarify the contract format with the customer.

  —Establish the order of precedence of contract documents incorporated by reference.

  —Set the date by which the contract will be available in final form for management review prior to execution.

  —Participate with the project manager in final briefing of management on the contract terms and conditions prior to signature.

Project Planning Phase

- Establish channels of communication with the customer and define commitment authority of project manager, contract administrator, and others.
- Integrate contract requirements and milestones into the project plan and schedule, including both company and customer obligations.
- Establish procedures for submission of contract deliverables to customer.
- Establish mechanics for monthly contract status reports for the customer and management.

Project Execution Phase

- Monitor and follow up all contract and project activities to assure fulfillment of contractual obligations by both the company and the customer.
- Assure that all contract deliverables are transmitted to the customer and that all contractually required notifications are made.
- Record any instance where the customer has failed to fulfill his obligations and define the cost and schedule impact on the project of such failure.
- Identify and define changes in scope, customer-caused delays, and force majeure, including:

  — Early identification and notification to customer.

  — Obtaining customer's agreement that change of scope or customer-caused delay or force majeure case has actually occurred.

  — In coordination with the project manager and the project team, prepare a proposal that defines the scope of the change(s) and resulting price and/or schedule impact for submittal to the customer for eventual contract modification.

- Assist in negotiation and definition of contract change orders.

- Participate in project and contract status reviews and prepare required reports.

- Arrange with the customer to review the minutes of joint project review meetings to assure that they accurately reflect the proceedings.

- Assure that the customer is notified in writing of the completion of each contractual milestone and submission of each contract deliverable item, with a positive assertion that the obligation has been fulfilled.

- Where the customer insists on additional data or work before accepting completion of an item, monitor compliance with his requirement to clear such items as quickly as possible.

Project Closeout Phase (See Chapter 14)

- At the point where all contractual obligations have been fulfilled, or where all but longer term warranties or spare parts deliveries are complete, assure that this fact is clearly and quickly communicated in writing to the customer.

- Assure that all formal documentation related to customer acceptance as required by the contract is properly executed.

- Expedite completion of all actions by the company and the customer needed to complete the contract and claim final payment.

- Initiate formal request for final payment.

- Where possible, obtain certification from the customer acknowledging completion of all contractual obligations and releasing the company from further obligations, except those under the terms of guaranty or warranty, if any.

Project/Contract Record Retention

Prior to disbanding the project team, the project contract administrator is responsible for collecting and placing in suitable storage the following records, to satisfy legal and internal management requirements:

- The contract file, which consists of:
    —Original request for proposal (RFP) and all modifications.
    —All correspondence clarifying points in the RFP.
    —Copy of company's proposal and all amendments thereto.

—Records of negotiations.

—Original signed copy of contract and all documents and specifications incorporated in the contract by reference.

—All contract modifications (supplemental agreements).

—A chronological file of all correspondence exchanged between the parties during the life of the program. This includes letters, telexes, records of telephone calls, and minutes of meetings.

—Acceptance documentation.

—Billings and payment vouchers.

—Final releases.

- Financial records required to support postcontract audits, if required by contract or governing statutes.
- History of the project (chronology of all events—contractual and noncontractual).
- Historical and cost and time records that can serve as standards for estimating future requirements.

9.6 PROJECT CONTROLLER DUTIES

The primary responsibility of the project manager is to plan and control his project. On some smaller or less complex projects, he may be able to perform all the planning and controlling functions himself. However, on most major projects, as defined in Chapter 2, it will be necessary to provide at least one person who is well qualified in project planning and control and who can devote full attention to these specialized project management needs. This person is the project controller. (A number of other equivalent job titles are in use for this position.) On very large or complex programs or projects the project controller may require one or more persons to assist in carrying out these duties and responsibilities.

If a centralized operations planning and control function exists in the company (discussed in Chapter 8), that office may provide the needed planning and control services to the project manager. In that case, the project controller would be a member of the Operations Planning and Control Office and would have available the specialists in that office. In other situations the project controller may be transferred from Operations Planning and Control to the project office for the duration of the project.

The duties of the project controller are described in the following sections.

- Perform for the project manager the project planning, controlling, reporting, and evaluation functions (described in following chapters) as delegated to him, so that the project objectives are achieved within the schedule and cost limits.

- Assist the project manager to achieve clear visibility of all contract tasks so that they can be progressively measured and evaluated in sufficient time for corrective action to be taken.

Project Planning and Scheduling

- In cooperation with responsible managers define the project systematically so that all tasks to be performed are identified and hierarchically related to each other, including work funded under contract or by the company, using the project breakdown structure or similar technique.
- Identify all elements of work (tasks or work packages) to be controlled for time, manpower, or cost, and identify the responsible and performing organizations and project leaders for each.
- Define an adequate number of key milestones for master planning and management reporting purposes.
- Prepare and maintain a graphic project master plan and schedule, based on the project breakdown structure, identifying all tasks or work packages to be controlled in the time dimension, and incorporating all defined milestones.
- Prepare more detailed graphic plans and schedules for each major element of the project.

Budgeting and Work Authorization

- Obtain from the responsible functional project leader for each task or work package a task description, to include:
  —Statement of work.
  —Estimate of resources required (work days, computer hours, etc.).
  —Estimate of labor, computer, and other costs (with assistance of the project accountant).
  —Estimate of start date, and estimated total duration and duration between milestones.
- Prepare and maintain a task description file for the entire project.
- Summarize all task manpower and cost estimates, and coordinate needed revisions with responsible managers and the project manager to match the estimates with available and allocated funds for the project in total, for each major element, and for each task.

- Prepare and release, on approval of the project manager and the responsible functional manager, work authorization documents containing the statement of work, budgeted labor, and cost amounts; scheduled dates for start, completion, and intermediate milestones; and the assigned cost accounting number.
- Prepare and release, with approval of the project manager, revised work authorization documents when major changes are required or have occurred, within the authorized funding limits and the approval authority of the project manager.

Work Schedules

- Assist each responsible manager or project leader in developing detailed plans and schedules for assigned tasks, reflecting the established milestone dates in the project master plan.
- Issue current schedules to all concerned showing start and completion dates of all tasks and occurrence dates of milestones.

Progress Monitoring and Evaluation

- Obtain weekly reports from all responsible managers and project leaders of
  —Activities started and completed.
  —Milestones completed.
  —Estimates of time required to complete activities or tasks under way.
  —Changes in future plans.
  —Actual or anticipated delays, additional costs, or other problems that may affect other tasks, the schedule, or project cost.
- Record reported progress on the project master plan and analyze the effect of progress in all tasks on the overall project schedule.
- Identify major deviations from schedule and determine, with the responsible managers and the project manager, appropriate action to recover delays or take advantage of early completion of tasks.
- Obtain monthly cost reports and compare to the estimates for each current task, with summaries for each level of the project breakdown structure and the total project.
- Through combined evaluation of schedule and cost progress compared to plan and budget, identify deviations that require management action and report these to the project manager.

- Participate in project review meetings, to present the overall project status and evaluate reports from managers and project leaders.
- Record the minutes of project review meetings and follow up for the project manager all resulting action assignments to assure completion of each.
- Advise the project manager of known or potential problems requiring his attention.
- Each month or quarter obtain from each responsible manager an estimate of time, manpower, and cost to complete for each incomplete task or work package; and prepare, in cooperation with the project accountant, a revised projection of cost to complete the entire project.

Schedule and Cost Control

- When schedule or budget revisions are necessary, due to delay or changes in the scope of work, prepare, negotiate, and issue new project master plans, schedules, and revised work authorization documents, with approval of the project manager, within the authorized funding limits and the approval authority of the project manager.
- In coordination with the project accountant, notify the Finance Department to close each cost account and reject further charges when work is reported complete on the related task.

Reporting

- Prepare for the project manager monthly progress reports to management and the customer.
- Provide cost-to-complete estimates and other pertinent information to the project accountant for use in preparing contract status reports.
- Prepare special reports as required by the project manager.

9.7   PROJECT ACCOUNTANT DUTIES

The basic function of the project accountant is to provide to the project manager the specialized financial and accounting assistance and information needed to forecast and control manpower and costs for the project. The project accountant duties are as follows:

- Establish the basic procedure for utilizing the company financial reporting and accounting system for project control purposes to assure that all costs are properly recorded and reported.

- Assist the project controller in developing the project breakdown structure to identify the tasks or project elements that will be controlled for manpower and cost.
- Establish account numbers for the project and assign a separate number to each task or work element to be controlled.
- Prepare estimates of cost, based on manpower and other estimates provided by the controller, for all tasks in the project when required to prepare revised estimates to complete the project.
- Obtain, analyze, and interpret labor and cost accounting reports, and provide the project manager, project controller, and other managers in the project with appropriate reports to enable each to exercise needed control.
- Assure that the information being recorded and reported by the various functional and project departments is valid, properly charged, and accurate, and that established policies and procedures are being followed for the project.
- Identify current and future deviation from budget of manpower or funds, or other financial problems, and in coordination with the project controller notify the project manager of such problems.
- Prepare, in coordination with the project manager and the project controller, sales contract performance reports as required by division or company procedures on a monthly basis for internal management purposes, and for submission to any higher headquarters.

9.8   MANUFACTURING COORDINATOR DUTIES

The general duties and responsibilities of the manufacturing coordinator (sometimes called the project leader—manufacturing) are to plan, implement, monitor, and coordinate the manufacturing aspects of an assigned project (or projects, where it is feasible to coordinate more than one contract).

Specific Duties

- Review all engineering releases before acceptance by manufacturing to insure they are complete and manufacturable (clean releases), and that all changes are documented by a formal written engineering change request.
- Participate in the development of project master schedules during proposal, negotiation, and execution phases, with particular emphasis on determination of requirements for engineering releases,

critical parts lists, equipment requirements, and so on, to insure meeting delivery requirements.

- Monitor all costs related to assigned projects to assure adherence to manufacturing costs and cost schedules. Analyze variances and recommend corrective action. Collect needed information and prepare manufacturing cost to complete.

- Develop or direct the development of detailed schedules for assigned projects, coordinating the participation of manufacturing and product support engineering, material planning, fabrication, purchasing, material stores, assembly, test, quality control, packing and shipping, in order to insure completion of master project schedule within budget limits; provide information and schedules to different functional groups in order for action to be initiated.

- Approve all shipping authorizations for assigned projects.

- Provide liaison between the project manager and manufacturing; diligently monitor manufacturing portions of assigned projects and answer directly for manufacturing performance against schedules; prepare status reports and provide information needed to prepare costs to complete as required.

- Take action within area of responsibility and make recommendations for corrective action in manufacturing areas to overcome schedule slippages; obtain approval from the project manager for incurring additional manufacturing costs.

- Coordinate requests for clarifications of the impact of contract change proposals on manufacturing effort.

- Participate in the preparation and approval of special operating procedures.

- Review and approve for manufacturing all engineering releases and engineering change notices affecting assigned projects, and participate in Change Control Board activity.

- Represent project manager on all Make/Buy Committee actions.

9.9   FIELD PROJECT MANAGER DUTIES

The field project manager (or equivalent) has overall responsibility for constructing required facilities and installing, testing, maintaining for the specified time period, and handing over to the customer all installed equipment and related documentation as specified by the contract. This includes direct supervision of all company and subcontractor field personnel, through their respective managers or supervisors.

Specific Duties

- Participate in the development of project master schedules during proposal, negotiation, and execution phases, with particular emphasis on determination of equipment delivery schedules and manpower and special test equipment needs.

- Monitor all field operations costs for the project to assure adherence to contract allowables. Analyze variances and recommend corrective actions. Collect needed information and prepare field operations cost to complete.

- Develop or direct the development of detailed schedules for all field operations: coordinating the equipment delivery schedules from manufacturing and subcontractors with field receiving, inspection, installation, testing, and customer acceptance procedures, with due regard for transportation and import/export requirements, to insure completion of the master project schedule within budget limits; provide information and schedules to different functional groups or departments in order for action to be initiated.

- Provide liaison between the project manager and installation and field operations; diligently monitor field operations portion of the project and answer for performance against schedules; prepare status reports.

- Take action and make recommendations for corrective action in field operations and other areas to overcome schedule slippages; obtain approval of the project manager for incurring additional installation costs.

- Coordinate requests for clarifications of the impact of contract change proposals on field operations.

These model statements of responsibilities can be used to develop additional statements for other project team members.

10

‹ ›

Planning and
Initiating Projects

The triad of project management concepts introduced in Chapter 1 consists of (1) identified points of integrative project responsibility (the project sponsor, the project manager, and the functional project leaders); (2) integrative and predictive project planning and control systems; and (3) the project team. This triad of project management concepts are interdependent. The project manager and the functional project leaders must direct the planning and control efforts, understand and believe in the systems and tools used, and actively use the results. If this occurs, good project teamwork will result. In this and subsequent chapters, we describe project planning and control (the related functions, tools methods and systems), and discuss how these are used by the project manager and project team members.

10.1 PROJECT MANAGER'S PLANNING AND CONTROL RESPONSIBILITIES

Effective project management requires having good planning, scheduling, estimating, budgeting, work authorization, monitoring, reporting, evaluation, and control methods and procedures in place, but also requires that the project manager:

- Understand and actually use these methods and procedures.
- Perform key planning work at the master schedule level, and give adequate direction to those who perform the detailed planning and control work.

226

- Establish and maintain effective control of the project.

- Assure that all plans and schedules are adequate and valid.

- Assure that the planning and control functions, as described in the various position descriptions in Chapter 9, are performed properly.

Integrated Planning and Control

Project control is established by:

- Mutually setting objectives and goals.

- Defining the tasks to be performed.

- Planning and scheduling the tasks on the basis of required and available resources.

- Measuring progress and performance through an established, orderly system.

- Taking proper corrective action by each project contributor when progress is not made according to plans, or when plans must be changed.

- Resolving schedule and resource conflicts and raising unresolved conflicts to successively higher management levels until a resolution is reached.

Integrated project planning and control means putting together all essential elements of information related to the products or results of the project, time or schedules, and cost, in money, manpower, or other vital resources for all (or as many as practical) life-cycle phases of the project.

The objective of the planning and control effort is to document current plans, schedules, and budgets; compare actual results with each of these and continually forecast the total project time and cost at completion to enable evaluation, the making of proper decisions, and follow-up of the effect of the decision.

10.2 PROJECT PLANNING AND THE PROJECT LIFE CYCLE

Where in the life cycle of a project does planning begin? In the early conceptual phase, the main emphasis is on the results to be achieved by the project, with only a rough estimate of how the project will be carried out, how much it will cost, and when it can be accomplished. During each subsequent phase, more information is obtained, assumptions are gradually replaced or at least narrowed with known facts, and more detail is added to the project plan and schedule. In these early phases, relatively small amounts of money are usually spent ("seed money"), so detailed plans are not usually justified. However, at some point in all projects there comes a time when significant commitment of money and other resources is required. In a life cycle that is defined as having four phases—concept, definition (proposal), execution, and close-out—the point of significant commitment is generally at the start of the execution phase. A rule of thumb is that the definition phase will cost 10 times that of the concept phase, and the execution phase 10 times that of the definition or proposal phase. In many cases, these factors may be even larger. The close-out phase should expend only a fraction of the execution phase, if it is well-planned and controlled.

The material in this and subsequent chapters is directed toward the comprehensive planning and control required *prior* to approval of the significant commitment of resources at the start of the execution phase, often identified by acceptance of the project proposal. These planning and control principles and tools are equally useful in earlier phases.

The Importance of Adequate Project Planning

Inadequate project planning is a frequently cited reason for project failures. There are many causes of inadequate planning, including the widely recognized aversion of technical and, in fact, many other people to performing planning work ("Do you want me to do planning, or do some productive work?"), the reluctance of many people to expose their plans and knowledge of the job (or lack thereof) to others, and the basic difficulties of planning complex projects. In some situations, the complexities of imposed planning methods, techniques, and tools themselves block the creation of good plans.

In spite of these difficulties, creating a sound project plan is extremely important to project success. Without an adequate plan, the required resources cannot be assured and committed at the proper time, the team members cannot be fully committed to the project, monitoring and control will not be effective, and success will be a matter of luck.

Rules for Effective Project Execution

Thamhain and Wilemon (1986), in a study involving 304 project managers and their superiors from U.S. companies in electronic, chemical, and construction industries, identified a number of problems adversely affecting project performance and recommended several actions to assure effective project planning and execution:

- Assure that each team member is personally "signed-on" to the project.
- Work out a detailed project plan, involving all key personnel.
- Reach agreement on the plan among the project team members, the customer and sponsor.
- Obtain commitment from the project team members.
- Obtain commitment from management.
- Define measurable milestones.
- Attract and hold good people.
- Establish a controlling authority for each work package.
- Detect problems early.

Some ideas for overcoming the barriers to integrated project planning were discussed in Chapter 3, and proven methods for project team planning are presented in Chapter 11.

10.3   PROJECT OBJECTIVES AND SCOPE

In Chapter 1, the hierarchy of objectives and strategies from the policy level to the strategic and operational levels is discussed. The specific objectives of each project must support one or more of these higher level objectives. It is important for the project sponsor, project manager, and functional project leaders to understand not only the project objectives but also the higher level objectives that the project supports. Only with this understanding can the best trade-off decisions be made when the inevitable conflicts between the time, cost, and technical results of the project occur.

Defining the Project Objectives

When a project enters the definition or execution phase, some statement of its objectives has normally been made. This is usually a description of the desired outcome of the project: *What* is proposed to be created; and a target date for its creation: *when* the results should be available. There usually will also be a statement of *how much* money can be spent in accomplishing the project. These three dimensions of the project objectives—results, time, and cost—form the core of the concrete, specific, or "hard" project objectives.

In addition, as discussed in Chapter 6, project objectives as criteria for project success can be viewed along a hard/soft dimension and an acceptable/excellent dimension. In addition to the classic "hard" time, cost, and technical performance objectives, the "soft" criteria are more subjective, and deal more with how the work is accomplished: attitudes, skills, behavior, and the more subtle expectations of the client. The acceptable/excellent dimension relates to the willingness of the project team to continually strive to exceed expectations. This does not mean that engineers should be encouraged to continually improve a design beyond the stated technical specifications (a practice that is frequently blamed for time and cost overruns on projects), but it does mean that the most successful project teams continually strive for improvement in all aspects of the project within the limits of time and cost that have been established. That includes improvement in the way things are done, to do them more quickly, efficiently and with higher quality results, as well as improvement of the project results themselves. The key phrase is *within the limits that have been established*. Planning is about defining those limits, and determining how to achieve the project objectives within the limits.

The hierarchy of objectives and strategies described in Chapter 1 continues within each project. Given a good set of hard and soft project objectives, as elaborated by a project team using the team planning approach described in Chapter 11, the project manager and functional project leaders will each develop their own lower level strategies for achieving their pieces of the overall project objectives. These strategies will in turn have more detailed, shorter term objectives, often tied to specific milestone events in the project master schedule.

Defining Project Scope

There is often confusion in project teams regarding the difference between the project objectives and the project scope. The term *project scope* refers to the "space or opportunity for unhampered motion, activity, or thought," "extent of treatment, activity, or influence," and "range of operation." A statement of project scope has been defined as "a documented description" of the project as to its output, approach and content. The terms *scope of work* or *statement of work* are often used, but they may or may not include the total definition of a particular project's scope. Project scope is given such importance in the project management literature that is recognized as one of the nine modules of the Project Management Body of Knowledge, as defined by the Project Management Institute. These modules are integration, scope, time, cost, quality, risk, human resources, procurement, and communications (PMI PMBOK®, 2000, p. 39).

The statement of scope of a specific project must include:

- *The project results:* What will be created, in terms of physical size and shape, geography, quantity, technical performance and operating specifications, cost characteristics, utility, and so on.

- *The approach to be used:* Technology (new or existing?), internal or external resources, definition of boundaries between the project and its environment.

- *Content of the project:* What is included and excluded in the work to be done, and definition of the boundary between the project tasks and other work that may be related to the project results or its environment.

Clear and complete definition of both the project objectives and the project scope are prerequisites for good project planning and control, and ultimate success of the project.

10.4   FORMAL PROJECT INITIATION

A certain amount of planning is required for any project to develop its concept, preliminary objectives and scope prior to its formal initiation. However, at some point in its concept life-cycle phase the project must be initiated formally. The document most commonly used for this is the *project charter.* The *project summary plan* is also prepared during project initiation, and then updated as required throughout its life cycle.

Project Charter

"A project charter is a document that formally authorizes a project" (PMI PMBOK®, 2000, p. 55). Without a charter, the project does not exist officially. Various documents may serve this purpose, but it is recommended that every project be given a well-defined charter. A good charter will include, directly or by reference, statements of project objectives and scope, the business case for the project, the higher level strategic objectives that the project supports, major assumptions and expectations, milestones and key dates, and major deliverables and their key performance objectives. It will also identify the project's relationship to corporate project portfolios and/or programs and name the project sponsor and project manager. The charter will describe the scope of and limitations to the project manager's authority and indicate the specific corporate project life-cycle management process that is to be applied to the project. It will also describe the major known risks and constraints to the project's success.

The project charter is used by the project sponsor and project manager to gain the needed commitment and support from the affected managers and the project team members to assure project success. It provides the authority needed to issue the various authorizing documents discussed in Chapter 12, including the project release, task work orders, and contracts. The charter is issued with the signature of an appropriate

senior executive holding corporate authority commensurate with the
cost and risks involved in the project.

Project Summary Plan

A written project summary plan should be prepared by the project manager prior to or at the time that work on the project is started. This plan
must explicitly define the objectives of the project, the approach to be
taken, and the commitments being assumed by the manager.

For internally funded projects, the project summary plan should be
approved before the work is started. For contractual projects, the manager typically has up to 30 days to complete the plan in order not to lose
valuable time during start up.

The project summary plan should cover the following general topics:

- Project scope.
- Objectives (technical, profit, other).
- Approach (management, technical, make/buy).
- Contractual requirements (deliverable items).
- End item specifications to be met.
- Target schedules.
- Required resources.
- Major contributors (key team members).
- Financial limitations and possible problems.
- Risk areas (penalties, subcontractor default, work stoppages, tech-
  nical exposures, etc.).

The plan must be complete, but not elaborate; precise, but not hair-
splitting; thorough, but not constrained by a rigorous format.

As soon as the plan is complete, it is submitted to management for approval. When approved, it gives the project manager authority to execute
and control the project to completion, following the general approach
outlined in the plan, in conjunction with the project charter and such
documents as the contract or project release (described later), which authorizes the expenditure of money and other resources.

For contractual projects, the proposal may form a large part of the project summary plan. However, a number of very important parts of the summary plan are not included in proposals submitted to potential customers.
Some companies require a complete project summary plan, accompanied
by a written statement by the general manager that he has personally reviewed the proposed project and accepts the risks that it represents, before the proposal can be submitted to the potential customer.

For new product development projects, the product plans and research and development case application documents will usually cover the major topics of the project summary plan. The same is true for a well-prepared project authorization request for capital facilities or new information systems.

Major changes in approach or other revisions to the plan made after initial approval must be communicated to management using the project evaluation and reporting practices described in Chapter 14.

10.5 PLANNING AND CONTROL FUNCTIONS AND TOOLS

This section lists the various planning and control functions and tools related to project management. No attempt is made to explain each of these many items in detail; rather, the intent here is to show how the numerous existing procedures and systems are interrelated to the several newer techniques developed to plan and control projects more effectively.

Product versus Project Planning and Control

It is beneficial to recognize the differences between the *product* (or results being produced by the project) and the *project* itself (or the process by which this product is being created). Table 10.1 lists the major product planning and control functions and tools, and Table 10.2 lists the functions and tools related to projects. These are presented to assure a comprehensive view of all the functions involved in effective project management. The project planning and control tools discussed more fully in this book are indicated by an asterisk in Table 10.2.

10.6 PLANNING DURING THE CONCEPTUAL, PROPOSAL, OR PRE-INVESTMENT PHASES

There are widely varying practices in the amount of planning performed before a project is authorized to begin. Inadequate planning during the proposal or preinvestment phase will result in funding and scheduling difficulties, and in some cases failure and cancellation of the project.

During preparation of the project proposal, considerable basic planning, estimating, and scheduling must be done to assure that the basic technical, cost, and schedule objectives to be proposed are attainable. A proposal team is formed, which ideally will be the nucleus of the future project team.

The ultimate project team organization is planned at this time, and the basic make or buy decisions are made for the major elements of the

Table 10.1   Summary of Product Planning and Control Functions and Tools

Concern *what* will be the end results of the project.

Encompass technical specifications and drawings defining physical and performance characteristics of the product, and related procedures and practices.

Functions	Examples of the Tools
Defining, designing, and controlling the product characteristics	Product plans Market analyses Specifications, drawings, and diagrams Analytical techniques, tests, and reports Design review procedures Models, mock-ups, and prototypes Cost estimating procedures Value engineering procedures
Defining and controlling product configuration	Drawing release procedures Design review procedures Configuration management practices Change order control procedures Change control board Production control systems Technical supervision
Establishing and controlling product quality	Quality control procedures Product assurance (reliability and maintainability) procedures Technical supervision Design review procedures Project evaluation meetings

project. All of the planning steps described in the remainder of this chapter are taken, although in a fairly gross way. After the project is authorized to proceed, the planning steps are repeated and carried to the full degree of detail required to execute and control the project. The project summary plan is developed in outline form during the preinvestment phase, and prepared in detail after receipt of the contract or other approval to proceed. The foundation for success of the project must be firmly established during this critical proposal/planning phase.

During these early phases, the decision to proceed with the project must reflect the overall strategic management objectives, strategies, and decisions of top management, as discussed in Chapter 1. Project selection and justification are more closely related to strategic management of an organization than to project management per se. However, Morris (1988, p. 810) makes a strong case for "bring[ing] project management more strongly back into the project initiation stage of projects." Souder

Table 10.2 Summary of Project Planning and Control Functions and Tools

Concern *how* the end results of the project will be achieved.

Encompass administrative plans, systems, procedures and information defining the project objectives, work plans, budgets, resource plans, expenditures, and other management information.

Functions	Examples of the Tools
Defining and controlling project objectives and target completion date	Product plans
	DCF and other financial analysis methods
	Project authorization request (PAR)
	R&D case documents
	The project file*
	Contract administration procedures*
	Project evaluation procedures*
	Risk analysis methods*
Defining the deliverable end items and major tasks	Contract, R&D Case and/or PAR
	Systematic planning techniques such as the Project Breakdown Structure*
	Task/Responsibility Matrix*
	Master Schedule or Master Phasing Charts*
	Product development process definition*
	Project management process definition*
Planning the work (tasks)	Project Breakdown Structure*
	Work control package (task) definition procedures*
	Network systems (PERT/CPM/PDM)*
	Bar charts and milestone charts
	Risk analysis methods*
Scheduling the work	Network systems*
	Bar charts and milestone charts
	Production control systems
Estimating required resources (manpower, money, material, facilities)	Working planning procedures
	Manpower and material estimating procedures
	Cost estimating and pricing procedures
Budgeting resources	Planning, scheduling, and estimating procedures*
	Budgeting procedures*
	Risk analysis methods*
Work assignment and authorization: Internal	Master Contract Release documents*
	Project Release documents*
	Work order documents*
External	Contracting and purchasing procedures

(continued)

Table 10.2 *(Continued)*

Functions	Examples of the Tools
Evaluating progress: Physical	Reporting procedures* Network systems (PERT/CPM/PDM)* Project management information systems*
Cost	Financial information systems (accounting, budgeting, etc.) Contract administration procedures* Project management information systems*
Manpower	Manpower reporting procedures Project management information systems*
Schedule and cost control	Budgeting procedures* Work order procedures Contract change procedures Project management information systems* Production control systems
Technical	Technical Performance Measurement procedures*
Integrated evaluation of time, cost, and technical performance	Project evaluation procedures and practices, using information produced by all the above tools*

*Discussed in some detail in the book.

(1988, pp. 140–164) describes a number of models (screening, evaluation, portfolio, organizational) for making the decision whether to proceed with a specific project or not. Pilcher (1973) gives several basic, practical methods for economic analysis and risk appraisal of projects. In the conceptual or proposal phases, formal project management practices may not be applied to all projects, simply because so many of them fail to proceed to execution. However, application of project management principles in these early phases is a good investment of the time and money required, especially for high-risk projects that have a high probability of being approved for execution. During these early phases, risk analysis and risk management methods are of critical importance.

The Successive Principle: A New Logic for Planning under Uncertainty

During the conceptual phase of any project, especially of a high-technology project, there will be many uncertainties concerning the project objectives, technologies, methods, schedules, and costs. The more concrete, quantified, and specific planning methods described in this book apply most appropriately to the later phases of a project when more specific information is available and the uncertainties have been reduced. When dealing with the rapid changes in today's world, managers have learned that the old, highly quantified methods of planning are no longer effective, and have adopted a planning logic that is more intuitive. Among the very few systems that are described in the literature, the Successive Principle is probably the most general and widespread. Lichtenberg (1990, pp. 137–154) summarizes his experience in applying this principle to project planning, and identifies four basic conditions of the new planning logic:

1. Uncertainty is handled correctly and as a matter of greatest importance.

2. All matters of potential impact on the project are dealt with, including difficult and highly subjective issues and situations.

3. Only matters of relevance are dealt with.

4. The project is seen and planned as a whole, interlinked with its environment. Its various aspects (time, costs, resources, risks, etc.) are also recognized as being tightly interlinked.

Lichtenberg reports that feedback from managers who have been using the Successive Principle in their project planning for a number of years shows that this principle:

- Enables managers and decision makers to have a more realistic and better qualified preview of the potential end results of the project plans, even at a very early stage.

- Supports the teambuilding process and the mutual creativity of goals and objectives.

- Links planning, estimating, timing, risk management, resources, profitability, and environmental considerations into a harmonic whole.

- Works significantly faster and more flexibly than conventional planning procedures do.

Description of the Successive Principle. The Successive Principle is an integrated decision support methodology or process that can be used to address a variety of business problems or situations, and is particularly well suited to conceptualizing, planning, justifying, and executing projects. Its purpose is to produce unbiased, realistic results (time or cost estimates, risk analysis, profitability calculations, key decisions, and understanding of other key aspects or parameters of a project), based on holistic, broad coverage of all factors influencing or involved with the project, including subjective factors, hidden assumptions, and especially areas of uncertainty or potential change (Lichtenberg and Archibald, 1992).

How it works.   The Successive Principle incorporates the concepts of holistic, whole-brain, systems thinking and the team approach with the mathematics of uncertainty and probability. The basic steps are:

1. *Identify the evaluation subject and purpose.* The *subject* may be a set of strategic plans, a project in the embryonic or early conceptual phase, a response to a request for proposal or bid on a defined project, a project encountering unforeseen problems, a project entering a later phase of its life cycle, as well as other situations requiring a disciplined decision-making support system. The *evaluation purpose* may be to decide (1) whether to proceed with the project, prepare a proposal and submit a bid, (2) what action to take in response to a particular change or problem, and/or (3) what risks are involved and what contingency plans are required to mitigate the identified risks, to name a few examples.

2. *Form the evaluation team.* Identify the most appropriate team of people for the evaluation purpose. The team should include persons with knowledge and experience in the major aspects of the evaluation subject, and if possible representing the most involved organizations.

3. *Identify, quantify, and rank the central factors of uncertainty.* The team, using its factual knowledge and intuitive hunches and guestimates, stimulated by open interchange of ideas and opposing points of view in a truly collaborative style, first identifies the factors which, in their collective judgment, reflect the greatest uncertainties or unknowns regarding the evaluation subject and purpose. Frequently, this results in a list of "top 20" items for further consideration. Second, the team members organize, define and quantify each identified factor using the so-called triple estimate (minimum, likely, maximum) and Bayesian statistics to calculate the total result as well as the relative criticality to the result from each factor. This is expressed as the factor's specific influence upon the uncertainty of the result. (Correct use of the methodology eliminates the need for correlation factors because the user deliberately creates stochastic independence between items and factors.)

4. *Successively break down the most critical factors to reduce uncertainty.* If any of the critical factors identified and quantified in Step 3 exhibit unacceptable levels of uncertainty (that is, the range between best and worst estimates is too great, or the mean value is too large or too small), the most critical factors are further broken down into their component parts (subsystems) by the team. These subfactors are in turn quantified and are included in the above

ranking in the same manner as before. This successive breakdown, quantification, and ranking is continued until the level of uncertainty is close to the minimum or unavoidable. Logically, no further reduction in uncertainty can be achieved.

5. *Present the results and make the decision.* The results of the evaluation are presented by the team to the decision maker, who may accept them or require a replanning. This systematic, disciplined, but wide-ranging and intuitive plus factual back-up for the results has proven to be extremely persuasive in many diverse settings, and the resulting decisions have proven to be well justified.

The results represent a realistic, largely unbiased total measure of the most likely values of the key parameters under consideration, and the related degree of uncertainty. Experience indicates that a list of the top ten areas of uncertainty will usually encompass all of the most critical items that need to be improved or kept under observation. Another very important but informal result from using the Successive Principle is attainment of a higher level of mutual understanding, trust, and consensus among the evaluation team members. This improved potential for cooperation is utilized during execution of the project, if the decision is made to proceed, for better commitment, teamwork, motivation, and more productive response to unforeseen events and changes.

Proactively Exploiting and Managing Risk and Uncertainty

Lichtenberg (2000, pp. 19–20) reports the following benefits from proactively managing risk and uncertainty using the Successive Principle:

1. Extremely realistic budget and schedule forecasts very early in the projects. No unplanned overrun has been reported since 1980 in the several hundred projects involved.

2. Increased mutual understanding and improved cooperation and consensus among the parties involved.

3. Responsible managers receive an innovative top 10 list of areas of potential improvement including risk reduction.

4. The needed planning effort is drastically reduced.

5. Risk assurance and risk management become a more integral part of the management process.

Lichtenberg goes on to say:

Instead of considering uncertainty as a necessary evil, it should be considered as an extremely important, inspiring and useful factor given its inherent opportunities for making improvements and taking measures against risk. In the author's opinion, uncertainty is likely to hold some of the greatest potential for improving management skills and efficiency today. (p. 21)

Lichtenberg's book (2000) is a practical manual for understanding and applying the Successive Principle to all types of projects. It includes many case studies, illustrations, exercises, and specimen solutions.

10.7 DEFINING THE PROJECT AND ITS SPECIFIC TASKS: THE PROJECT/WORK BREAKDOWN STRUCTURE

For complex projects, it is necessary to use a disciplined, systematic approach to define the total project in such a way that all elements have the proper relationship to each other and that no element is overlooked. If this is properly done the result is very useful in a number of ways.

The most effective method of accomplishing such a definition of a project is the creation of a Project Breakdown Structure (PBS), also commonly called the Work Breakdown Structure (WBS). In the following paragraphs, the PBS is described, its use is discussed, and several simplified examples are presented.

Description of the Project Breakdown Structure

The PBS is a graphic or word model of the project, exploding it in a level-by-level fashion down to the degree of detail needed for effective planning and control. It must include all deliverable end items (consumable goods, machinery, equipment, facilities, services, manuals, reports, and so on) and includes the major functional tasks that must be performed to conceive, design, create, fabricate, assemble, test, and deliver the end items.

Although the original impetus for defining projects systematically in this way came from large U.S. military and aerospace programs and projects, the concept has been adopted by virtually all areas of application of project management for complex projects. The basic U.S. Department of Defense definition is:

1.6.3 Work Breakdown Structure

This term is defined as:

- A *product-oriented family tree* composed of hardware, software, services, data, and facilities. The family tree results from systems engineering efforts during the acquisition of a defense material item.

- A WBS displays and defines the product, or products, to be developed and/or produced. It *relates the elements of work* to be accomplished to each other and to the end product.
- A WBS can be expressed down to any level of interest. However the top *three levels* are as far as any program or contract need go unless the items identified are high cost or high risk. Then, and only then, is it important to take the work breakdown structure to a lower level of definition. (U.S. DOD 1998, p. 4)

The PMI Practice Standard for Work Breakdown Structures (PMI, 2001) presents useful discussion of project/work breakdown structures—what they are, the reasons they are used, and how to create them—plus eleven industry-specific project examples: oil, gas, and petrochemical; environmental management; process improvement; pharmaceutical; process plant construction; service industry outsourcing; Web design; telecom; refinery turnaround; government design-build; and software implementation. Fleming and Koppelman (2000, pp. 50–59) provide several illustrative examples of project/work breakdown structures for various project categories, and emphasize the importance of the use of the P/WBS for planning and controlling projects using the earned value approach.

Extended P/WBS Dictionary

"The problem with a WBS is that deliverable elements are usually defined with very short descriptions.... This brevity often leads to confusion, miscommunication, and unclear expectations for various stakeholders.

"By linking each WBS element to a dictionary-like item that contains descriptive text, the problem can be eliminated. If we extend that concept just a little further by adding several descriptive fields driven by an electronic database system, an extremely beneficial tool can be created. This tool not only addresses the brevity problem, but also can significantly enhance communication and project control. Any size or type of project could benefit from this tool" (Ward 2001).

Ward defines the extended WBS dictionary as "an electronic database system that links a variety of information to each element of the WBS." This information provides clarity so that everyone fully understands the deliverable and has similar expectations regarding its scope. A copy of this database system can be obtained from greg.ward@compaq.com.

Various Types and Uses of Breakdown Structures

The concept behind the project/work breakdown structure tool that originated in the 1960s within aerospace/defense programs and projects has spawned a number of different breakdown structures that are useful in managing complex projects. The more widely used of these include breakdown structures for the deliverables and work or tasks (P/WBS), organization (OBS), cost (CBS), schedule (SBS), and product. Liberzon and Lobonov (2000, p. 3) report the use of many breakdown structures in Russia and give examples for project objectives, project processes, project resources, and "responsibilities of implementers," which appears to be the same as an OBS. Others describe using this technique to break down project scope. While most of the presently available commercial project management software application packages limit the user to one P/WBS, one OBS, and one CBS, the most widely used commercial package in Russia, called Spider Project, allows an unlimited number of breakdown structures to be used, with estimating, summarizing, and reporting capabilities for each of them. Liberzon and Lobonov say "It should be stressed that the structure of responsibilities successfully substitutes for the responsibility matrix that is usually elaborated as part of the project plan. Responsibilities are usually distributed hierarchically and only in small projects the responsibility structure becomes flat and can be reduced to a matrix" (p. 3).

Automating the Project/Work and Other Breakdown Structures

Most of the planning and scheduling software applications referenced in Chapter 5 have provisions for automating the preparation and use of the P/WBS, although most leave much to be desired in that respect. As noted earlier, most can also handle the OBS and CBS. Add-on software products enable creating and displaying a P/WBS chart in many alternative formats. One example of these is WBS Chart Pro (see www.criticaltools.com), which provides two-way interaction with one of the most widely used PM planning and scheduling packages, Microsoft Project, and can be linked to others.

Because the term *work breakdown structure* is imbedded in the U.S. government project management directives and literature, this term has been used extensively in other industries. This name actually is somewhat misleading and causes confusion with practitioners, since it infers that only "work," or tasks, are involved. The tendency therefore is to look at a large project and immediately identify the work activities to be done—design, procurement, construction, commissioning, in a construction project. However, in most large projects, this is not a satisfactory second-level breakdown. Therefore, the term *project breakdown structure* is used in this book, to emphasize that the many elements of the project must first be broken out, and then the functional work tasks identified for each deliverable element, at the proper level.

The Project/Work Breakdown Structure

Prior to the advent of the project breakdown structure approach (which emerged in the early 1960s), the many different functional specialists who contributed to a project each broke the project down in different ways, to suit their particular needs. Many differing frameworks were developed, and still exist, for planning, estimating costs and other resources, budgeting, cost accounting, financial analysis, assigning responsibilities, purchasing, scheduling, issuing of contracts and subcontracts, material handling and storage, and many others. Often these frameworks are themselves different for the different functions of finance, marketing, engineering, procurement, manufacturing, field construction, and operations, to name a few. Bitter experience on many large projects showed that it was impossible to properly correlate and integrate the planning and control information on a large project in this hodgepodge of differing definitions of the same project. What was needed was one systematic project breakdown structure that all parties could agree to and understand for a given project, and to which all the other frameworks listed above could be cross-referenced. The PBS can be viewed as the Rosetta Stone of project management, because it enables the correlation of many diverse elements of information and coding schemes, like the diverse Egyptian languages that the Rosetta Stone enabled scholars to understand.

Creating a project breakdown structure.   The project breakdown structure is developed by a judicious combination of the *product breakdown structure* with the *product development process* of the organization. The term *product* here refers to any result being created by the project, including hardware, software, equipment, facilities, services, staffed organizations, documents, data, and other tangible project results. The product development process, discussed earlier in this chapter, is the series of phases, steps, tasks, and activities that the organization uses in creating the various products of the project. Although this development process links the various phases and tasks together in a chronological flow, the PBS does not attempt to portray such chronological linkages. These will be identified in a subsequent planning step, when the project master schedule and action plans and schedules are prepared.

The PBS chart is created by starting at the top-level element, which identifies the total project, and breaking out the major, natural elements of the project (systems, facilities, categories of end items, etc.) at the next lower level. Each of these elements is then subdivided into its component elements. This level-by-level breakdown continues, reducing the scope, complexity, and cost of each element, until the proper practical level of end-item identification is reached. These are then subdivided into the major functional tasks that must be performed to create the end item in question. The objective is to identify elements and tasks that are in themselves manageable units clearly the responsibility of a functional project leader, and that can be planned, estimated, budgeted, scheduled, and controlled. This approach assures that the project is completed defined and that useful summaries of project information can be made.

During the creation of the PBS, which should be performed on a team basis as discussed in Chapter 11, the results or product breakdown plays a dominant role, but the product development process is also reflected at appropriate points. At the top level, the major phases of the development process are often identified, either directly or in terms of the major deliverables for a particular phase. For example, a major deliverable for the conceptual phase is often a *Conceptual Design Package* or a *Concept Feasibility Report*. Each of these might be broken down into sections or components, and then the functional tasks required to create each of those would be identified at the next lower level. The product development process heavily influences the definition of specific functional tasks or work packages at the lowest level of the PBS, and the organizational breakdown structure (OBS) will also influence the task definitions.

When first developing a PBS chart, many persons tend to think of it as an organization chart. This results in a confused PBS overly influenced by the particular structure of the company involved. The PBS is *not* an organizational structure, although it may superficially resemble one depending on its drafting on paper. As discussed later, each element in the PBS can be identified as the responsibility of a particular person. One person may be responsible for a number of elements scattered throughout the PBS. The functional organization structure of the sponsoring company will have some influence on the PBS, especially at the level where deliverable end items are divided into functional tasks.

U.S. Department of Defense project/work breakdown structure guidance.

Elaborate and detailed guidance has been issued officially by the U.S. Department of Defense (DOD) and the several individual DOD services for projects to develop and acquire their weapon systems, information systems, and other defense material items (U.S. DOD, 1998). The basic standard provides general breakdowns for seven defense systems: aircraft, electronics, missile, ordnance, ship, space, and surface vehicle. Definitions are provided of the hardware and work breakdown through three levels for each system type. Work continues by a government/industry taskforce to reflect new technologies and more recent business practices. A separate standard has been issued for information system and software projects (U.S. DOD, 1988). The U.S. Department of Energy has also issued a guide for use in defining its major projects (U.S. DOE, 1987).

Level		
1	2	3

Information system development project
        Concept study
                Feasibility study
                Requirements study and conceptual design
                Information system proposal
                Detail design specification
        Support software
                Compiler/assembler
                Database control
                Test support software
        Operating system
                Executive
                Input/output control
                File management
                Message handling
                Control management
                Maintenance and diagnostics
        Application software
                Application program A
                Application program B
        Data
                Technical publications
                Engineering data
                Support data
        System test and evaluation
                Equipment
                Services
                Facilities
        Training
                Equipment
                Services
                Facilities
        Operations and maintenance
                Operations
                Maintenance
        Project support
                Project management
                System engineering

Figure 10.1   First three levels of a project breakdown structure for an information system development project. Adapted from Frank D. Postula, "WBS Criteria for Effective Project Control," *1991 Transactions of the American Association of Cost Engineers,* AACE, Morgantown, WV, ISBN 0-930284-47-X, 1991, p. I.6.4.

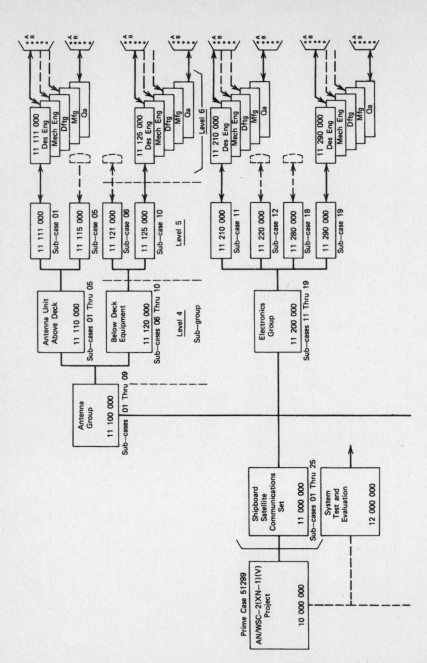

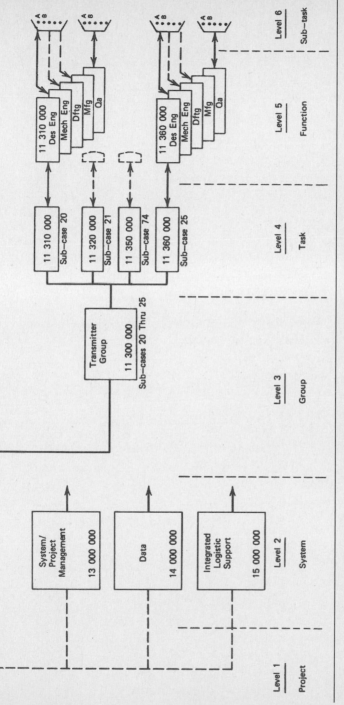

Figure 10.2   Breakdown structure for a large communications project (showing financial accounts assigned to project elements).

247

PBS Examples

Figures 10.1 through 10.4 illustrate various ways of depicting a PBS for several types of projects. Actual breakdowns of large projects are usually carried to four or five levels and often are presented on several pages to avoid excessively large charts. Several examples of varying usefulness are given in PMI (2001).

Using the PBS

The process of creating the PBS produces, in itself, important benefits. In the process of breaking down the project, the project manager, the supporting planners, and key project team members are forced to think through all elements of the project. This helps to avoid omissions and clarifies the scope of work assigned to each functional project leader. The PBS is a means for visualizing the entire project in a meaningful way. Significant insight into the project and the interrelationships between its elements is often gained by creating and using the PBS. The following steps outline its customary use:

- Develop the initial PBS in a top-down fashion, through direct effort by the project manager and supporting planners, with appropriate inputs from the key project team members.
- Review and revise the completed PBS with all affected managers and team members and until agreement is reached on its validity.
- Identify work control packages (tasks) to be planned, estimated, budgeted, scheduled, and controlled.
- Identify for each PBS element down to and including each task:
  —Responsible and performing organizations and functional project leaders.
  —Product specifications.
  —Prime and subcontracts and major purchase orders.
  —Resource (people, funds, material, facilities, equipment) estimates and budgets.
  —Work order numbers.
  —Cost account numbers (task level only).
  —Milestone events and related activities in PERT/CPM/PDM network plans, with scheduled dates.
- Summarize resource information up the PBS, comparing estimates, budgets, commitments, expenditures, and actual accomplishments for each element and for the project as a whole.

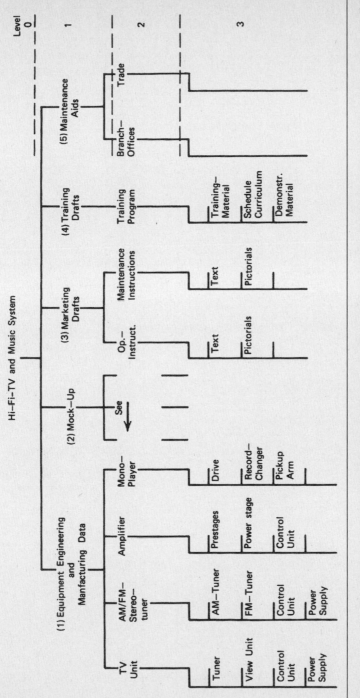

Figure 10.3 Sample format of project breakdown structure (PBS). RD and E portion of product development project: (1) RD and E has prime responsibility; (2) responsibility shared between RD and E and E Model shop; (3) responsibility shared between RD and E (first drafts of documents) and Marketing (final drafts); (4) responsibility shared between RD and E Marketing Service.

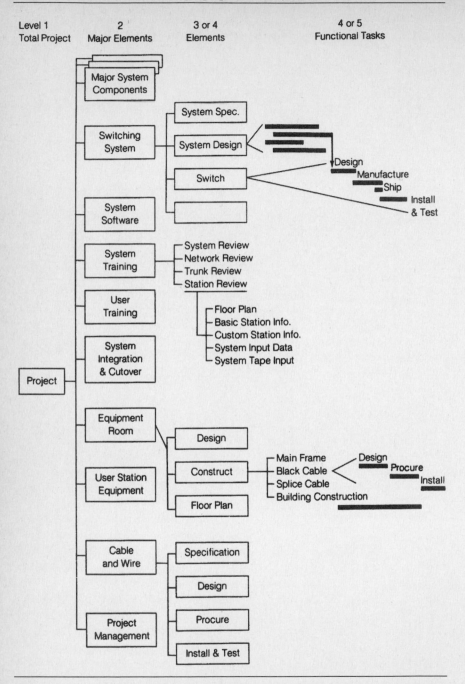

Figure 10.4   Project breakdown structure for a telecommunications-information system project.

- Add expenditures to date to latest estimate to complete (ETC) for each task to obtain estimate at completion (EAC), and summarize the PBS.

- Evaluate results to identify problems and initiate appropriate corrective action.

- Reiterate the above cycle as needed to replan and balance schedules, resources, and scope of work.

The PBS thus becomes a framework of the project that enables all management information (from various systems and sources) to be correlated and summarized for planning and control purposes.

Controlling the PBS

When properly used, the PBS is a vital communication tool. It evolves and reflects current plans as the project matures. More detail is added to particular areas as the actual execution of those areas approaches. Thus, a procedure for revising and controlling the distribution of the PBS is usually necessary to prevent unauthorized change and to assure that all managers are working with the latest issue. The PBS is, in a sense, the top assembly drawing of the project from the management point of view.

10.8   DEFINITION OF TASKS (WORK CONTROL PACKAGES)

Tasks are the final elements identified in the PBS, and thus are found at the end of the breakdown of a particular part of the project. Usually they emerge at several different levels of the PBS. These control packages may represent a total subcontract for work to be performed by an outside firm, but they usually represent a functional task for which a particular functional project leader is responsible. To be useful for control purposes, functional tasks should be of relatively short duration and small total cost compared to the total project duration and cost.

The cost accounting system is correlated to the PBS through the work control packages. A separate cost account number is established for each package or task, and expenditures are then recorded for each. The cost accounting coding scheme (chart of accounts) does not have to carry the summary structure of the PBS. Summarization can be accomplished outside the cost accounting system for project management purposes, using the relationships established by the PBS.

Task Statement of Work

Each task is best defined by a concise statement of the work to be accomplished. This should include:

- Summary statement of the work to be accomplished.
- Inputs required from other tasks.
- Reference to applicable specifications, contractual conditions, or other documents.
- Specific results to be achieved: deliverable or intermediate items of hardware, software, documents, test results, drawings, specifications, and so on.

Types of Tasks and Effort

Several varieties of tasks can be identified, each requiring different treatment for scheduling and budgeting purposes. These include:

- Design/development tasks.
- Manufacturing tasks.
- Construction or installation (field operations) tasks.
- Procurement (purchased and subcontracted) tasks.
- Management tasks.

Within these categories, three basic efforts exist as follows:

1. *Readily identified tasks.* Specific start and end events associated with an end product or result.
2. *Level of effort tasks.* Activities that cannot be associated directly with a definable end product or result, and that are controllable by time-phased budgets established for that purpose. Example: A project management task, including salaries and travel costs for the project manager and supporting staff when charged directly to the project.
3. *Apportioned effort.* By itself not readily divisible into short-span tasks but related in direct proportion to other tasks. Example: Inspection activity for manufacturing tasks.

Numbering Schemes

The numbering sequence applied to the PBS must be carefully designed to enable summarization of the schedule, cost, resource, and technical information from the task/work package levels to each intermediate level and up to the total project. Many organizations extend the numbering scheme to multiproject and corporate levels, to enable appropriate summarization across the entire organization, especially of resource information. The PBS numbering scheme should be kept separate from other corporate coding arrangements and not, for example, incorporated directly into the cost accounting numbering system. The PBS numbers must be compatible with the software capabilities of the project management information system, in terms of numbers of digits and summarization procedures. A typical PBS numbering system is illustrated in Figure 10.2.

Computer Software Support

An important feature of a project management computer software package is its ability to handle the PBS for scheduling, resources, and costs. Some of the packages allow the user to define the PBS on the screen, interactively and graphically, and provide for development of the project master schedule with milestones identified, intermediate level schedules, and task level schedules, all with appropriately integrated resource and cost information. This is an important capability to consider when selecting a project management software package, as discussed in more detail in Chapter 5.

10.9   TASK/RESPONSIBILITY MATRIX

The task/responsibility matrix is a planning tool for relating the work defined the by PBS to responsible organizational units, subcontractors, and individuals. With a given company organization breakdown structure (OBS) on one hand, and the work to be performed as depicted by the PBS on the other, the objective is to couple the two. Since the PBS will never exactly match the OBS, the matrix provides a mechanism for assignment of prime and supporting accountability in the typical, functionally organized company.

Figure 10.5 illustrates this tool. Developing such a matrix will verify whether there is too much or too little detail in the PBS. It will also provide the planner with at least one activity on the PERT/CPM/PDM network plan for each entry.

When completed, the matrix provides a simple framework for further planning and control. In the planning process, each prime task assignee should provide schedule, manpower, cost, and technical information on the assigned task, including the contributions required from those in supporting roles. The application of task and organization code numbers allows unique identification of each matrix entry. The logical and

| | | Project Team Members | | | | | |
Project Breakdown Structure:	Wade S. Proj. Mgr.	Bob B. Mktg.	Paul F. PSC	Larry H. FSO	Ken H. MMS	Tom L. Eng.	Etc.
Level							
1 2 3 4 5							
New Telecommunications Project							
Electronic Switch System							
System Specifications							
—							
System Design							
—							
Switch Manufacture	I						
Place Orders	C	W					
Manufacture Switch Equipment	(Factory)						
Ship Switch Equipment	N			N		W	
Stage Switch Equipment On Site	N			N		W	
Switch Installation	I						
Make Area Ready	N			N		W	
Equipment On Site/Inventoried	N			W		W	
Install Switch	N			W		N	
Install Peripheral Equipment				W			
Test Remote Fibre Links				W			
(Etc)							

LEGEND

W—Does Work
C—Must Be Consulted
A—Must Approve
N—Must Be Notified/Copied
I—Integrative Responsibility

Figure 10.5   Example of a task/responsibility matrix.

coherent framework of the matrix and associated technical information, schedules, and cost estimates provide the basis for work authorization and the necessary measurement criteria for control purposes. These points are discussed further in following sections.

The task/responsibility matrix is frequently referred to as a "linear responsibility chart (LRC)." Cleland and King (1988, pp. 374–393) provide an excellent discussion of the use of this important tool in project management.

10.10   INTERFACE AND MILESTONE EVENT IDENTIFICATION

As an important part of the project planning effort, the major interface events to be managed by the project manager must be identified and incorporated into the detailed project plans and schedules. Milestone events are also important in developing the project master plan, evaluating overall progress, and reporting to higher management, Many, but not necessarily all, milestone events are also interface events.

Basic Definition of an Event

Poor project plans frequently result from improper or ambiguous event identification. An event is *not* a task or activity. *An event is an occurrence at a point in time that signifies the start or completion of one or more tasks or activities.* To be useful for project planning, scheduling, and control, an event must be understandable to all concerned, clearly and unambiguously described in precise terms, and its occurrence must be immediately recognizable. The occurrence of an event cannot be planned and scheduled to the hour, minute, and second of a specific day. But it must clearly be pinpointed to one specific day, month, and year; in other words, a calendar date.

Several dates may become associated with one event:

- *A scheduled date.* The currently agreed and committed time of event occurrence.

- *A predicted (earliest or forecast) date.* The currently predicted event occurrence time if the present plans are carried out without deviation or change.

- *A latest allowable (or required) date.* The time the event must occur, if the following tasks and events take place according to present plans, so that the project will be completed on schedule, or some intermediate contractual commitment will be met.

- *A target date.* The desired occurrence time.

- *A commitment date.* The time an event must occur, representing a customer or formal management commitment.

- *An actual date.* The time that the event actually did occur.

Not all of these dates are necessary for any given event, but confusion about the type of event date under discussion can cause serious communication problems.

Checklist for Interface and Milestone Event Identification

Table 10.3 presents a checklist for key event identification. This is recommended for use in stimulating thought about interface or milestone events to be identified, planned, scheduled, and controlled.

To qualify as an interface event, an occurrence must denote a change of responsibility or a point of interaction between two or more elements of the project breakdown structure. A milestone event identifies a significant accomplishment in the project. Further discussion of interface events is given in Chapter 13.

10.11 PROJECT MASTER SCHEDULE AND THE SCHEDULE HIERARCHY

Schedule planning ensures that all contract or other requirements, including hardware, software, and support items, are delivered on time. Fundamentally, there are two levels of schedule planning: the project level and the task level. The project level schedules integrate all tasks, interfaces, and milestones. Task level schedules and budgets are discussed later in this chapter. In very large projects, intermediate levels of master schedules and budgets may be required, but these are considered to be extensions or subdivisions of the project schedules. (Although the word *task* is used here to denote a package of work that is the basic unit of project control, it is recognized that this word will have different meanings in various organizations. In adapting these practices, each organization should use the best term possible to avoid confusion and ambiguity.)

Types of Schedules

Many types of schedules are useful in managing projects, as indicated in Table 10.4. The project manager and contributing functional project leaders should review this list to select those types of schedules required for each specific project. The various schedule types reflect emphasis on a specific element or function of the project, or combination of these. They are all derived from and consistent with the project master schedule.

Project master schedule. The project master schedule interrelates all elements and tasks of the project on a common time scale. It should:

- Be based on the PBS.
- Be complete and comprehensive in scope.

Table 10.3   Checklist for Interface and Milestone Event Identification

1. *Things or objects moving through the interface or milestone events*
   Unique identification of

General	Projects, systems, subsystems, project elements, requirements, funds.
Documents	Contracts, subcontracts, specifications, drawings, plans, budgets, schedules, charts, reports, work orders, procedures, bills of materials, parts lists, manuals.
Equipment (hardware)	Models, test boards, components, materials, parts, subassemblies, assemblies, modules, deliverable hardware items, intermediate hardware items, equipment lots, spare parts.
Software (operating)	Flow charts, coding lists, assemblies, packages, card decks, listings, tapes, source programs, object programs, compilers, simulators, systems, deliverable software items, intermediate software items.
Services	Training, field support, operating, management, or administrative.
Facilities	Buildings or structures, test equipment or machines, tools and tooling, operating or production equipment, or machines.

2. *Operations performed on the things or objects*

   Begin, start, establish, define, analyze, design, modify, release, issue, procure, purchase, fabricate, assemble, wire, test, pack, ship, receive, inspect, hang, mount, place, install, adjust, accept, approve, operate, negotiate, write, prepare, compile, correct, collect, construct, complete, finish, end.

3. *Event designator*

   Past tense of any verb in Section 2 associated with one or more objects in Section 1.

   Examples: "Contract XY funds released"
   "Hardware lot 2 received on site"
   "Tests complete on software package no. 3"
   "Building complete and available"

- Reflect contractual commitments and customer obligations.
- Assist in planning the buildup and effective use of manpower and other resources.
- Include key interface and milestone events linking all tasks.
- Be useful for progress evaluation and management reporting.

Table 10.4   Types of Schedules Used on Projects

1. Project master schedule (Master Phasing Schedule)
2. Major milestone schedule
3. Master development schedule
4. Master production schedule
5. Master summary schedules—PBS level 2, 3, etc.
6. Near term milestone schedule
7. Project trend charts (cost/milestones)
8. Project network plan (management logic diagram)
9. Task schedules
10. Functional element schedules
11. Detailed PERT network(s)
12. Major product schedules
13. Hardware utilization schedules
14. Unit hardware delivery schedules
15. Pre-award subcontract schedules
16. Subcontractor submitted engineering, manufacturing, and procurement schedules
17. Drawing release schedule
18. Contractually required review schedules
19. Flight test schedule
20. Government or customer furnished property schedule
21. Government or customer data or other obligation schedule
22. Training equipment and maintenance demonstration hardware schedule
23. Technical publication schedule
24. Material support test schedule
25. Contract data requirements schedule
26. System demonstration schedules

The project master schedule is initially established during the proposal (or equivalent) phase. It is continually refined as the project progresses. It is developed in an iterative top-down, bottom-up fashion by the project manager and supporting planners, working with the concerned functional project leaders as the task schedules and budgets are developed.

A *management schedule reserve* should be established at the outset of the project by setting the planned completion date ahead of the critical commitment date by some reasonable amount of time. This provides a contingency reserve to be carefully allocated by the project manager when specific tasks encounter unavoidable delays that affect the project critical path. This reserve is analogous to the management budget reserve discussed later.

The project master schedule may take the form of a bar chart, a bar chart with selected interface and milestone events, or a time-scaled summary PERT network or logic diagram. If the last, it will usually appear as a bar chart or "bar-net" with selected interface and milestone events, and with logical dependencies shown between the events. Where intermediate level master schedules are required, different formats may be needed for different schedules, as indicated. Figure 10.6 shows a typical master schedule format.

Computer-generated master schedules.   Many of the better project scheduling computer software packages will produce high quality, multicolor project master schedules on plotters and printers. The best of these also portray milestones and interface events, with user control of the symbols used.

10.12   THE PERT/CPM/PDM PROJECT LEVEL NETWORK PLAN

Application of the PERT/CPM/PDM network planning and critical path analysis technique to the overall project can produce significant benefits, if done properly. These benefits include:

- Integration of all tasks with interface and milestone events.
- Reduction in total project duration through improved overlapping of tasks and activities, where feasible and necessary.
- Identification of the chain of events and activities leading to project completion, which forms the *critical path*. These are the activities and events that, if delayed, will delay the project completion; and that, if accelerated, will enable earlier project completion.
- More effective integrated evaluation of actual progress by all contributors.

The basic elements of a network plan are:

- *Events.* The start or completion of one or more activities or tasks; represented graphically by a circle, square, or other geometric figure.
- *Tasks or activities.* Time-consuming jobs or actions; represented graphically in one of two ways: (1) in CPM (critical path method) and PERT (Program Evaluation and Review Technique), as lines or arrows

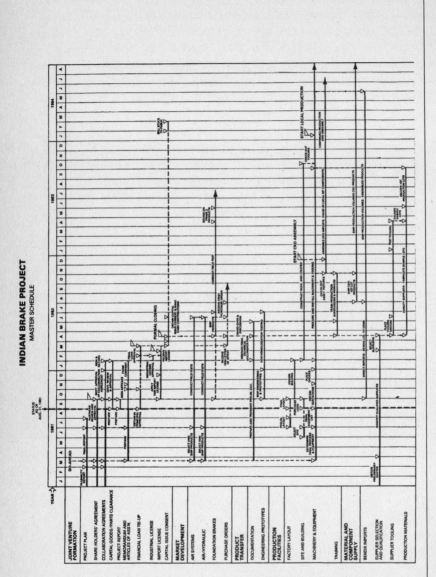

Figure 10.6 The project master schedule for a complex joint venture project involving a new company, technology transfer, a new manufacturing plant, new suppliers, and new customers.

between events, with the arrowhead showing the sequential dependencies involved; and (2) in PDM (precedence diagram method), as enclosed geometric shapes, usually rectangles. In CPM plans, the events are usually small circles with numbers only; in PERT plans, the events are described and coded. Hence, CPM plans are often termed "activity oriented" and PERT plans "event oriented."

- *Dependencies.* The logical constraints between the events and activities. On CPM and PERT network plans, the dependencies are indicated by the graphic connections made between the events and activities. On PDM plans, arrows are drawn between the activity boxes to indicate the dependency relationships. Dependencies in CPM and PERT plans are simple: when the preceding activity is 100 percent complete its end event has occurred and the succeeding activity can start. In PDM plans, more complex dependency relationships can be shown: finish-to-start (as in CPM and PERT notation), finish-to-finish, start-to-finish, and start-to-start, and these can have lead and lag times associated with them. PDM plans generally require fewer activity boxes than CPM or PERT plans to portray a complex project plan.

Time Analysis of Network Plans

After the tasks or activities in a project have been defined and the network plan developed showing the logical sequence of the work, the durations and required resources for each task or activity are estimated. Then by simply adding up the times from left to right (the "forward pass"), the time required to complete the project *according to this plan* can be determined, together with the "expected" start and completion dates for each activity and event. Next, by starting with a given date at the end of the network plan and subtracting the durations, working backward through the plan (the "backward pass"), the "latest allowable" dates for each event and activity can be calculated. The *critical path* consists of the chain(s) of activities whose expected and latest allowable dates are equal; these have zero "float" or "slack" time (delay allowable without delaying project completion). Since on average about 15 percent of the activities in a project are on the critical path, all others have some float or slack time, which can be used to balance the resource requirements.

There is a large quantity of published literature concerning PERT/CPM/PDM network planning and critical path analysis and the application of the technique to projects in various industries. Mulvaney's (1969) short book on preparing and using PDM network planning provides a complete description of this powerful technique, and O'Brien (1984) provides an in-depth treatment of its use in the construction industry.

Effective application of this technique for project planning and control can be difficult. In brief, the following principles should be observed:

- Maintain the master schedule emphasis in the project network plan:
  - —Incorporate all interface and milestone events.
  - —Organize the network to reflect the PBS.
  - —Assure that all specific tasks are represented, but exclude level-of-effort and apportioned tasks.
  - —Avoid detail more appropriate to the task schedules (see Section 10.14) or short interval schedules (production control).
  - —Include customer and other external obligations and constraints.
- Use the project network plan to validate, substantiate, and determine ways to recover to the master project schedule; change the master schedule only by appropriate management decision, not automatically to reflect the current network plan.
- When using electronic data processing support, choose the software package carefully; inflexible or inadequate software can be the source of extreme aggravation, delays, and extra costs (see Chapter 5).
- Display the results produced by the analysis of the project network plan on a fixed time scale for higher management review; use graphic display whenever possible.
- Conduct adequate indoctrination of all concerned to assure understanding and use of the results.

Project network plans are usually rather large charts and vary considerably in method of documentation, hence it is not feasible to reproduce examples in this book. Further discussion of the use of PERT/CPM/PDM network plans at detailed task levels is given in Section 10.14.

10.13 PROJECT BUDGET AND RESOURCE PLANS

The resources to be planned, budgeted, and expended or otherwise used to carry out the project include: time, money, people, facilities, equipment, and materials.

The nature of each specific project dictates which resources are critical to the project and therefore must be scheduled carefully. Time is budgeted on a gross basis by the project master schedule, and in detail by the task schedules. Facilities, equipment, and material are planned, budgeted, and controlled by special procedures set up for those purposes within each organization. The project master schedule establishes the key dates to be used in those procedures, and in setting up the detailed task schedules. The resources of money and people require special attention for effective project planning and control.

The *project budget* is equivalent to the operating budget for an organizational unit. A key difference is that, rather than being on an annual recurring basis, the project budget covers the entire project through to its completion. The project budget should be divided into direct and indirect project budgets for effective control.

The *direct project budget* is a primary control tool for the project manager and the contributing functional managers. It includes the costs (labor, travel, etc.) incurred by all project team members performing specific project tasks, as well as:

Cost of resale material.

Standard manufacturing cost.

Manufacturing variances.

Engineering expense.

Installation (field operations) expense.

Freight and delivery.

Other direct cost.

An example of a direct project budget summary is given in Figure 12.2. The direct project budget should:

- Be broken down following the PBS exactly to the task (work control package) level.
- Include for each task and intermediate level project element the labor, material (purchased or subcontracted), and other costs as discussed later under tasks schedules and budgets, on a weekly basis.
- Include overhead or burden on direct labor or material.
- Be summarized also by the contributing or performing organization, cutting across the various tasks.
- Provide management reserves, as discussed in the following paragraphs.

The *indirect project budget* includes warranty or penalty costs; research and development assessments; service charges and commissions; financing, marketing, and general administrative costs; inventory adjustments; and other allocations. These are generally set up for the total project without further breakdown. They should be extended by quarter through the life of the project to assist in preparation of the project funding plan, if required.

The *total project budget,* combining both direct and indirect budgets, includes the *gross and net profit projections.*

The project budget is established during the proposal (or equivalent) phase. Initially it is a gross target. As the project breakdown is developed, more detailed estimates are made at the task level by the functional managers responsible for performing the work. Through reiterative top-down, bottom-up cycles, the project and functional managers negotiate mutually agreeable cost estimates and budgets for each task. When the project is authorized to proceed (contract award, or approval of research and development case or project authorization request), further negotiations reflect any changes from the proposal estimates. The project budget, supported by the individual task budgets, is then established and approved, and the work is authorized to proceed as described in Chapter 12. It is recommended that existing budgeting formats be adapted within each unit to serve its project management needs.

Management Reserves

It is a natural tendency on the part of every person to provide a certain amount of cushion or reserve in his or her time and cost estimates. If this tendency is not strictly controlled, overall project cost estimates become substantially inflated. If approved, then each person will tend to expend all the time and cost available to him, including his reserve for contingencies. As Parkinson (1957) has said:

- The work at hand expands to fill the time available.
- Expenditures rise to meet the budget.

The project manager must strive to identify all such reserves for contingencies, both in time and cost. As a general rule, these should be collected and held at the highest possible aggregate level in the project. Each task should be scheduled and estimated realistically. It should be recognized that only a few tasks should encounter major unforeseen difficulties. The management problem is that it is not possible to predict which tasks will have such problems. Therefore, by establishing a central management reserve, the comptroller and project manager have the freedom to allocate funds from the reserve to overcome the unforeseen problems. This will minimize rebudgeting funds for all other tasks. If the reserve is not totally used, the balance is then available as added profit.

For these reasons, it is recommended that only one contingency reserve account be established on each project, with appropriate procedures for allocation to various tasks as needed during execution of the project. This requires setting tight but realistic targets for every task. A figure of 10 percent of direct costs is commonly used for the initial contingency on complex projects.

If unrealistically low initial budgets are established or large cost increases are experienced, the contingency reserve may be negative. The project manager must then seek additional funds from his management, while attempting to find places to reduce the scope or quality of the work to reduce the task budgets to the level required.

A *management reserve transaction register* is necessary to assure adequate control of the reserve. Appropriate procedures for approval and control of reserve transactions must be established, with the project manager as one of the approving authorities. These principles should be observed:

- Reserve transactions do not affect the original task budgets, which should remain fixed.
- *All* transfers between tasks should go through the reserve transaction register, including transfers from tasks where underruns are experienced, as well as transfers to tasks requiring additional funding.
- Specific approvals should be established for:
  —Contractually authorized increase or decrease in scope of work.
  —Cost savings realized, either during or after task completion.
  —Cost expenditures over budget.

The previous comments relate primarily to money, but the concept is equally valid when applied to people and other resources. The resource buffers that are an important feature of the critical chain method (discussed later in Section 10.16) represent a sophisticated approach to the allocation of management reserves.

Project Funding Plan

It is the responsibility of the company controller to assure the adequacy and validity of funding proposals. However, in some cases, the project manager will be responsible for preparing and obtaining approval of a *project funding plan.* This is based on a cash flow analysis of the project budget coupled with the project master schedule, to identify expenditure levels by month and thereby establish the funding requirements. The project manager would then identify the sources of funds for the life of the project, based on contract payment terms, related research and development cases and PARs (project authorization requests), with assistance and approval of the comptroller. The project funding plan would thus indicate the working or invested capital required to be provided by the unit each month or quarter in support of the project. The funding plan should include termination costs, if any, over and above the project budget, should the project be terminated before completion.

Project Chart of Accounts

During the development of the project master schedule and budget, the project chart of accounts should be established. This is necessary to assure proper work authorization, accounting for expenditures, and cost control, as discussed later.

By analyzing the task/responsibility matrix (Figure 10.5), the project manager, project accountant, contract administrator, and project controller, working with the functional managers as appropriate, can establish the project chart of accounts so that all accounting and reporting requirements can be satisfied. Important considerations here include the following:

- Each task (or work package) that is to be scheduled, budgeted, and controlled should be assigned a unique cost account number within the corporate chart of accounts.

- Summaries by elements of the project breakdown structure do not *necessarily* have to be produced by the accounting system; in other words, the project chart of accounts and the accounting numbers assigned do not have to reflect the PBS, although this is desirable if possible.

- Summaries by PBS elements can be prepared manually or by EDP programs outside the basic cost accounting system, but using data produced and controlled by the accounting system.

- A reasonable balance must be maintained between the improved controls that a large number of cost accounts provides and the added cost and administrative burden resulting from more numerous accounts.

Further discussion of this area is given in Chapter 12.

10.14   TASK SCHEDULES AND BUDGETS

A task schedule covers all key activities that must be carried out to complete the task as defined in the task statement of work. It should:

- Be prepared by the responsible performing manager or functional project leader and negotiated with the project manager.

- Incorporate all related interface and milestone events from the project master schedule.

- Show a reasonable number of specific activities that can be related to cost, manpower, material, or other resource requirements.

- Enable monitoring and evaluation of progress on the task.

- Reflect not only the project schedule requirements, but also the functional organizational requirements and resources considering all other tasks in the organization.

Task Budgets

The budget for each task is based on the cost and resource estimates to accomplish the work, together with the task schedule. In practice, the schedule and budget are usually developed simultaneously with the objective of meeting the limitations imposed by the project master schedule and budget. The task budget should:

- Be prepared by the responsible performing manager, using available estimating and pricing procedures and specialists, in negotiation with the project manager.

- Be related directly to the activities shown in the task schedule, to the extent possible.

- Enable collection of and comparison to actual expenditures of money, manpower, and other critical resources.

Design/Development Task Schedules and Budgets

The design/development category includes tasks involving purchasing, engineering, drafting, model shop, product engineering, engineering test, prototype fabrication and assembly, and similar functions as related to design and development of the end product or services.

A suggested design/development task schedule and budget format for labor hours, and material and other direct costs is shown in Figure 10.7. Various detailed estimating forms and procedures are ordinarily used to assist in completing the design/development task schedules and budgets. Labor cost and labor and material overhead cost should be added to the information given in Figure 10.7 to produce a complete task budget.

Manufacturing Task Schedules and Budgets

Based on the product design as specified in the proposal, contract, research development case (if any), and available engineering documentation, manufacturing prepares the cost estimates and budgets for each

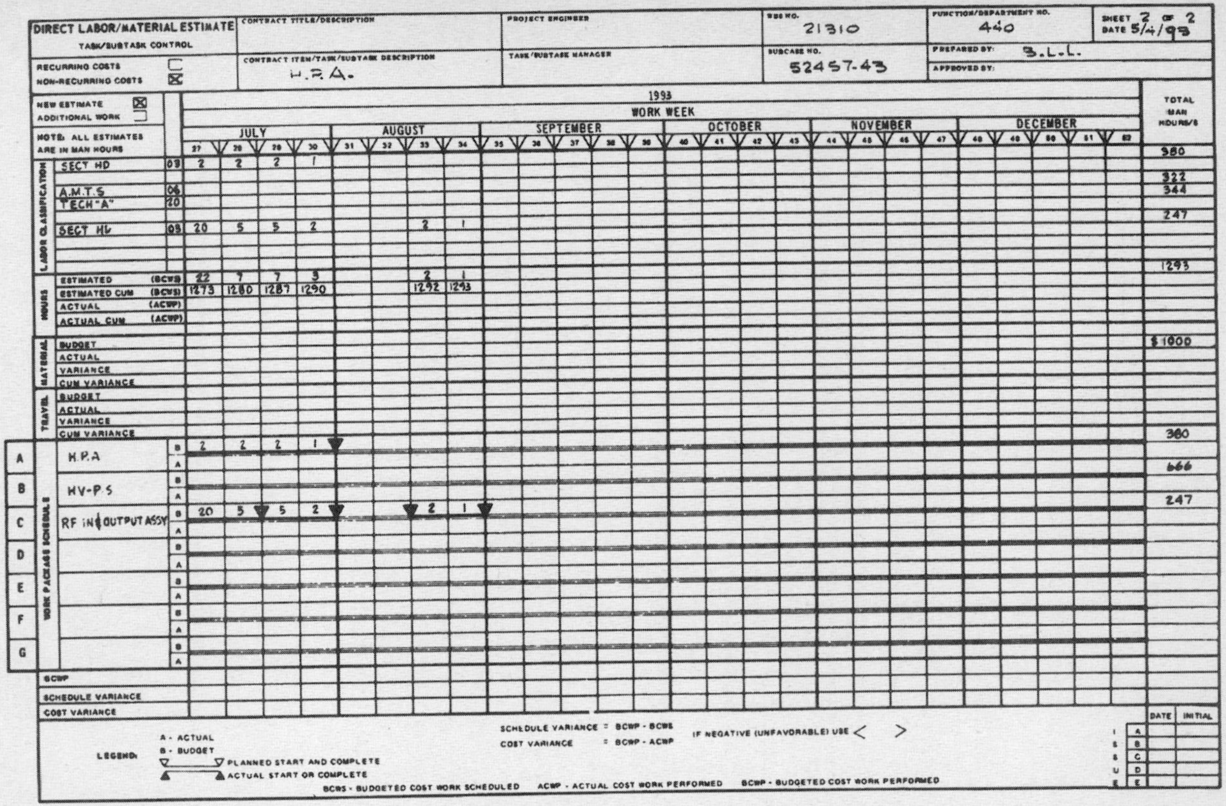

Figure 10.7 Example of a task budget and schedule for design development tasks.

manufacturing task. The production control group establishes the manufacturing delivery schedules. Both of these actions are accomplished in a negotiating process between the manufacturing project leader and the project manager, with appropriate involvement of the project engineer and other project team members. Both the budgets and schedules must be consistent with the project master schedule and budget. Variances in time or cost must immediately be referred to the project manager or higher line authority for resolution.

Manufacturing tasks may involve either recurring or nonrecurring costs, or both. Recurring costs are those associated with normal production operations for specific tasks, as indicated in Figure 10.8. Nonrecurring costs are associated with tooling and special test equipment, and similar special items, as well as industrial fabrication, test, packing, and product engineering for a specific task, as indicated in Figure 10.9.

Other established manufacturing estimating procedures and forms are used to develop the labor and material costs for each manufacturing task in the project. Where standard production costs are available for manufactured parts or assemblies to be used on the project, detailed estimates such as shown in Figures 10.8 and 10.9 would not be required.

Manufacturing task schedules will generally show deliveries of the parts or assemblies produced by the task on a quantity per week basis by part number. These should be correlated to budgeted costs for control purposes.

Installation (Field Operations) Tasks

Installation or field operations tasks may be scheduled and budgeted using formats similar to those applicable to design/development tasks (Figure 10.7).

Procurement Task Schedules and Budgets

For complex tasks being performed under subcontract or purchase order by outside organizations, detailed schedules and budgets are required. These may be for design/development, manufacturing, or installation (field operations) tasks, and the requirements stated in the preceding paragraphs would apply. Usually, however, less detailed schedules and budgets will be provided by subcontractors and vendors. If detailed schedules are required, the contract or purchase order should clearly stipulate such requirements.

Budgeted and Actual Cost for Work Scheduled and Performed

Budgeted cost for work scheduled (BCWS) is the budgeted amount of cost for work scheduled to be accomplished, plus the amount of level

MANUFACTURING FUNCTIONAL COST—TASK BUDGET		

PROPOSAL TITLE
CUSTOMER
ITEM/TASK DESCRIPTION

PROPOSAL NO.   DATE
ITEM NO./TASK NO.   QUANTITY

MATERIAL INCLUDING SUB-CONTRACTING

PURCHASED PARTS	UNIT COST	TOTAL COST	FREIGHT & SHRINK. @ _____ %	TOTAL INCLUDING FREIGHT & SHRINKAGE
PACKING				
SUBCONTRACTING				

REMARKS	TOTAL W/O OPERATION BURDEN	
	OPERATION BURDEN @ _____ %	
	TOTAL LOADED MATERIAL	
	REVIEWED AND APPROVED BY AND DATE	

DIRECT LABOR

NO.	FUNCTION	LABOR CODE	UNIT HOURS	TOTAL HOURS	RATE	DOLLARS		DOLLARS
	PROGRAM MANAGEMENT						DIRECT LABOR W/O ECONOMIC FACTOR	
70	FABRICATION MACHINIST	41					ECONOMIC FACTOR @ _____ %	
70	FAB. INSPECTION _____ %	71					TOTAL DIRECT LABOR	
60	ASSEMBLY "A"	51					OVERHEAD @ _____ %	
60	ASSEMBLY "B"	52						
53	ASSY. INSPECTION _____ %	71					TOTAL LOADED LABOR W/O OPERATION BURDEN	
71	PACKING AND SHIPPING	55					OPERATION BURDEN @ _____ %	
30	INDUSTRIAL ENGR'G.	61					TOTAL LOADED LABOR	
20	PROD. CONTROL PLANNER	62					TOTAL LOADED MATERIAL	
52	TEST	72					TOTAL FACTORY COST	
			TOTALS				UNIT FACTORY COST	

REMARKS	PREPARED BY DATE
	CHECKED BY AND DATE
	REVIEWED AND APPROVED BY AND DATE

RECURRING COSTS	ITEM NO./TASK NO.	QUANTITY

MK 5064 12/67

Figure 10.8   Manufacturing functional cost-task budget for recurring costs.

of effort or apportioned effort scheduled to be accomplished, within a given time period.

Budgeted cost for work performed (BCWP) is the budgeted amount of cost for completed work, plus budgets for level of effort or apportioned effort activity completed within a given time period. This is sometimes referred to as the "earned value."

MANUFACTURING FUNCTIONAL COST–TASK BUDGET

PROPOSAL TITLE		PROPOSAL NO.	DATE
CUSTOMER			
ITEM/TASK DESCRIPTION		ITEM NO./TASK NO.	QUANTITY

MATERIAL INCLUDING SUB-CONTRACTING

TOOLING AND TEST EQUIPMENT	UNIT COST	TOTAL COST	FREIGHT & SHRINK. @ _____ %	TOTAL INCLUDING FREIGHT & SHRINKAGE
TOOLING (VENDOR)				

OTHER

TOOLING (ASSEMBLY)				
TOOLING (FABRICATION)				
SPECIAL TEST EQUIPMENT				
REMARKS			TOTAL	
			OPERATION BURDEN @ _____ %	
			TOTAL LOADED MATERIAL	
			REVIEWED AND APPROVED BY AND DATE	

DIRECT LABOR

NO.	FUNCTION	LABOR CODE	TOTAL HOURS	RATE	DOLLARS		DOLLARS
30	INDUSTRIAL ENGINEERING	61				DIRECT LABOR W/O ECONOMIC FACTOR	
70	FABRICATION ENGINEERING	61				ECONOMIC FACTOR @ _____ %	
51	TEST ENGINEERING	72				TOTAL DIRECTOR LABOR	
71	PACKING ENGINEERING					OVERHEAD @ _____ %	
40	PRODUCT ENGINEERING					TOTAL LOADED LABOR W/O OPER. BURDEN	
						OPERATION BURDEN @ _____ %	
						TOTAL LOADED LABOR	
						TOTAL LOADED MATERIAL	
	TOTALS					TOTAL FACTORY COST	
REMARKS/ADDITIONAL CAPITAL EQUIPMENT				PREPARED BY AND DATE			
				CHECKED BY AND DATE			
				REVIEWED AND APPROVED BY AND DATE			

NON - RECURRING COSTS | ITEM NO./TASK NO. | QUANTITY |

MK5065 ISS. 12/67

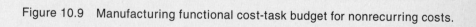

Figure 10.9   Manufacturing functional cost-task budget for nonrecurring costs.

Actual cost for work performed (ACWP) is the amount reported as actually expended in completing the work accomplished within a given time period.

These costs apply to individual tasks or work packages (completed, in-progress, or future, as appropriate), to summaries of several tasks within a higher level element in the project budget structure, or to the total project. They are identified in Figures 10.7 and 14.1.

These values are useful in calculating schedule and cost variances in dollars or other monetary units at each level of summarization on the project (task, intermediate elements, and total project):

$$\text{Schedule variance} = \text{BCWP} - \text{BCWS}$$

$$\text{Cost variance} = \text{BCWP} - \text{ACWP}$$

The use of these values for control and evaluation purposes is discussed further in Chapter 12.

10.15 INTEGRATED, DETAILED TASK LEVEL PERT/CPM/PDM PROJECT NETWORK PLAN AND SCHEDULE

For some projects, considerable improvement in overall scheduling and control will result if all appropriate tasks are planned in network fashion, and all such task networks are integrated by placing them into the appropriate parts of the project master network. Level of effort and apportioned activities would be excluded from the detailed, integrated network.

Although this approach is desirable in general, careful planning and control of the planning effort is required to avoid or overcome a number of potentially serious difficulties:

- If the task networks are too detailed, the resulting integrated project network becomes costly and difficult to maintain on a current basis.
- Electronic data processing procedures are usually required; useful, flexible software must be available, and quick response processing of results must be provided.
- Thorough indoctrination and training must be given to all task leaders and other users.
- The project control group must realize they are serving the functional task managers and leaders in providing them with the

scheduling information produced, and not controlling the internal schedules of each task.

- The "rolling wave" technique (detailing plans only for the next few months) is a useful way to avoid excessive detail.

Despite many years of experience in the application of PERT/CPM/PDM network planning through many industries, its successful use at the detailed, integrated level for large projects is difficult to achieve. It is recommended that such application be limited to the project master schedule level until considerable experience is gained with its use. Then, selected critical tasks should be added on a detailed basis. Experience on successive projects will indicate the practical limits within particular environments and for specific types of projects.

For many tasks or work packages, simple bar charts, production rate charts with trend analysis, or checklists are all that is needed, *provided* that the key task interface events (start, complete, other) are included in the project network plan discussed earlier.

10.16 RESOURCE-CONSTRAINED PLANNING, SCHEDULING, AND CONTROL

In the 1990s, Goldratt's theory of constraints (TOC) started making an impact on project planning, scheduling and control (Goldratt 1994, 1997). Leach (2000, pp. 23–26) reports impressive improvements in schedule performance, efficiency, and other areas of project management, and Patrick (2001) extols the ability to manage risk and uncertainty using critical chain project planning and control.

Also in the 1990s, the Western world began to learn more about resource management on projects in Russia and other former members of the USSR. Voropajev (1997, first published in Russian in 1994) provides a detailed, well-documented history and discussion of the development of the project management profession in Russia from the 1930s to the mid-1990s. "Modern project management methods development as a whole in our country was in step with world project management development, but we were a little behind the West. This was caused by lack of information and computer technologies and historical conditions related to the planned economy, administrative style of management, and isolation from 'the world of project management'" (p. 115). One of the most noteworthy developments in project management coming out of Russia is the concept of the *resource critical path,* which closely resembles the definition of the *critical chain.* This concept is further discussed, following a brief summary of the important characteristics of the critical chain approach.

Critical Path versus the TOC Critical Chain

Debate continues in the project management literature concerning exactly what is new and different in the critical chain approach compared to the well-known critical path technique of project planning, scheduling, and control. These differences are summarized as follows:

- *Resources:* While resources have always been a consideration in developing a PERT/CPM/PDM network plan, TOC focuses more intensively on resource constraints in creating the network plan logic. "The critical chain identifies the project constraint" (Leach 2000, p. 123). The TOC approach provides quantified "resource buffers" that helps to ensure that critical resources will be available when required to avoid project delays. Quantified resource buffers are certainly a new addition to project planning and control practices.

- *Duration estimating:* The early PERT approach in the 1950s provided for probabilistic activity and project durations based on three time estimates. The question of whether the lower level task or activity time estimates were optimistic, most likely, or pessimistic, and of how much "padding" was included in each estimate has been debated for over 50 years now. The critical chain approach "bases its schedule on the mean value (M) (that is, estimate with a 50 percent probability of being achieved) and proposed a distribution with a worst-case value of $M + 0.5 \times M$ for any task or sequence of tasks" (Crispin, 2000, p. 51, citing Goldratt 1997). Crispin argues that this approach is statistically inconsistent and proposes that the critical chain use the old PERT formula for calculating the "most likely" task or activity duration.

- *Float/slack and management reserves versus buffers:* PERT/CPM/PDM has always provided these two important types of float:

  —*Total float:* The amount of time an activity can be delayed without affecting the project duration. This is available only one time in a chain (or path) of activities although it is available (until used) to each activity in the chain.

  —*Free float:* The amount of time an activity can be delayed without affecting any other activities or delaying the project. It is only available to the last activity in a chain before the chain joins a more critical chain.

  —*Management reserves:* Practitioners have for decades advocated various techniques for eliminating excess padding in time and cost estimates when planning projects (see for example Archibald and Villoria, 1967, pp. 76–90). The establishment of management reserves for both schedule and cost has also been a well-known best practice since the early days of modern project management, as discussed earlier in this chapter and in the previous editions of this book. The TOC buffers are a method of formalizing, quantifying, and managing such management reserves.

—*Critical chain buffers:* "Time or budget allowance used to protect scheduled throughput, delivery dates, or cost estimates on a production process or project. Buffers are sized based on the uncertainty in the protected group of activities. Therefore, the schedule buffers are not the same as float or slack that occur as an accident of the activity logic in the critical path schedules" (Leach, 2000, p. 300). They may not be the same, but schedule buffers are analogous to free float as defined above; you could argue that they convert the free float into a new "a buffer activity" in the network plan. "*Float* is an outcome of the task dependencies; *buffers* are an input to schedule planning" (Piney, 2000, p. 53). However, you need to know where to place the buffers, and float—or the lack thereof—is a good indicator of that.

Buffer Management in Critical Chain Project Planning and Control

The addition of critical chain buffers to the project plan may be a significant development in the art and science of project planning, monitoring, and control, although it has not as yet been accepted in widespread application. While the use of buffers requires additional detailed planning, estimating, and reporting information to achieve its benefits, those organizations that have implemented the critical chain approach report satisfaction with the results (Leach, 2000, pp. 23–26).

There are various types of buffers: constraint, cost, drum (constraint resource), and schedule (Leach, 2000, pp. 302, 304). Buffer management consists of:

- *Planning:* Identifying the need for and the type and location of buffers.

- *Quantifying:* Calculating the size and content of each buffer.

- *Monitoring and control:* Updating progress, revising the project plan and buffers, and evaluating and directing the project using established methods and procedures (see Chapter 14).

Detailed explanations of how to implement the TOC critical chain approach are presented in Leach (2000).

Table 10.5   Outline of the Project File

1.0 *General Project Information*
    1.1   The project summary plan: scope, objectives, approach
    1.2   Project appropriation requests (PAR) (product development, capital facilities, data processing systems projects)
    1.3   Research and development cases (R & D or product development projects)
    1.4   Product plan (product development projects)
    1.5   Contract documents (sales projects)
        1.5.1   Request for proposal and all modifications thereto
        1.5.2   Proposals
        1.5.3   Original signed contracts and modifications, and all documents and specifications incorporated in the contract by reference
        1.5.4   Contract correspondence
        1.5.5   Acceptance documentation
    1.6   Statement of work
        1.6.1   X Company
        1.6.2   Y Company

2.0 *Management and Organization*
    2.1   Key organization chart
    2.2   Linear responsibility chart
    2.3   Key project personnel
        2.3.1   X Company
        2.3.2   Y Company
    2.4   Project manager and key team member job specifications
    2.5   Key functional managers and staff assigned to project
    2.6   Policies and directives

3.0 *Technical*
    3.1   Technical approach
    3.2   System specifications
    3.3   Component specifications
    3.4   Production specifications
    3.5   Drawings
    3.6   Reports
    3.7   Design review minutes
    3.8   Production plans
    3.9   Configuration status
    3.10 Engineering change notices
    3.11 Change control board minutes
    3.12 Quality assurance
    3.13 Reliability, maintainability, supportability, assurance
    3.14 Field service and engineering
    3.15 Value engineering

(continued)

Table 10.5 *(Continued)*

4.0 *Financial*

 4.1 Estimates
 4.2 Budgets
 4.3 Cost accounting reports
 4.4 Project Profit and Loss statement
 4.5 Contract status reports
 4.6 Project chart of accounts
 4.7 Billings and payment vouchers

5.0 *Work Plans and Schedules*

 5.1 Project breakdown structure
 5.2 Master schedule and milestone charts
 5.3 Network plans or bar charts
 5.4 Detailed schedules

6.0 *Work Authorization*

 6.1 Work orders—internal
 6.2 Work orders—other affiliated companies
 6.3 Major purchase orders
 6.4 Subcontracts

7.0 *Evaluation and Reporting*

 7.1 Project evaluation reports and charts
 7.2 Project evaluation meeting minutes
 7.3 Management reports
 7.4 Customer reports
 7.5 Trip reports
 7.6 Audit reports

8.0 *Communications*

 8.1 Internal communications
 8.2 External communications

9.0 *Project Security*

 9.1 Work classification
 9.2 Visitations
 9.3 Clearance lists

Resource Critical Path versus Critical Chain

A detailed description of the resource critical path/RCP concept together with a comparison of RCP with the traditional critical path and new critical chain method is given in the Appendix.

In summary, resource constrained project planning, scheduling, and control continues to evolve and develop and represents an important frontier in project management.

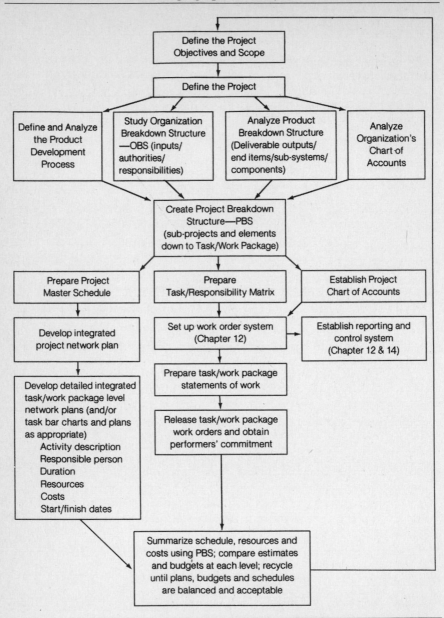

Figure 10.10   Summary of project planning steps. *Source:* Robert Youker, "A New Look at Work Breakdown Structure (WBS) (Project Breakdown Structure—PBS)," *Proceedings of the Project Management Institute Seminar/Symposium,* Calgary, Alberta, Canada, October 1990, Project Management Institute, Drexel Hill, PA. Adapted from Figure 3, p. 712.

10.17   PROJECT FILE

The project file is an orderly collection of documents reflecting all aspects of the project. Its purpose is to assure that all pertinent information is continually available to the project manager and others regarding any matter related to the project, and it is important for a number of reasons, including:

- When a change in the project manager (or a key project staff member) is necessary, the project file is a valuable aid in achieving a rapid, smooth transition of assignment.
- When litigation occurs or is threatened, the file provides vital information that may not otherwise have been recorded or retained.
- When a similar project is to be undertaken at a later date, it provides data for use in proposal preparation, pricing, and management planning.
- Upon project completion, the postcompletion audit or other study of the project file will reveal weaknesses and strengths in the unit's project management or other capabilities and thus indicate where improvements are needed.

The basic content of the project file is outlined in Table 10.5. As the final step in the initial project planning effort, the project file is established with procedures to assure that all documents are properly retained within the file.

10.18   SUMMARY OF PROJECT PLANNING STEPS

To summarize the key points of this chapter and link it to those that follow, the steps required in planning any phase of a project are shown in Figure 10.10.

11

‹ ›

Project Team Planning and Project Start-Up

Ⅰn recent years, the importance of the multidisciplinary project team has been recognized more widely and the power of project team planning has been discovered by many practitioners. This is becoming evident in the increased emphasis on systematic project start-up using team planning workshops at the beginning of each phase of the project life cycle.

Additionally, as the world immerses itself into the "Internet New World" way of doing business, the imperative for speed—Internet speed—has intensified. This imperative adds more significance to using the project start-up process because it sets the requirement for collaborative planning. The usual approach to speeding up things is to eliminate or overlap numerous activities. Unfortunately, with each dropped and overlapped activity, an increase in project risk occurs. Instead of dropping activities, the proper approach is to reduce the number of times each activity is done. For instance, consider a typical planning scenario between a subcontractor (sub), a prime contractor (prime), and an end-user client. The subcontractor or supplier drafts a proposed plan and presents it to the prime contractor, then the prime asks for changes and the sub goes back and reassesses those areas. The sub submits the amended plan for approval, the prime approves and presents the plan to the end-user client. The end-user client asks for some changes, the prime delivers the end-user client changes to the sub; the sub makes the changes and resubmits to the

Adapted from Daniel P. Ono and Russell D. Archibald, Chapter 28, "Team Infrastructure Management: Project Team Planning and Project Start-Up," *Project Management for Business Professionals*, Joan Knutson (Ed.) (New York: John Wiley & Sons, 2001), pp. 528–549.

prime and the prime resubmits to the end-user client. This process represents three iterations of this plan. Collaborative team planning will get this plan done once through.

11.1   NEED FOR COLLABORATIVE PROJECT TEAM PLANNING

Recognition of the need for project team planning has grown out of the increased awareness of the following:

- Weaknesses in the more traditional project-planning approaches.
- Difficulties in getting functional managers and team members to be committed to a plan that has been created by others.
- Need to accelerate the project-planning and team-building processes at the very beginning of a project, or at the beginning of a new phase of a project.

Team planning can also be used effectively when any major change in scope is required or when a major, unforeseen problem is encountered.

Traditional Project-Planning Approaches

Traditionally, project-planning activities are considered to be a primary function of the project manager. On smaller projects and within organizations that have relatively little experience in formalized project management the project manager is typically expected to put together whatever plans and schedules may exist for the project.

In larger organizations, especially when they have considerable experience in project management and have formalized their approaches to managing their projects, project-planning specialists often create the project plans, schedules, and budgets. The basic tools used by such specialists are described in this book and elsewhere in the project-management literature. Ideally, these project-planning specialists (planners, schedulers, cost estimators, cost engineers, and software and computer operations specialists) carry out their work for a specific project under the direction of the project manager assigned to that project. In other situations, they may work independently of the project manager, as discussed later in this chapter.

Weaknesses in the Traditional Approaches

Several critical weaknesses often can be observed in the traditional approaches including:

- *Project plans, schedules, and budgets do not reflect the realities of how the work will actually be done.* There are always many ways to plan and execute a project; even the best plans will not be followed if they do not reflect the methods that the people doing the work will actually use.

- *The functional managers and other team members, and even at times the project manager, are not committed to the plans and schedules.* If the plans do not reflect how the work will actually be done, the people doing the work will not have a sense of commitment to the plans, with the result that they will not be committed to the project itself.

- *More than one plan exists.* It is not surprising to find many situations where more than one plan exists, either for the entire project, or for many portions of it. The project manager who does not believe in and is not committed to the "official" plans and schedules produced by a central planning department will produce his or her own "real" plans as a result. Many functional managers and project leaders often do the same thing.

- *The planning process is inefficient in the use of key persons' time.* A project manager or the planning specialists who recognize the need for involvement of the key project team members in creating the plans will often meet with each individual team member one-on-one to obtain the needed information. After meeting with other team members, a second or even several more rounds are usually needed to work out various conflicts or discrepancies. This "round robin" process is inefficient and consumes much time of all concerned, compounding the dislike most people have for planning in the first place. This "round robin" approach slows down the critical start-up period of the project, and does not enhance teamwork or communication.

- *Plans created either without involvement of the key people, or with their involvement through the "round robin" approach, will generally be based on a bottom-up view of the project.* This bottom-up approach results in project plans and schedules that are often poorly integrated, and harbor unrecognized conflicts that will be identified later when there is insufficient time to avoid them through more integrated, top-down planning.

- *Standardized project templates are used improperly.* Corporate attempts at "templating" project plans generally do not work. Using overall project templates contradicts the definition of a project, namely, that each project is unique. However, the use of templates for lower level, specific, repetitive functional tasks within the overall unique project plan can be a useful technique, if properly used.

These weaknesses have led to a growing realization that there is a better way. That is the use of project team planning during intensive project start-up workshops.

11.2   PROJECT START-UP WORKSHOPS AND THE PROJECT TEAM PLANNING PROCESS

Many organizations regularly hold project kick-off meetings to inform key participants that a particular project is being launched (contract or go-ahead received, project proposal approved, etc.). Often such meetings are limited to rather formal presentations—giving the good news and marching orders to the troops. However, by integrating the concept of project team planning with the kick-off announcement, significant benefits can be realized as described in the remainder of this chapter.

Project Start-Up Workshops

Although the importance of getting a project off to a good, well-planned start has long been recognized, it has only been within the last 15 years that the concept of systematic, intensive, well-planned project start-up (also called project kick-off) workshops has been widely accepted and used. The Committee on Project Start-Up of the International Project Management Association (IPMA) has been instrumental in promulgating and documenting this concept. The Committee's *1989 Handbook of Project Start-Up* (Fangel, 1989) provides detailed information on the concept, the methods, and many examples of experience in its application in various industries and geographic areas. Pincus (1989) presents a persuasive case for using the intensive workshop approach to developing execution plans on a team basis for design and construct projects. Valencia (1997) emphasizes the importance of using a systematic start-up planning process for new projects at Bombardier-Concarril in Mexico.

The fundamental essence of these systematic project start-up workshops is *project team planning*. Start-up workshops, when properly conducted, provide the setting and well-planned processes that enable the project team to work together effectively to produce integrated plans and schedules in a very short time period.

With functional groups handling simultaneous, multiple projects, often in different parts of the world, the project team must focus on and use common processes, communication methods, and standards.

The phrase *project start-up* may be misleading because the concept applies not only to the very first start up, say, at the beginning of the conceptual phase of a project, but also to the beginning of each subsequent phase: definition, planning or proposal; execution or implementation; and project closeout. The term *project phase transition workshop* may be more appropriate than *project start-up workshop*. This is not to be confused with starting up the facility, system, or product being created by the project.

The Team Planning Process

The basic elements of an effective team planning process are:

Adequate preparation.

Identification of the key project team members.

Interactive exchange of information.

Physical setting conducive to the process.

Capturing the team memory.

Appropriate planning aids.

Use of a planning process facilitator.

Each of these is discussed in the following sections.

Adequate preparation.   Prior to bringing together a project team for a team planning session, it is vital to prepare adequately for the meetings. This preparation includes:

- Defining the specific objectives of the team sessions and the results to be achieved.
- Establishing a well-planned agenda for each session.
- Preparing sufficient project planning information in preliminary form (project objectives, scope definition, top levels of the PBS/WBS, team member list, established target schedules—if any, etc.).
- Setting the session date sufficiently in advance to ensure that all team members can attend.
- Announcing the session through appropriate authoritative channels to ensure higher management interest and support, and to assure that all team members show up.
- Defining and understanding the planning process to be used, and the roles and responsibilities of the project manager and the planning process facilitator.
- Arranging for a suitable meeting facility and related logistical support.

Pincus (1989, p. 351) states that "The workshop approach should not be considered without the full endorsement and participation of the project manager. The project manager must control the planning and decision making."

Identification of the key project team members. It seems obvious that to have a project team planning session, it is necessary to identify the team members. However, this is often not a simple task. Who are the *key* project team members? Which functions must be included, and what level of manager or specialist from each function should be identified and invited to the team planning session? How many people can participate effectively in such a session? The following basic rules can be helpful in answering these questions:

- Each of the important functional specialties contributing to the project must be represented. This may include people from within and outside of the organization (contractors, consultants, major vendors, etc.).

- The persons holding responsibility and accountability for the project within each functional area (the "functional project leader") must be present.

- If a functional project leader cannot make commitments of resources for his or her function, that person's manager (who *can* make such commitments) should also be invited to participate in the team planning session, or at least be available by telephone when resource decisions are required.

- If the key team members number more than 20 people, special efforts are needed to assure appropriate interaction (such as plenary sessions combined with breaking into smaller working team sessions).

- The project manager plays a vital role in the team planning sessions, and, if available and assigned, project planning, scheduling and estimating specialists should also participate in—but not dominate—the sessions.

Interactive exchange of information. Central to the collaborative project team planning concept is the need for intensive interaction between the team members during the planning process. The session preparation, the information provided, the physical setting, and the methods of conducting the planning sessions must be designed to promote, not inhibit, this interaction. If the project manager goes too far in preparing planning information prior to the meeting, and presents this information as a *fait accompli* to the team in a one-way presentation, there

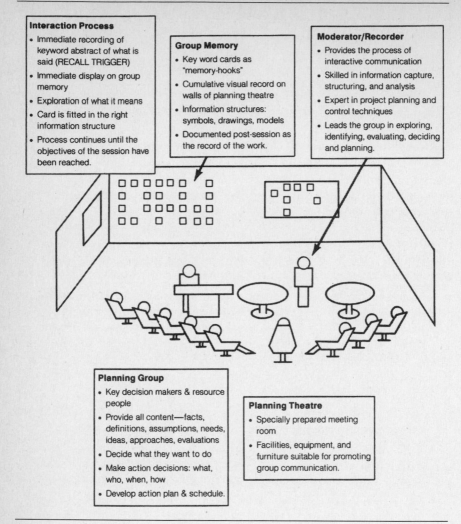

Interaction Process

- Immediate recording of keyword abstract of what is said (RECALL TRIGGER)
- Immediate display on group memory
- Exploration of what it means
- Card is fitted in the right information structure
- Process continues until the objectives of the session have been reached.

Group Memory

- Key word cards as "memory-hooks"
- Cumulative visual record on walls of planning theatre
- Information structures: symbols, drawings, models
- Documented post-session as the record of the work.

Moderator/Recorder

- Provides the process of interactive communication
- Skilled in information capture, structuring, and analysis
- Expert in project planning and control techniques
- Leads the group in exploring, identifying, evaluating, deciding and planning.

Planning Group

- Key decision makers & resource people
- Provide all content—facts, definitions, assumptions, needs, ideas, approaches, evaluations
- Decide what they want to do
- Make action decisions: what, who, when, how
- Develop action plan & schedule.

Planning Theatre

- Specially prepared meeting room
- Facilities, equipment, and furniture suitable for promoting group communication.

Figure 11.1   Team planning session using a planning theatre. *Source:* Robert Gillis, "Strategies for Successful Project Implementation," in *Handbook of Project Start-Up,* Morten Fangel (Ed.), 1989. Section 4. Used by permission.

will be little or no interaction, and the objectives of the team planning session will not be met.

Gillis (1989) has pioneered the development of such sessions over several decades in his work in Canada, the United States, and Europe. Figure 11.1 illustrates several important factors in achieving the interactive exchange of information that is needed for effective project team planning. As indicated, the interaction process is based on the following:

Immediate recording of keyword abstracts of what is said (recall trigger).

Immediate display of the group memory.

Exploration of what the group memory means (through interactive discussion).

Fitting the keyword card in the right information structure.

Continuing the process until the objectives of the session have been reached.

The project master schedule is typically developed on the wall of such a planning theater using the PBS/WBS and the major milestones and interface events that have been identified. This team development achieves very effective integration of all functional tasks with simultaneous understanding by all team members of how their contributions fit with those of the other team members. Serious conflicts are quickly revealed and become the subject of later, more detailed planning and analysis involving only the specific parties concerned.

Physical setting conducive to the process.   As shown in Figure 11.1, Gillis uses the term *planning theater* for the room in which the interactive team planning sessions are held. Such a facility is an important factor in achieving the interaction desired. It does not have to be an elaborate design, but it must provide the following:

- Plenty of wall space with good lighting for display of the team memory and planning results.
- Open access to the walls by the team members (elimination of large tables and other impediments to individual movement and interaction to fill in keyword cards and place them on the walls).
- Sufficient space to enhance individual comfort, movement to view other walls, and open communication.

Capturing the team memory.   The *group* or *team memory* is based on:

- Using the keyword cards as "memory hooks" to recall specific ideas.
- Creating a visual record on the walls of the planning theater or meeting room.
- Proper information structures that are appropriate to the planning work being done: models, matrices, drawings, symbols, and charts.

The team memory resulting from capturing and structuring the information exchanged and produced during the planning sessions provides an agreed, understood, postsession record of the plans created by the team.

Appropriate planning aids.   These include:

- Notebook computers and digital projectors to enable interactive team planning by joint viewing of all information, capture of the team memory, and instant analysis of proposed plans.
- Preformatted output files in PowerPoint, Excel, or other spreadsheet software, MS Project or other scheduling software, and so on, for the following:

  —PBS/WBS responsibility matrix.

  —High-level schedule in selected areas.

  —Contact/team member lists.

  —Agendas and minutes.

- Portable color printers to produce usable hard copies for all team members during the planning sessions.
- Whiteboards that can produce xerographic copies of what is written on them.
- Plastic-coated, adhesive paper for wall-planning work with marker pens.
- Preprinted adhesive forms (symbols, calendars, etc.).

Use of a planning process facilitator.   The facilitator (moderator/ recorder in Figure 11.1) is a crucial player in the project team planning process. This person does the following:

- Supports and enables the process of interactive communication.
- Is skilled in information capture, structuring, and analysis.
- Is expert in the application of project planning, control methods, and techniques; and other aspects of project management.
- Leads the team during the planning sessions in the processes of exploring, identifying, evaluating, decision making, and planning.
- Maintains the process discipline to adhere to the established agenda for the planning session.

Project Manager's Role in Team Planning

A key characteristic of the project manager's role in planning is that of *integration.* The project manager must assist the project team members in developing acceptable plans and schedules that achieve the objectives of the project and reflect the plans and available resources of the various team members. The project manager usually holds the lead responsibility for preparing for the team planning sessions, as discussed earlier.

The project manager plays a vital role in the project start-up team planning sessions, to accomplish the following:

- Establish his leadership position.
- Create the management paradigm (or overall model) that the project team will use on the project.
- Establish the proper focus of the project team.
- Make the project "special" among the contributing functional managers.

In today's environment, where most functional groups are handling multiple projects, the project manager has to create some type of distinction for his project to get the proper attention.

During the planning sessions, the project manager must be alert to real or potential conflicts in plans, and bring these to the surface for resolution. He must concentrate on identification of the key project interface events, or those points of transition of responsibility from one team member to another. This is because one of the key tasks of the project manager is to manage these interfaces properly. The project manager begins to establish discipline within the project team by maintaining the schedule for the project start-up meetings. Finally, he starts to build an effective project team during these planning sessions.

The key role of the process facilitator can also be taken by the project manager. However, experience shows that it is much more effective on all but very small projects for another person to carry out the facilitator's role, especially when an organization is just beginning to use this approach.

Setting the Stage for Detailed Planning

The plans, schedules, and other planning documents created during a team planning session should be limited to integrated plans at the overall project level. These will require definition of the project down to the major functional task level so that responsibilities can be assigned, agreed upon, and understood among the team members. The team-produced project master schedule will show the agreed-upon target dates for key milestones, reflecting the team's judgment on the overall allocation of time to accomplish the intermediate and final objectives.

Team planning sessions are not intended to produce detailed, functional task plans, schedules, or budgets. To attempt to do so would be an extravagant waste of valuable time. Rather, these team sessions set the stage for truly effective detailed planning, scheduling, and budgeting. The stage is set very effectively for the ensuing detailed planning needed to validate the team's efforts and prove whether its collective judgments are correct. This outcome is based on the results of the top-down planning performed by the project team under the integrating influence of the project manager and guided by the planning process facilitator.

After completion of the start-up sessions the project manager, often with the assistance of planning, scheduling, and estimating specialists, can proceed with the more detailed, integrated planning that is necessary to assure effective monitoring and control of the project. The top-level project plans produced by the team can be entered into the computer software to be used on the project, often during the team planning sessions themselves. The more detailed functional task plans and schedules can also be entered in the planning and control system, usually shortly after the team planning sessions, to the extent that this is warranted and practical.

11.3   PROJECT START-UP WORKSHOPS IN THE TELECOMMUNICATIONS INDUSTRY— A CASE STUDY

Experience in the use of project team planning and project start-up workshops over the past 20 years within what is now the Business Communications Systems (BCS) strategic business unit of Lucent Technologies (formerly a unit within AT&T). With annual worldwide sales of several billion dollars within this business unit, there is a wide variety of projects of all sizes, degrees of risk, complexity, and character of the end result. For the projects involved in this case study, Lucent Technologies agreed under fixed-price contract to companies, institutions, and agencies, that it will design and manufacture hardware; develop software; install, test, and cutover into operation complex, high-technology voice/data/video communications and related systems together with required training and documentation.

Such projects usually must be completed within a few months to perhaps one year, although some multiproject contracts cover several years. They involve global voice/data/video networks, call center technologies, and global voice messaging networks.

Within Lucent Technologies, there are many projects of this type under way at any one time, ranging from small implementations to systems covering an entire state government. There are also a small number of mega-projects for federal, state, and local government agencies or nationwide and multinational corporate facilities. Such projects must be executed so that the new facilities are in place and tested to enable a rapid cutover from the old to the new, usually over a weekend, with minimum disruption to the ongoing operations of Lucent's customer. Achieving the agreed cut-over date is almost always of extreme importance to the customer, and once the cut-over date has been agreed upon, it is very difficult to change. Cost is fixed by the contract, but changes in project scope often affect the total system cost. The technical and functional performance specifications to be met by the system are spelled out in great detail in the contract terms.

Project Management in Lucent Technologies' Business Communications Systems (BCS)

Over the past 25 years, Lucent-BCS had been moving toward more formalized project management practices. In the 1980s, a national director of project management held responsibility for the management of all contractual projects. This national project director had three project directors (each responsible for a region of the United States) and specialized staffs reporting to him. The three project directors each had a number of program and project managers and project scheduling specialists reporting to them. A full-time project manager was assigned to a project when its value exceeded a few million dollars. Some projects exceeded a value of $100 million. In some cases, a project manager was assigned for smaller contracts if the project was unusually complex, either technically or organizationally. Other exceptions were made for smaller projects which are parts of a larger program. A program manager held responsibility for multiproject contracts with one customer, and usually had several project managers or site managers (a step below project manager) reporting to him.

In 1988, because of the rapid growth of this business segment, a cadre of experienced project managers was not available. There was a continual need to indoctrinate and train new people who were experienced within other parts of the company in the requirements of the project manager assignment and in project planning and control principles, practices, and tools. As a result, the AT&T forerunner of Lucent-BCS established a broad-ranging education and training program in project management and has for a number of years stressed the certification of its project managers and supporting staff as project management professionals (PMPs) with the Project Management Institute. This broad program continued after the divestment by AT&T of Lucent Technologies in the mid-1990s.

Two important points regarding the project management challenges within Lucent-BCS are the following:

1. *Detailed performance specifications.* These are spelled out in the project contract. They consist of both technical and functional specifications. While the technical specifications are still important, the functional specifications are more critical to customer satisfaction and their willingness to pay. In today's environment, customers expect vendors to provide systems that do what the customers need in order to achieve their strategic objectives. Customers rarely care about the type of equipment or the technical aspects of the systems as long as the systems provide the functionality that will create a competitive advantage for them.

2. *Schedule achievement is dependent on customer actions.* These communication systems are deeply intertwined with the customer operations and physical facilities. The customer must carry out significant actions during the life of a project that directly affect schedule achievement. Therefore, to be successful the project schedules must be developed collaboratively with the customer. If the project is positioned correctly with the customer and the other vendors the people involved with the project from all aspects will realize that the biggest challenge is for the project team to overcome the difficulties provided by the environment, and not by each other.

Today, the Lucent Technologies project manager continues to operate within a classic matrix organization, usually as a one-person project office but using specialized staff support as required. In very large projects, the project manager has several people on her direct staff. Many different parts of Lucent located in different geographic regions contribute to each of these projects, including several engineering and technical disciplines, purchasing, manufacturing, field installation and testing, provisioning and logistic support, software development, training, and various other services and operations departments. The project manager is charged with providing full project management deliverables in order to mitigate risk as much as possible. There is a continuing need to train new people and a project coordinator group has been established as a feeder pool for project managers.

Identifying the Need for Project Start-Up Improvement

In the mid-1980s, Lucent-BCS (then a part of AT&T) director of projects for Southern California and Hawaii identified a need for ways to accelerate the planning, learning, and team-building processes that take place on every project. He saw this need for his own project managers as well as the functional managers who carried out the specific tasks on each project.

Very importantly, he also saw this need within the customer's people who were involved with the project. In addition to this acceleration, he wanted to prevent or quickly resolve any adversarial attitudes that may be encountered at the start of a project with the customer's assigned people or among the BCS project team. Such attitudes, when encountered, took some time to overcome and had sometimes caused delays and avoidable added costs.

Typically, after a new project had been under way for a few months, good teamwork emerged. The director of projects wanted to achieve that teamwork in a few days or weeks, due to the short duration of many of his projects.

Finally, the projects were not meeting financial and customer satisfaction objectives.

Satisfying the Need with Project Start-Up Workshops

The projects director decided to initiate project start-up workshops on his new projects to see whether these needs could be met in this manner. The workshops were structured as discussed next.

Approach.   A three-meeting start-up workshop format was designed. The first two meetings, usually spaced at least a week apart, involves only BCS people. The third meeting, following the second by at least a week, includes the customer people who were involved directly in the project, and also involves senior customer managers.

Workshop objectives.   The start-up workshop objectives are:

1. To apply proven project management methods to the project, and develop—as a team—jointly agreed-upon project plans, schedules, and control procedures.
2. To assure good understanding of the roles and responsibilities of all BCS and customer project team members, thereby enhancing effective teamwork.
3. To identify additional steps needed to assure project success.

While team building was not stated specifically as an objective, it obviously is one of the most important results to be achieved.

Start-up workshop planning deliverables.   Emphasis throughout the workshop sessions is on the deliverables to be produced by the team. These are:

- Agreed list of key project team members.

- List of key concerns and major open issues.

- A well-defined project/work breakdown structure (PBS/WBS).

- A task/responsibility matrix based on the PBS/WBS, and reflecting all identified contributors to the project, including the customer and outside agencies (such as the involved local telephone operating companies).

- A list of key project interface events, linked to the PBS/WBS, and showing the initiator and receiver(s).

- A project master schedule, based on the PBS/WBS, reflecting the key project interface events, and based on the consensus of the project team on the overall allocation of time.

- Agreed procedures for project monitoring and control, including dates for periodic project review meetings.

- A mutually agreed upon escalation plan that takes into account how key problems or conflicts will be escalated through organizational channels for prompt resolution.

- Action items resulting from the start-up workshop discussions, with assigned responsibility and agreed upon due dates for each.

The sessions.   The workshop sessions are the responsibility of the assigned project manager. She plans and prepares for the sessions with the assistance of a staff or outside consultant acting as the facilitator. For each topic listed in the agenda, the consultant/facilitator briefly presents the underlying concept to be applied. Then the project team members roll up their sleeves and create the deliverable item for the project: the PBS/WBS, PBS/WBS/responsibility matrix, key project interface event list, and project master schedule, and so on.

Some of these items, especially the PBS/WBS, matrix and interface event list, are usually developed by breaking into five or six person teams with each team covering assigned parts of the project. These small teams then report their results back to the full project team (usually 15 to 20 people) to assure total team buy-in of the plans.

In this process, the assisting staff member or consultant acts as the process facilitator, assuring that the overall process is adhered to and acting as a source of industry-proven project management knowledge. After a project manager has experienced several such start-up sessions, she will often take on the facilitator role, especially when most of the other team members have also been through several project start-up/kickoff sessions.

One of the overall objectives of the start-up workshop is to position the project manager properly in the eyes of the other team members, and also of the customer team members. The project manager thus must be seen as basically running the start-up workshop sessions with the assistance of the facilitator, when one is used.

Continued Application of Project Start-Up Workshops

Since the initial application of this approach in the mid-1980s, the objectives and deliverables have remained essentially unchanged. The approach has been embedded as a key element of the Lucent-BCS project management process.

Results Achieved

The most direct indication of the overall benefits of using a well-organized process for starting up projects is that the system *cut-overs*—project completions—are on schedule and of better quality on projects using this approach compared to the projects that did not.

Better project and functional planning. The start-up workshops get the project team started quickly with a good understanding of *what* needs to be done, *who* does each of the many tasks, and *when* each must be completed. This approach gets all of the functional organizations thinking about what kind of planning is required—before getting into the thick of the action. Previously, some functional managers would leave the planning to the last minute, or would not do any planning at all.

Improved financial performance. From the corporate viewpoint the primary benefit achieved was improved financial performance. When the job was done on schedule and met the customer requirements without rework to correct quality problems the payoff in financial terms became very obvious.

Better communications and teamwork. After the start-up workshops, all project team members use the same semantics and planning terms. By jointly working through the planning deliverables, good teamwork is achieved much earlier on each project. This joint planning shows each team member that everyone on the team has important tasks to perform and how these tasks are interrelated. There is a better realization that they all need to be involved in the planning effort to assure project success. The success achieved during the start-up meetings gets the team working together in an effective way that is immediately carried into the actual work on the project.

Improved customer relations. There are very positive reactions from customer team members and higher management to the start-up workshop sessions and the resulting deliverables. Lucent Technologies marketing managers give similar positive reactions and point to the fact that the workshops provide a vehicle for the company's team members to work closely with the customer team members very early in the project. This has avoided the adversarial attitudes that were experienced previously on some projects. An important result of the external meeting with the customer team members and managers is quick escalation and resolution of open issues that threaten to delay the cutover.

Benefits to the project manager.   Several important benefits to the project manager are:

- *Positioning the project manager.* Typically the marketing people work on the sale to a particular customer for months if not years preparing the proposal and negotiating the contract. The project manager, who is often involved during the proposal preparation stage, takes over implementation when the contract is signed. Before using the start-up workshops, it would usually take the project manager some time to establish her position with both the customer and internal team members, especially with the marketing people who naturally felt a strong proprietary interest in the project. By the end of each start-up workshop process, all team members have a good understanding of the need for a project manager and are ready to give him the required support.

- *Detailed planning and scheduling.* Another benefit to the project manager is that she can immediately use the project breakdown structure, the project master schedule, and the project interface event lists produced by the team as the basic framework for the detailed PERT/CPM/PDM network plan and schedules.

- *Project manager as project interface manager.* A key benefit is that the team members understand the project manager's role as the project interface manager. Since the team has identified the key project interface events and understands how the project manager will manage these project interface events while each functional manager manages his assigned tasks between these events, good acceptance of the project manager role is achieved. The functional managers quickly realize that this is a valuable asset to their getting the job done successfully to specification, on schedule, and within budget.

- *Earlier establishment of the project manager as the leader of the project.* The start-up sessions provide the project manager with the opportunity to demonstrate that she is the real leader of the project. Previously, it would take a number of weeks or even months for this to be established in the minds of the project team members.

Hidden Agenda Items within the Start-Up Workshop Process

In addition to the deliverables and other results described previously, there are several important hidden-agenda topics and related results involved in the start-up workshop process. The most important of these—not listed necessarily in order of importance—are as follows:

- Introducing uniform, proven industry project management practices with common terminology.
- Providing hands-on training to all project team members in effective project planning and control methods.
- Tapping the wisdom of the group to develop the best overall project plan.
- Creating a shared vision of the total scope of the project, its challenges, and its objectives at several levels.
- Demonstrating and gaining the power and benefits of open team planning and communications.
- Establishing early project discipline and the management model for the project.
- Exchanging experience and developing planning skills and understanding among the team members of all aspects of what goes into a complex communications/information systems project.
- Building a working team and getting individual team members to commit to, and be enthusiastic about, the project through involvement, understanding, and promises made to the peer group—the project team—and not just to the project manager.

Learning and Development at Four Levels

The approach used—short presentations, small team assignments, and team reports to the full group—has proven to be effective in exchanging and transferring knowledge and experience. Using this approach individual and team development takes place at four levels:

1. The facilitator and project manager convey a certain level of knowledge with the initial presentation on a given topic.
2. The members of the small teams work together for periods of one or more hours and interchange ideas and experience; there will always be diverse levels and types of experience and knowledge in each small team and the team members learn from each other.

3. As each team reports its results to the full project team, exchange and learning takes place as the team members see what their peers have done. Team members also get the experience of making presentations to the full team.

4. The workshop facilitator and the project manager add to and expand on the information presented or show where it may need further improvement. Additional knowledge and development occurs during these discussions.

After completion of the three project start-up/kick-off meetings, the project team has been put through several experiences that provide first-hand demonstration of the team's ability to work together effectively and to produce valuable deliverables that will be used for the life of the project.

Modifications Made for Smaller Projects

To achieve the same objectives on smaller projects, and on larger projects that are very similar to or use the same team members as other recent projects, the following modifications have been made to the procedures described earlier:

1. Reduce the duration of the internal sessions from two days to approximately four hours.

2. Condense the formal presentations to fit the reduced time.

3. Prepare more detailed drafts of the project breakdown structure, the task/responsibility matrix, the interface event lists, and the project master schedule before the workshop is started, and incorporate any changes introduced by the team members during the workshop sessions.

4. Shorten the client workshop to four hours or less.

5. Address only areas of relatively high risk.

The objectives, preparation, invitations, and workshop deliverables for smaller projects do not vary from large projects. However on some smaller projects the full set of project planning deliverables may be limited to the areas of greatest risk. If the small project workshops are conducted with the same professionalism as large projects the project manager can instill the same team spirit, generate the same quality plans, and use the same monitoring of progress and quality while demonstrating sensitivity to the functional managers' workloads.

11.4   BENEFITS AND LIMITATIONS OF PROJECT TEAM PLANNING

The basic benefits of project team planning are:

- Plans produced are based on how the work will actually be accomplished.
- Persons responsible for performing the work have a greater sense of commitment to the plans and to the project.
- Only one set of plans exist: Those that the project team has created and is following.
- The overall time required for planning by the key project team members is reduced.
- The project plans reflect a top-down approach using the total wisdom of the project team, which then sets the stage for more effective, detailed, bottom-up validation, and elaboration of the plans.
- The project manager gets an early indication of where to spend his or her time to begin mitigating the risks of the project.

The decision to use project team planning should be based on the characteristics of the project in question. The following factors may indicate some limitations to project team planning. It would not be appropriate to insist on the type of team planning described here if projects:

- Are of the type that is very well known to the organization.
- Are very repetitive of many previous projects.
- Have project team members who are all experienced in this type of project.
- Have planners available who can produce plans and schedules that are valid and acceptable to all concerned.
- Satisfy top management with their financial and technical results.

There appears to be no upper limit in project size for the use of the project team planning approach. At the top of a massive mega-project, as one extreme, the objectives of the top-level project team planning session would be to:

1. Define the appropriate major subprojects into which the mega-project should be divided.
2. Identify the key milestones and interface events that will link these subprojects.

3. Assign responsibilities as appropriate.

4. Lay out the target project master schedule.

5. Identify and assess the key risk areas.

At each subordinate level, the project team must recognize the appropriate level of detail below which they must not attempt to develop plans and schedules. Each team must concentrate on handing down the structured plans and schedules within which the next level teams must in turn develop their plans.

The primary limitation in project team planning is probably the time required of the project team members to devote to the team planning sessions. Although planning should be given a high priority in any organization, planning is viewed frequently as unproductive and even wasteful, hence it is difficult to convince the project team members that they should devote even a few days to developing the project plans. Top management understanding and support is required to overcome these ingrained attitudes and habits. A successful project team planning session can also do a lot to demonstrate the power and usefulness of this approach.

For team planning as described here to be most successful, the project manager must have a thorough understanding of the project start-up process and its objectives, as well as the project's objectives, political attributes, and the personal aspirations and motivations of the project team members.

12

‹ ›

Authorizing and Controlling the Work, Schedule, and Costs

If the planning actions described in Chapters 10 and 11 are properly carried out, and the project and task plans, schedules and budgets are well documented, then it will be possible to exert good control over the work, schedule, and costs. Simultaneously, technical progress monitoring and performance measurement are required to enable overall evaluation of the project

The definition of project control given in the introduction to Chapter 10 should be reemphasized here. The project and functional project leaders achieve cooperative control by:

- Establishing a joint understanding of the project objectives and goals.
- Jointly defining, planning, scheduling, and budgeting the tasks.
- Using established procedures to authorize the work, to control changes and scope of work, and to control schedules and costs (as described in this chapter).
- Measuring and evaluating performance in cost, schedule, and technical terms on a joint basis to identify current or future variances from plan and to initiate appropriate corrective actions (as described in this and the following chapters).

12.1 WORK AUTHORIZATION AND CONTROL

After a project has been defined, planned, scheduled, and budgeted, effective project management requires that the individual tasks be communicated in *written, documentary form* to the persons who will direct and perform the work, authorizing them to expend money, labor, and other resources on the project. This authorization will specify the required schedule and agreed budget. The project manager must obtain agreement and commitment (preferably by signature) that each manager or supervisor accepts the assignment. Such agreements may of course be modified, revised, or cancelled when conditions change.

This process is referred to as work authorization and control. It is required for tasks performed within the sponsoring organization and also by outside contractors, suppliers, or vendors. The general flow of work authorization is:

- Contract is awarded (or PAR, research and development case, or other go-ahead approval granted), and master contract release is issued.
- Project release document is issued.
- Project and task schedules and budgets are revised as necessary and time phased to reflect the date of go-ahead and changes made during the approval process.
- Task work orders are agreed upon and issued for all initial tasks.
- Subcontracts and purchase orders are issued as required.
- Cost accounts are authorized and opened for active tasks; budgets are entered into EDP system (if used).

At this point, work is initiated. New work orders, subcontracts, and purchase orders are issued as their scheduled start dates approach. Expenditures are recorded against the proper cost accounts for monitoring and control purposes. When a task or subtask is complete, its cost account is closed and further charges to it are rejected, unless special late charge authorization is made.

Figure 12.1 illustrates the work authorization flow described and shows the correlation of the functional organization with the Project Breakdown Structure.

Contract and Project Releases

Upon contract award, the *master contract release* (or equivalent) document is prepared by the contract administrator and distributed to the key managers concerned.

In one company, as an illustration, this document consists of 12 pages, with appropriate attachments:

1. Summary sheet.
2. Statement of work.
3. Items and prices—hardware.
4. Items and prices—data requirements.
5. Drawings.
6. Delivery schedule.
7. Inspection, packaging, shipping, and billing data.
8. Replacement orders.
9. Property requirements.
10. Tooling and test equipment.
11. Contract requirements.
12. Support requirements.

Additional or alternative items would be required for other companies.

The *project release* document is issued next. This authorizes the total funding of direct costs for the actual execution of the project. Although it may carry different names in various organizations, its purpose is still the same. For new product development projects, for example, the research and development case document itself may serve the purpose of the project release, with appropriate approvals or cover sheet.

Figure 12.2 illustrates a typical project release document. This requires approval of the project manager, contract administrator, director of operations or manager of projects, and comptroller.

If additional funds are required to complete the project because of unforeseen problems or a change of scope, a revised project release is required prior to expenditure of such funds. In overrun situations, a *management release* is used to provide the needed funds either by reducing the gross margin on the contract or from some other source.

Task Work Orders

A formal procedure is required for authorizing and controlling tasks and their related budgets and schedules. The key document in this procedure is usually referred to as a *work order*. Frequently, companies have a rigid work order procedure for relatively trivial expenditures, such as building maintenance, but no equivalent procedure for authorization and control of much larger project funds, including research and development cases. This is an obvious weakness in their ability to control a

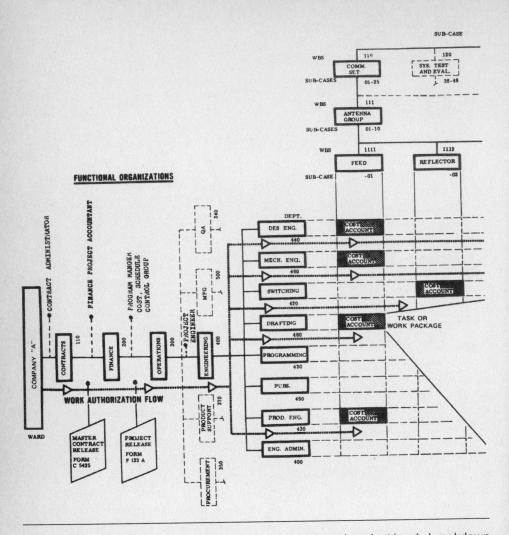

Figure 12.1   Integration of functional organizations and project/work breakdown structure. *Source:* ITT Defense Communications Division. Used by permission. See also Figure 10.7.

project's scope, schedule, and budget. Work orders should contain at least the following:

- Brief, but complete, *statement of work*.
- Relationship to the *project breakdown structure*, with appropriate code numbers (if used) for the work package and parent element in the project breakdown structure.

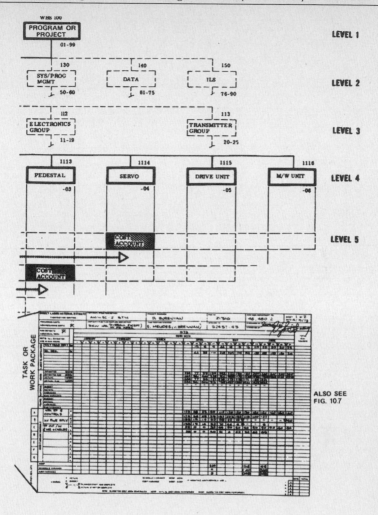

Figure 12.1   *(Continued)*

- *Budget,* divided into labor and material dollars, labor hours and quantities, and other direct costs by time period, if appropriate.
- *Schedule,* including task start and completion, and known intermediate milestone and interface events, with indication of interfaced (interrelated) work control packages.
- Reference to applicable product *specifications,* drawings, and other documents.

PROJECT RELEASE

ISSUE NO. _____ ACCOUNT NO. _____

CONTRACT NO. _____ TYPE _____ DATE OF ISSUE _____
CONTRACT DATE _____ PRODUCT CLASS _____ DEPT. NO. _____
CONTRACT COMPLETION DATE _____ PROPOSAL NUMBER _____
PROGRAM/PROJECT MANAGER _____ CONTRACT ADMINISTRATOR _____

TITLE/QUANTITY _____

TOTAL AUTHORIZED COSTS

DIRECT LABOR
   1. ENGINEERS .... $ _____
   2. TECHNICIANS .... _____
   3. DRAFTSMEN AND TECHNICAL WRITERS .... _____
   4. MACHINISTS .... _____
   5. BENCH MACHINISTS .... _____
   6. CLERICAL .... _____
   7. TEST AND INSPECTION .... _____
   8. OTHER .... _____
      TOTAL DIRECT LABOR .... $ _____

DIRECT LABOR - FABRICATION
   4. MACHINISTS .... $ _____
   5. BENCH MACHINISTS .... _____
   6. CLERICAL .... _____
   7. INSPECTION .... _____
   8. OTHER .... _____
      TOTAL DIRECT LABOR - FABRICATION .... $ _____

OVERHEAD - OTHER (%) .... _____
OVERHEAD - FABRICATION (%) .... _____
DIRECT MATERIAL .... _____
SUBCONTRACTED SERVICES - MATERIAL .... _____
SUBCONTRACTED SERVICES - OTHER .... _____
PREMIUM TIME .... _____
        COMPANY CHARGES - MATERIAL .... _____
        COMPANY CHARGES - OTHER .... _____
TRAVEL .... _____
SPECIAL FACILITIES - TOOLS AND TOOLING .... _____
SPECIAL FACILITIES - CAPITAL .... _____
OTHER .... _____

   TOTAL AUTHORIZED FOR EXPENDITURE .... $ _____

   LESS: MANAGEMENT FUNDING PER RELEASE NO. .... $ _____

   TOTAL CUSTOMER FUNDED COSTS .... $ _____

REMARKS _____
_____
_____
_____

APPROVAL _____ APPROVAL _____
        PROGRAM/PROJECT MANAGER   CONTRACT ADMINISTRATOR

_____ _____
      DIRECTOR OF OPERATIONS   COMPTROLLER

Figure 12.2   Example of a project release document.

- *Cost account code,* with provisions for subaccount codes for control of further delegation of assist work, if possible and desirable.
- *Signature of the initiator* (the project manager or a task manager for subsequent assist work orders).
- *Signature of person authorized to accept responsibility* for performance of the work as specified and his organization identification name or code (e.g., functional project leader or task leader).
- Any *special terms or conditions.*

Figure 12.3 is an example of a typical work order document. As indicated, the task schedule and budget, plus other appropriate documents, should be attached.

Lower level authorization of work is frequently needed. Subordinate work assist orders, releases, fabrication orders, shop orders, purchase orders, requisitions, test requests, and so on, should be issued or approved by the person holding responsibility for the basic work order. Provision for cost accumulation back to the basic work order cost account number is required.

Subcontracts and Purchase Orders

Formal authorization to perform work and/or expend funds externally is usually required by established policies. Procedures and documents are well established in this area. The project manager must understand and know how to use the company's subcontracting and purchasing departments and procedures to assure effective project control.

12.2   BASELINE PLAN, SCHEDULE, AND BUDGET

The project baseline plan, schedule, and budget is the officially approved set of documents that define the project objectives, scope, target technical performance specifications, master schedule, key milestone dates, and budget allocations. The baseline concept is similar to the "design freeze" point on the product design side: Once established, changes to the baseline targets can only be made after considered review and approval using established change control procedures. Some baseline changes may fall within the scope of authority of the project manager, especially if they can be handled by allocating time or money from the management reserve accounts, but many will require approval of the project sponsor, project owner, or the customer providing funds for the project.

ENTER X X WHERE ENTRY OR SIGNATURE NOT REQUIRED

DATE: _____ PAGE 1 OF ____

	GIVER	CONTRACT NO.	PROGRAM/PROJECT NAME		CONTROL LEVEL	SUMMARY ACCOUNT NO.
TASK WORK ORDER			TASK TITLE (27 SPACES)			
	RECEIVER	REF. NO.	CONT. ITEM NO.	TASK NO.	START DATE	COMPLETION DATE	DELIVER TO

ALL CLASSIFIED MATERIAL REQUIRED TO SUPPORT THIS FORM MUST BE HANDLED IN ACCORDANCE WITH PROCEDURES. THIS FORM IS NOT TO BE CLASSIFIED, NOR ATTACHED TO ANY CLASSIFIED MATERIAL.

SECURITY

QUALITY ASSURANCE	INSPECTION POINT	CONTRACT–PECULIAR INSPECTION REQUIREMENTS:

STATEMENT OF WORK: (IF THIS SPACE IS INADEQUATE, USE ATTACHMENT(s))

SUPPLEMENTS

1. STATEMENT OF WORK
2. SCHEDULES
3. BUDGET
4. DATA REQUIREMENTS
5. GIVER–RECEIVER PLAN
6. SPECIFICATION REQUIREMENTS
   A. APPLICABLE DOCUMENTS
   B. REQMTS – PERFORMANCE
   C. REQMTS – DEFINITION
   D. REQMTS – DESIGN–CONSTR.
7. PRODUCT EFFECTIVENESS
8. ACCEPTANCE REQUIREMENTS
9. SCN FORM
10. PROVISIONABLE ITEMS LIST
11. OTHER

CODE APPLICABLE
U – UNCLASSIFIED ATTACHED
C – CLASSIFIED SEPARATE COVER
N – NOT APPLICABLE

SIGNATURES AS REQUIRED – * INDICATES MANDATORY

REVISION	BUDGET		GIVER						RECEIVER			
		$(000)	INITIATOR	PROD. EFF.*	APPROVAL *	DATE	CONTROL POINT *	DATE	CONTROL POINT *	DATE	APPROVAL *	DATE
		ORIG						OUT		IN		
								IN		OUT		
		A						OUT		IN		
								IN		OUT		
		B						OUT		IN		
								IN		OUT		
		C						OUT		IN		
								IN		OUT		
		D						OUT		IN		
								IN		OUT		
		E						OUT		IN		
								IN		OUT		
									SUMMARY ACCOUNT NO.			

DISTRIBUTION. WHITE RECEIVER: CANARY REC. CONTROL POINT: PINK GIVER CONTROL POINT: BLUE GIVER. GREEN PROD. EFF

Figure 12.3 Example of a work order document.

The more useful project scheduling software packages show the baseline plan on the schedule charts they produce, and compare the current plan and schedule graphically against the baseline schedule.

Figure 12.4 illustrates the relationships between a number of directives and planning documents and the baseline plan for a large, complex, high-technology project. Highly visible in the portrayed process of building the baseline plan for this project are many of the planning documents described in Chapter 10, and the work authorization and control documents discussed in this present chapter.

12.3   CONTROLLING CHANGES AND PROJECT SCOPE

Projects involve accomplishing an objective that has not been achieved before under the same circumstances or conditions. Changes, therefore, are inevitable since every problem or circumstance cannot be predicted or anticipated at the time the project is originally planned.

Procedures are required to evaluate and control changes in scope, schedule, and cost. Decisions to make a change may be made at the task project leader, at the project level by the project manager in coordination with affected functional project leaders, by higher management, or by the customer.

Project Scope Control

A primary cause of delay and cost overrun on projects is the uncontrolled, frequently unnoticed, increase in scope of the work being performed, compared to the original project plan. People tend to want to produce the best possible result, regardless of the agreed upon objective. Engineers, if not properly managed, often continue to improve their designs beyond the specification requirements. Customer representatives often exert pressure to perform additional work to correct an oversight on their part, respond to changes in requirements, or improve the product beyond the terms of the contract. Continual surveillance and discipline at the task and project levels is required to control the scope of work.

The project manager plays a key role in this effort, by the following:

- Insisting on well-documented task statements of work, schedules, and budgets, with signatures.

- Monitoring results with the functional project leaders to assure that the specifications and contract conditions are being met—no more, no less.

BASELINE COMPONENTS

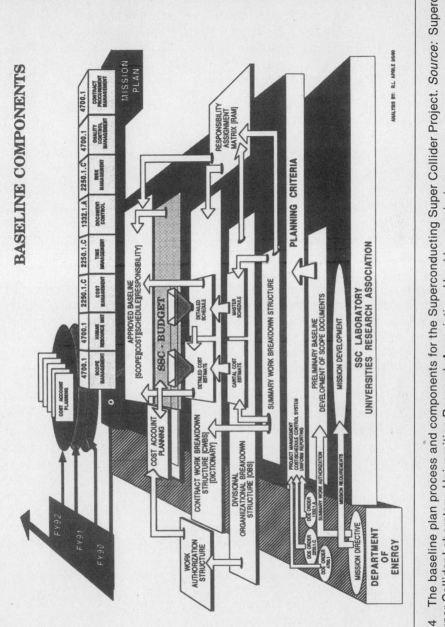

Figure 12.4 The baseline plan process and components for the Superconducting Super Collider Project. *Source:* Superconducting Super Collider Laboratory, Universities Research Association. Used by permission.

- Monitoring schedule and budget variances with the functional project leaders to identify tasks where the scope of work may have expanded, and initiating appropriate corrective action.
- Insisting on revised work statements, schedules, and budgets where an increase in scope is required by the customer or for other considerations. (Contract price changes should be initiated when justified.)
- Controlling and monitoring direct contact with customer representatives at the working level, and preventing company personnel from making unauthorized agreements that change the scope of work on any task.
- Personally participating in any trade-off agreements made between task managers and with customer representatives.
- Insisting that the contract administrator be fully involved in the above actions.

Task Work Order Control

Since the task work orders are in effect contracts between the project manager and the functional managers and project leaders performing the tasks, and since the task schedules and budgets are a part of the work orders, these documents are vital to overall project control.

Procedures are required to govern the approval and issuance of work orders, or equivalent documents, and for their revision and administrative close-out. It is important that task work orders be:

- Released for a given task only when the start date of the task is near. (However, the functional managers would have preliminary copies of the work orders earlier for planning purposes.)
- Used as the basis for evaluation of progress in schedule and cost, determination of cost and schedule variances as described later, and estimation of the cost to complete.
- Updated and revised periodically to reflect actual progress and new knowledge.
- Terminated, and the associated cost accounts closed, immediately upon completion of the task.
- Retained as part of the project file for record purposes and for use in estimating future tasks of a similar nature.

Subcontract and Purchase Order Control

Established procedures should be used to carry out similar control actions related to subcontract and purchase orders. The project contract administrator is responsible for the duties specified in Section 9.5 for all subcontracts. The designation of a purchasing project leader will simplify control of all purchase orders for the project.

Engineering Change Control and Configuration Management

Ineffective control of engineering changes is frequently the cause of delay and cost overruns on projects. To manage this:

- Procedures for controlling engineering changes must be in operation.
- A *Change Control Board* must be established for the project, with voting membership to include the project manager (who may act as chairman in some cases) and key managers and/or functional project leaders from engineering, manufacturing, marketing, purchasing, contract administration, and possibly other areas.
- A *design freeze point* must be established, corresponding to the "baseline" design, and all subsequent design changes rigidly controlled and documented by the Change Control Board, which also determines the point of effectivity of each change (model or serial number to be affected).
- A disciplined procedure must be established and followed for controlling and documenting the functional and physical characteristics of the products being designed and produced. This is referred to as configuration management.

Contract Administration and Control

The contract administrator plays a key role in controlling the project during its execution, as detailed in Section 9.5, and assists in controlling the scope of work.

12.4   SCHEDULE CONTROL

Schedule and cost control must be performed on an integrated basis to achieve effective project control. In addition, technical progress on performance must be measured (see Section 12.8) and correlated to schedules and costs. Concentrated effort is necessary in each of these areas to achieve control of schedules and costs, integrate schedules and costs, and to measure technical progress and correlate with schedules and costs.

Correlation of Schedules, Costs, and Technical Progress

Schedules and costs are correlated at the task or work package level by the task schedule and budget document, as a part of the task work order. The correlations can be summarized in several ways, or a combination of these, for higher level control purposes. Examples include:

1. By elements of the project breakdown structure.
2. By organization (section, department, etc.).
3. By financial ledger accounts (engineering expense, manufacturing, etc.).
4. By type of cost (labor, material, overhead).

The project manager generally finds the summary by elements of the project breakdown structure the most useful for project control purposes.

Figure 12.5 illustrates the correlation of schedules and costs with the project breakdown structure. The PBS is arranged on the left side, and the work packages or tasks are shown by the bars, in line with their parent level PBS elements, in this case, level 3. The project master network plan is partially illustrated, linking the tasks through milestone and other events. Budgets, actuals, and estimates-to-complete and estimates-at-completion are indicated for a few tasks and for the total project. Intermediate level summaries are also made for each level and element. Technical progress is measured by correlation of technical objectives to specific milestone events, as discussed in Section 12.8.

Requirements for Control

Summarizing a number of the points in previous paragraphs, effective control of project schedules and costs requires:

- *Thorough planning* of the work to be performed to complete the project.
- *Good estimating* of the time, labor, and costs.
- Clear *communication* of scope of required tasks.
- Disciplined *budgeting and authorization* of expenditures.
- *Timely accounting* of physical progress and cost expenditures.
- *Periodic reestimation* of the time and cost to complete remaining work.
- *Frequent, periodic comparison* of actual progress and expenditures to schedules and budgets, both at the time of comparison and at project completion.

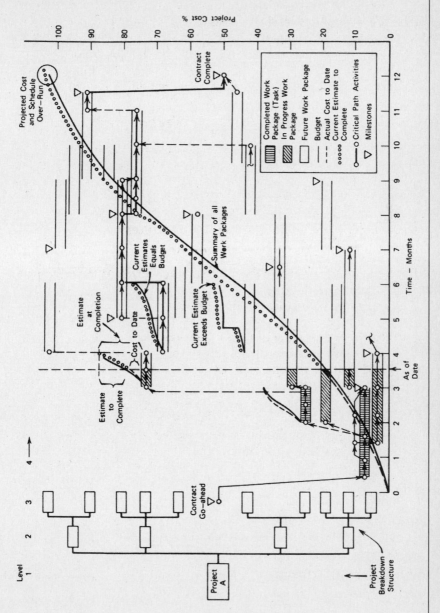

Figure 12.5 Correlation of schedules and costs with the project breakdown structure.

315

This process identifies deviations from plan that indicate the need for controlling action to recover to schedule and/or budget.

Measuring Progress against Schedule

Each functional project or task leader or manager must measure progress against the task schedule on a regular basis. This is usually done at the end of every week, since the weekend is then available for evaluation, special recovery effort, and replanning as needed for the following week.

Whether the task schedule is in the form of a bar chart or network plan, progress measurement is basically the same:

- *Progress to date is recorded:*
  —Completed activities noted.
  —Work accomplished on in-progress activities is noted.
- *Remaining work is estimated:*
  —Time to complete in-progress activities is recorded.
  —Future activities are reestimated or replanned as required.
- *Impact on task completion* and other key interface and milestone events is determined.

For in-process work, the emphasis should not be on "percent complete," but rather on *time remaining to complete* each activity and task.

The next step in progress measurement is to look at all tasks within the next higher level element of the project breakdown structure, with emphasis on intertask interfaces. Does a delay in one task affect other tasks? If so, what is the effect? This is where the use of PERT/CPM/PDM network plans provides powerful analysis of each level of summary, and of the total project master schedule.

The objective is to identify the currently critical activities and tasks that must be completed on schedule to meet key commitment dates. In a typical project network plan, about 15 percent of all activities form the critical path. When these are identified, management attention can be concentrated on them to assure on-schedule completion of the project.

Interface Event Control

Interface management is discussed in Chapter 13. On very large, complex projects, formal interface event planning and control procedures are required. On smaller projects, less formal methods can be used. In either case, the project manager should:

- *Establish interface event lists:*

  —Interface event coordination list.

  —Approved interface event list.

  —Interface event revision list.

- *Provide each task manager with lists* of the incoming and outgoing interface events for his task(s).

- Provide each task manager with the *current predicted dates* for all *incoming interface events,* based on overall integrated evaluation of the project master schedule, on a weekly or monthly basis, as appropriate.

When incoming interface events are delayed, the task manager usually must replan the work to attempt to avoid delay of subsequent outgoing interfaces, including task completion. This often incurs added cost, and the project manager analyzes the trade-off between schedule and cost with the concerned functional managers. If necessary, a portion of the project management reserve may be allocated to cover the increased cost to recover the delay.

The earlier a delay of an interface event is made known to the affected managers, the greater the chances are of replanning to overcome the delay without added cost.

12.5   COST CONTROL

Project cost control, like schedule control, is exercised primarily at the task (work package) level by the functional manager or project leader responsible for each task. The project manager's basic responsibility is to monitor costs at the task and higher levels of summary, to identify significant variances between actual expenditures and budgets, and to initiate corrective action so that the total final project cost is equal to or less than the total budget. Cost control for project management purposes consists of:

- *Setting budgets* for specific tasks (Section 10.14).
- *Measuring expenditures* against budget and identifying variances.
- Assuring that *expenditures are proper.*
- Taking *appropriate controlling actions* where budget variances exist.

Measuring Expenditures against Budget

Reports are required weekly, or at a minimum, monthly, to show direct labor, material, and other costs on each in-progress task. These data can be entered directly onto the task schedule and budget document (Figure 10.7), for use by the task leader or manager. Variances will then be apparent, coupled with information on actual progress against schedule.

Monthly actual versus budget reports are required at the total project level, intermediate project breakdown structure levels, and the task level, showing direct costs, burden costs, and total project costs.

Recording and Controlling Commitments

Outstanding commitments that are not yet booked must be included in the actual versus budget costs reports for project control purposes. Procedures must be established to identify and report such commitments as early as possible, even though their final values may change when booked. This would include reconciling the commitments to the actual costs when the bills are paid. Failure to record and control commitments is a frequent cause of cost overruns, especially where large purchases or contracts are required.

Late Charges

Late charges may result from disputes on invoices, correction of administrative errors, late submittal of invoices, and similar actions. Good commitment reporting and control will eliminate many late charges, but some are unavoidable. Any substantial apparent budget underruns should be analyzed carefully before reallocating the funds, to prevent surprise by late, forgotten charges.

Assuring That Expenditures Are Proper

Each task manager must continually assure that expenditures of labor or money charged to a task account number are proper and are for effort actually contributing to that task. There is a continual temptation for functional managers to charge costs for work done on a project where an overrun exists to another task (usually just beginning) that still has an unexpended budget balance. This hides real problems and distorts the cost records for analysis and future bidding purposes.

Persons performing the work may not realize the importance of properly recording their time against the charge (account) number for each task, and as a result simply fill in their time sheets or cards in a careless fashion. The project manager must continually watch for such erroneous charges to his project, whether or not they are intentional. Internal auditors should be asked to verify periodically that established policies and procedures are in fact being followed.

Cost to Complete and at Completion

Cost to complete should be reestimated monthly on in-progress tasks, and quarterly on all incomplete tasks. This is commonly termed the *estimate to complete* (ETC).

Cost at completion must be forecast at least monthly at the task, intermediate, and total project levels. Cost at completion is the sum of:

- Cost of all completed tasks.
- Cost to date plus estimate to complete on all in-progress tasks.
- Current estimate to complete each future task.

This is commonly termed the *estimate at completion* (EAC).

Controlling the Management Reserve

As discussed in Section 10.13, all reallocations of authorized funds for individual tasks must be recorded in the management reserve transaction register. The project manager should approve such transactions together with other approvals as required by established policies.

Causes of Cost Problems

Some of the primary causes of cost problems on projects are:

- Unrealistic, low original estimates, bids, and budgets.
- Management decision to reduce bid price and budgets to meet competitive pressure or offset assumed inflated estimates.
- Uncontrolled, unnoticed increase in scope of work.
- Extrascope work on proposals for change or extensions, or in response to customer or management inquiries.
- Unforeseen technical difficulties.
- Schedule delays that require overtime or other added cost to recover, or charging of idle labor time to the project.
- Inadequate cost budgeting, reporting, and control practices and procedures.

Analysis of cost control experience for specific projects should be made by each company to identify the sources of cost problems and initiate the needed corrective actions.

Project Cost Accounting Problems

If the company cost accounting and reporting system and practices are inadequate, good project cost control will be difficult. Typical problems in this area are:

- Information is not timely.
- Project chart of accounts is not set up to meet project management needs.
- Commitments are not properly recorded and reported.
- Manufacturing costs are difficult to identify until item is shipped, or to allocate and compare to budget.
- Project summaries (using the PBS) are not produced.
- Cost to complete and cost at completion are not handled in the accounting system or reporting procedures.

12.6 INTEGRATED SCHEDULE AND COST CONTROL: THE EARNED VALUE CONCEPT

Experience over the years on many projects in many industries, as reported in the extensive project management literature available today, has shown that trying to control physical progress and schedules separately from costs usually results in ineffective project control. However, achieving integrated schedule and cost control is a complex and demanding task. The planning principles and methods described in Chapter 10 are designed to enable such integrated control. The systematic definition of the project down to the work package or task level provides the key. For each task/work package, the start, completion, and any intermediate interface events are linked directly to the task estimates and budgets, as shown in Chapter 10.

Earned Value

As the term implies, the earned value of a task is the approved budget allocated to perform the task. When the task is complete, the value of the budget has been earned. The concept is simple and powerful, but there are many difficulties in using it effectively, especially on large projects. It is most effective when there are a large number of tasks and they are relatively short in duration compared to the status reporting period, since that would provide a number of task completions for variance analysis. However, breaking down a project into a large number of tasks may create such an administrative workload that it is too cumbersome and costly to maintain the information up to date. If the number of tasks is too few, they will all be of long duration, which erodes the effectiveness of the earned value measurement. With a task of long duration, if the value is not earned until its completion, substantial effort and money will be expended before any measure of progress can be made. If one resorts to estimates of how far along the task is prior to completion, the measurement loses its objectivity. This dilemma has led to various rules that may be dictated or allowed for a given project.

Fleming and Koppelman (2000, pp. 89–95) identify eight rules for planning and measuring earned value:

1. *Weighted milestones:* Within long duration work packages, objective milestones are identified that reflect definite divisions of work, preferably one or more in each measurement period. Each milestone is assigned a specific budgeted value that will be earned when the milestone is reported physically complete. The total of all weighted milestones equals the total work package budget.

2. *Fixed formula by task:* 25/75, 50/50, 75/25, and so on: The first figure is earned when the task is started, and the second is earned when it is completed. Any set of values can be assigned. ". . . it requires very detailed and short-span work packages to make it work successfully" (p. 90).

3. *Percent-complete estimates:* This is the easiest for the people involved and probably most widely used method, and is also the least reliable. "Typically such estimates are made purely on a "subjective" basis, that is, one's personal and professional yet unsubstantiated estimate. Thus, if people want to play games with earned value by claiming more value than they actually have, the subjective percent-complete estimate is where it will happen" (p. 90).

4. *A combination of percent-complete estimates with milestones used as gates:* With this method, objective milestones are used to at least partially overcome the subjectivity of the percent-complete estimates. This combination allows the use of fewer milestones, thereby reducing the progress reporting workload.

5. *Equivalent completed units:* This method is practical when a task is producing units of work that can easily be measured. The preestablished value of each work unit is then earned as it is reported complete. This is widely used in the construction industry.

6. *Earned standards:* This is similar to the above rule and is applied to repetitive, production-type work. Preestablished standards of earned value are set for the performance of the subject tasks. The unit standard may be for one labor hour, for example, or for completion of each of a series of operations.

7. *Apportioned relationships to other tasks/work packages:* In using this rule, a task receives earned value credit in proportion to the reported earned value of another task (called the *measurement base task*) that is being measured using one of the previous six rules. An example of this is *factory inspection* receiving an earned value credit in some proportion to the earned value of the *factory fabrication* (the measurement base) task.

8. *Level of effort (LOE):* Level of effort work packages or tasks are frequently made a part of project plans so that a budget item exists for such things as the salary for project manager and her direct staff. "We recommend that zero LOE be used on projects. If a given work package cannot be planned as discrete work, or simultaneously cannot be apportioned to other discrete tasks, then perhaps it should be considered as a candidate for indirect work, or perhaps eliminated altogether. LOE is not performance measurement. LOE is only the measurement of time" (pp. 95–96).

The organization's project management process, as tailored to each project category and classification, must describe which of these rules are to be used in measuring earned value for various type of tasks or work packages during the life of each project.

Measurement of Schedule and Cost Variances

The key terms used in the earned value approach were introduced in the 1960s by the U.S. Department of Defense (DOD) with its Cost/Schedule Control System Criteria (C/SCSC). The original 35 criteria were replaced in 1996 by the DOD's 32 earned value management system criteria. The terms as they have evolved today are defined as follows (Fleming and Koppelman, 2000, pp. 193–207):

- *Planned value (PV):* "The sum of the budgets for all work scheduled to be accomplished within a given time period." This was previously called the *budgeted cost of work scheduled* (BCWS), a term that continues to be used.

- *Earned value (EV):* "The sum of the budgets for completed work and the completed portions of open work" This was previously called the *budgeted cost of work performed* (BCWP), also still in widespread use.

- *Actual cost of work performed (ACWP):* "The costs actually incurred in accomplishing work performed."

- *Cost Performance Index (CPI):* "The cost-efficiency factor representing the relationship between the actual cost expended and the value of the physical work performed."

- *Cost variance (CV):* "The numeric difference between the earned value (BCWP) less the actual costs (ACWP)."

- *Schedule Performance Index (SPI):* "The planned schedule efficiency factor representing the relationship between the value of the initial planned schedule and the value of the physical work performed, earned value."

- *Schedule variance (SV):* "The numeric difference between earned value (BCWP) less the planned value (BCWS)."

Variance and Trend Analysis

Both the schedule and cost variance can be either favorable or unfavorable. Careful analysis is required to assure that the information being reported is reasonable and consistent. It is generally useful to set up simple charts to monitor the trends over several reporting periods, rather than jump to conclusions base on one-time reports. Examples of typical charts used in monitoring and progress evaluation are given in Chapter 14. A graphic portrayal of schedule and cost variances is shown in Figure 14.2.

Compliance with the DOD earned value criteria on large military and aerospace programs is complex. Fleming and Koppelman (2000) provide a comprehensive description of these criteria and practical guidelines for complying with them and reaping the substantial benefits from the effective application of the earned value concept. The College of Performance Measurement of the Project Management Institute (see www.pmi.org.cpm) is also an excellent source of current information in this regard.

Earned Value Software Applications

Many of the project management software applications discussed in Chapter 5 automate the preparation of the earned value calculations and the preparation of the related cost, schedule, and performance reports. Figure 12.6 is an example of one useful chart produced by one of these applications, showing the bimonthly rates and variances together with cumulative totals.

Earned Value versus the Critical Chain Approaches to Project Planning and Control

Peterson and Filiatrault (2000) have compared the earned value methods (briefly described earlier) that have many years of successful application

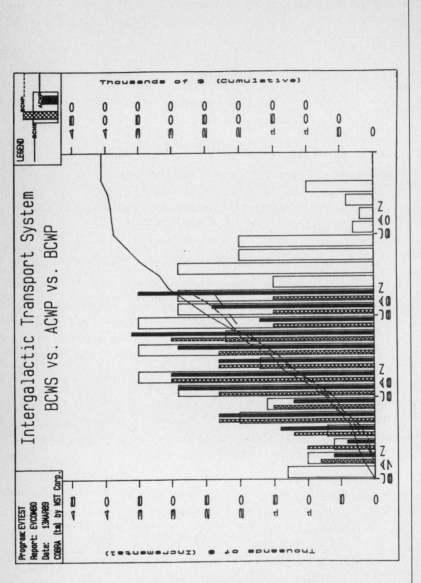

Figure 12.6 BCWS versus ACWP, bimonthly, and cumulative. (Plotted by the Cobra™ software package from Welcom Software Technology). Used by permission.

on large and small projects, with the relatively new critical chain approach to project planning and control. There is far less documented experience in the project management literature with the application of the critical chain approach. These authors propose that both can be used on an integrated basis:

> So, how would these two techniques be integrated? The key is for the PM to use them for the purposes in which they were best suited. EVMS (earned value management systems) should be used for contract performance issues, such as:

> - Supporting progress payments by documenting cost incurred versus value of work completed to date.
> - Reporting progress against key project/program milestones.
> - Validating the estimating methodology on which the project was based, so that future estimates are more accurate and any estimating risks yet to be encountered within the project are identified early.
> - Variance analysis for project performance issues.
> - Providing information to those charged with financial oversight.

> CCPM (critical chain project management) should be used to get the most from the project's process relative to work to be performed:

> - Managing the constraint(s) for maximum throughput, benefiting the project and the organization.
> - Protecting the constraint from lost time by ensuring work arrives ahead of its needs.
> - Ensuring critical resources arrive when expected.
> - Frequent monitoring, forecasting, and protecting of the project's completion date.
> - Providing information to those charged with overall project performance.

It will be interesting to see in a few years' time whether the predictions of the proponents of the critical chain approach regarding its benefits are verified by experience with its widespread use. Perhaps an integrated system blending both of these approaches will evolve.

12.7 TECHNICAL PERFORMANCE MEASUREMENT

Technical performance measurement (TPM) is the continuing prediction or demonstration of the degree of anticipated or actual achievement of technical objectives. It includes an analysis of any differences among the *achievement to date, current estimate,* and the *specification require-ment.* It is generally the most difficult of the three basic areas of project planning and control: schedule, cost, and technical.

Achievement to date is the value of a specified technical parameter esti-mated or measured in a particular test and/or analysis.

Current estimate is the value of a specified technical parameter to be achieved at the end of a project or contract if the current plan is followed.

Purpose of Technical Performance Measurement

The purpose of TPM is to:

- Provide visibility of actual versus planned technical performance for correlation to schedules and costs.
- Provide early detection or prediction of technical problems that re-quire management attention.
- Support assessment of the impact on the project of proposed change alternatives.

Relationship to Cost/Schedule Performance Measurement

Schedules, costs, and technical results are always interrelated. Cost/schedule performance measurement may reveal problems in the techni-cal area, and technical problems revealed by TPM can surface in-adequacies of time or money. However, the cost/schedule measurement methods previously described basically assume that the technical effort and results are adequate for project success. A disciplined approach to TPM is therefore necessary to avoid the problem of completing a project on time and within budget but with a product that is not acceptable.

TPM assessment points should be planned to coincide with the planned completion of significant design and development tasks, or aggregation of tasks. This will facilitate the verification of the results achieved in the completed task in terms of its technical requirements.

Technical Parameters

The parameters to be tracked and reported must be:

- Key indicators of project success.
- Interrelated by construction of tiered dependency trees similar to the specification tree.
- Correlated to an element of the project breakdown structure.

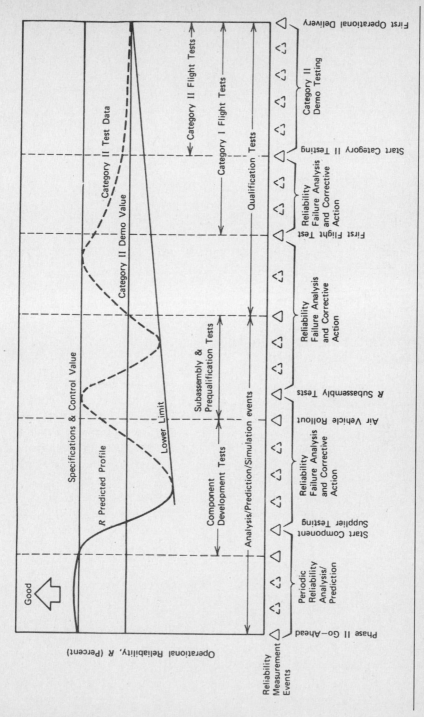

Figure 12.7   Reliability planned profile.

327

PROGRAM
CONTRACT NO.
ITEM
SPEC NO.
WBS NO.

Data Item
S−C584−001B

TABLE I
TECHNICAL PERFORMANCE MEASUREMENT REPORT

SUPPLIER NAME
RESP. ENGINEER
PROJECT MANAGER
DATE ISSUED
REVISED

*PARAMETER REQUIREMENTS

*PARAMETER	SPEC PARAGRAPH REFERENCE	PARAM UNITS	SPEC VALUE	CONT-ROL VALUE	EVENT NO. *DATE	EVENT NO. DATE	EVENT NO. DATE	EVENT NO. DATE	EVENT NO. DATE	EVENT NO. DATE	EVENT NO. DATE	EVENT NO. DATE	EVENT NO. DATE
Dection	3.1.1.3.2.4													
Antenna Pattern	3.1.1.3.5.2.1													
Missile Illumination	3.1.1.3.2.4.9													
Range Accuracy	3.1.1.3.2.9.1													
Angle Accuracy	3.1.1.3.2													
Range Rate Accuracy	3.1.1.3.2.													
Angle Track Rate	3.1.1.3.2.4.4													
Mov-up-Date	3.1.1.3.2.4.1.1													
Power Input	3.1.1.1.1.3													
Reaction Time	3.1.1.4													
Reliability	3.1.2.1.1													
Maintainability	3.1.2.2													
Weight	3.2.2													
Volume	3.2.2													

Figure 12.8 Technical performance measurement report.

For each technical parameter to be tracked, the following data, as appropriate, should be established during the planning of the related task:

- Specification requirement.
- Time-phased planned value profile with a tolerance band (illustrated in Figure 12.7). The profile must represent the expected growth of the parameter, and the boundaries of the tolerance band must represent the inaccuracies at the time of the estimation, and also indicate the region of budget and schedule within which the required specification is expected to be achieved.
- Project interface or milestone events significantly related to the achievement analysis or demonstration.
- Conditions of measurement (type of test, simulation, analysis, etc.).

Conducting Technical Performance Measurement

As the design and development activity progresses, achievement to date is tracked continually on the planned value profile for each technical performance parameter. In case the *achievement to date* value falls outside the tolerance band a new profile or current estimate is developed immediately.

The current estimate is determined from the achievement to date and the remaining schedule and budget. Any variation outside the tolerance band is analyzed to determine the causes and assess the impact on higher level parameters, interface requirements, and system or product cost effectiveness.

For technical performance deficiencies, alternate recovery plans are developed with cost, schedule, and technical performance implications fully explored. For performance in excess of requirements, opportunities for reallocation of requirements and resources are assessed.

Technical Performance Measurement Report

For a given subsystem or element in the project, a summary technical performance measurement report is prepared, as illustrated by Figure 12.8. Each parameter is listed, with the specification reference and the parameter units, specified value and control value. As key events are reached the current estimate is recorded for each parameter.

13

‹ ›

Project Interface
Management

13.1 WHY PROJECT INTERFACE MANAGEMENT

Planning and executing projects is challenging work for all persons involved: the project manager; the project planning and control staff (if any); the contributing functional managers, project leaders, and specialists (including outside contractors, consultants, vendors, and others); and the senior managers to whom these people report.

In spite of decades of experience in positioning the project manager within our organizations, and the availability of and experience in using powerful planning and control systems and procedures in project management, there are many areas that could be improved. Often there is too much conflict, too little acceptance of the role of the project manager, too little real use of the advanced planning and control systems that are available today, and projects that are not planned and controlled as effectively as they can and should be.

One approach to attacking these areas of need in project management can be found in the practice of *project interface management*. Experience in the application of this approach shows that it can lead to significant improvements in the following respects:

- Better definition of roles and responsibilities:
  —Improved understanding of the role of the project manager and better acceptance of the need for that role.
  —Clarification of the roles and responsibilities of the functional contributors to the project.

—Reduction in conflicts between the project manager and the functional contributors, as well as among the individual functional managers, project leaders, and specialists.

- Project planning and control improvements:

—Provision of good, logical linkage points between the levels in the schedule hierarchy, and between subprojects and subnetwork plans.

—Better identification of the proper degree of detail at each schedule level.

—Wider acceptance and use of project planning and control systems.

- Teamwork and team building improvement:

—Improved teamwork through clear identification of the points of interaction between functional tasks.

—More effective team building through joint identification of the key project interface points.

13.2   THE CONCEPT: THE PROJECT MANAGER AS THE PROJECT INTERFACE MANAGER

The basic concept of interface management is that the project manager plans, schedules, and controls—in a word, manages—the key interface events on the project, while the responsible functional project leaders manage the tasks or work between these interface events. This is no more than recognition, systemization, and formalization of how the project manager and functional contributors should divide their responsibilities, and how they should work together on any given project. The project manager must plan, schedule, and control the project interfaces in close cooperation with the contributing functional project leaders.

Various Meanings of Interface

The word *interface* can mean different things to different people. Often you see *interface agreements* as part of the project procedures, especially on large engineering/construction projects. These agreements establish the ground rules governing the relationships between the owner, the project manager, the architect engineer firm, and major contractors. In other words, they deal with the ongoing organizational relationships (or interfaces) between the major parties involved in a project.

Another meaning relates to the interaction between phases of a project, and there are many references in the literature to the engineering/construction interface, for example. This is closer to the meaning of "project interface management" used in this book, but not exactly the same thing.

Project Interface Management

While the management of these kinds of *interfaces* could be considered a form of *interface management,* this term refers more specifically to managing the specific project interfaces, as defined next. As used here, it is therefore somewhat different from managing on-going interfaces between organizations in a general sense, or generally managing the interface between engineering and construction, or other *interphase* management activities.

13.3   PROJECT INTERFACE MANAGEMENT IN ACTION

For a specific project, implementation of project interface management involves these activities during project start-up, execution, and closeout:

- Project or new phase start-up planning.
    - —During the initiation of the project, or of one of its major phases, the key project interface events are identified and described, planned, scheduled; outgoing and incoming responsibilities are assigned to specific individuals.
- Project or phase execution.
    - —During project execution, the project interface events are monitored and controlled as part of the on-going procedures used to manage the project.
- Project closeout.
    - —During the close-out phase, the project interface events that occur at the end of the project form important elements of the closeout checklists, and assist the project and functional managers in assuring that all the loose ends of the project are tied up so that the project can be completed cleanly.
- Identifying project interfaces through input-output analysis.
    - —The key project team members, once they have studied and understood the project objectives and scope, can usually identify most if not all of the key interfaces by performing an input-output analysis of the tasks they will be responsible for on the project.

This analysis simply requires each task leader to think through two questions:

1. What inputs do we need (information, resources, approvals, other) to initiate and then complete this task, and who will provide these? This will identify the *incoming* interfaces for that task.

2. What intermediate and final outputs will we generate in the performance of this task, and who should receive these? This will identify the *outgoing* interfaces related to the task.

An effective practice is to ask the functional managers, project leaders, or task leaders to prepare a memorandum for each major task they are responsible for on the project, listing the identified incoming and outgoing interfaces, with the expected sources and recipients for each. These memos should then be distributed to all affected project team members. It is sometimes surprising, at least to some team members, to see what others are expecting of them. In other cases, a task leader may not be aware that a particular team member needs to receive the output from a given outgoing interface. By sharing these memos with the other team members, each person has the opportunity to verify who is expecting what input from whom, and who is planning to give what output to whom. Better teamwork, improved communications, and fewer omissions and mistakes are the result.

A useful form for task input-output analysis enabling a more rigorous approach to identifying key interface points is given in Figure 13.1.

This approach also helps to position the project manager as the project interface manager. In this role, she is seen by all members of the project team as fulfilling a vital function that will aid the entire team in achieving success.

13.4 PRODUCT AND PROJECT INTERFACES

It is useful to differentiate between product and product interfaces. *Product* interfaces deal specifically with the things being created by the project activities: the intermediate and final results or products of the project. *Project* interface deals with the process of creating these products.

Product interfaces fall into two categories: (1) *Performance interfaces,* which exist between product subsystems or components; and (2) *Physical interfaces,* which exist between interconnecting parts of the product.

Note that the products or results of the project can be hardware, software, services, new consumable products, physical facilities, documents, and information. Performance and physical interfaces exist in all of these types of products.

For engineering products, procedures for managing the product design, quality assurance, and product configuration will provide the required

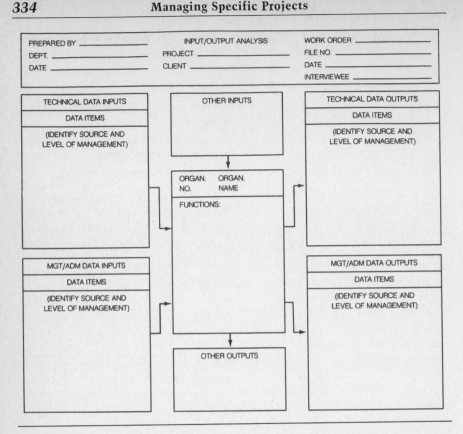

PREPARED BY _____
DEPT. _____
DATE _____

INPUT/OUTPUT ANALYSIS
PROJECT _____
CLIENT _____

WORK ORDER _____
FILE NO. _____
DATE _____
INTERVIEWEE _____

TECHNICAL DATA INPUTS

DATA ITEMS

(IDENTIFY SOURCE AND
LEVEL OF MANAGEMENT)

OTHER INPUTS

ORGAN.   ORGAN.
NO.   NAME
FUNCTIONS:

TECHNICAL DATA OUTPUTS

DATA ITEMS

(IDENTIFY SOURCE AND
LEVEL OF MANAGEMENT)

MGT/ADM DATA INPUTS

DATA ITEMS

(IDENTIFY SOURCE AND
LEVEL OF MANAGEMENT)

MGT/ADM DATA OUTPUTS

DATA ITEMS

(IDENTIFY SOURCE AND
LEVEL OF MANAGEMENT)

OTHER OUTPUTS

Figure 13.1 Input/output chart. *Source:* John Tuman Jr., "Development and Implementation of Project Management Systems," Chapter 27, *Project Management Handbook* (2nd ed.), David I. Cleland and William R. King (Eds.) (New York: Van Nostrand Reinhold, 1988), p. 666. Used by permission.

management of the product interfaces, both performance and physical. For other types of products, equivalent procedures must be provided.

Types of Project Interfaces

Six categories of project interfaces can be identified, although the lines of distinction between some of these can be rather hazy:

1. *Change of responsibility:* One task is completed and the task product is handed over to another team member or organization for further work. A large percentage of project interfaces are of this type.

   Example: Engineering completes a specification, then Purchasing initiates procurement of the items specified. Transmittal of the specification from Engineering to Purchasing is an interface event (outgoing for Engineering, incoming for Purchasing). This example is also an information interface.

2. *Result of action:* Results from one task are required before another task can begin.

   Example: Foundations must be completed by the concrete contractor before the process equipment can be set in place by the equipment erection contractor. This could also be considered a change of responsibility interface.

3. *Management:* Key decisions, approvals, and other management actions affecting other project interfaces, specific tasks, or the overall project.

   Example: Senior manager approval of the contract award for development of a software system needed for the project.

4. *Customer:* Actions similar to management interfaces, but involving the customer or client.

   Example: Customer approval of the conceptual system design in a software development project.

5. *Information:* Information or data developed in one task and needed by one or more other tasks.

   Example: Information on the soil conditions obtained during site investigations by the geologic survey engineering consultant is needed by the civil engineers designing the foundations.

6. *Material:* Equipment, supplies, facilities, or other physical items must be available at a specific location for work to proceed.

   Example: A mobile crane needed to hoist a major piece of equipment into place must be removed from another area of the project.

13.5 PROJECT INTERFACE EVENTS

All of these six types of project interfaces can be represented as *project interface events.* Events are points in time associated with specific dates (predicted, scheduled, or actual) that indicate when an action has taken place. Many project interface events represent doing something to a product interface, as for example, "Product XX Specification Released," or "System YY Design Approved." The specification released by engineering contains performance and physical information on a specific part of the product being created, enabling the purchasing department to procure the item in question so that it will perform and fit within the total project result and schedule.

Interface events are important elements of any comprehensive project plan. The most important ones must be included in the project master plan and schedule, and all key interface events must be included in the integrated project network plan. Interface events provide the means for integrating subnets at the second, third, or lower level planning tiers into the overall project plan and schedule. Many management milestone events are also interface events.

13.6   THE FIVE STEPS OF PROJECT INTERFACE MANAGEMENT

Project interface management consists of five steps:

1. Identification.
2. Documentation.
3. Scheduling.
4. Communication.
5. Monitoring and controlling the key interface events.

Identification

The first step in interface management is to identify the key project interface events. Clear, unambiguous event identification is required. An event occurs at a point in time and is different from an activity or task, which consumes time. An event signifies the start or completion of one or more activities or tasks. Events must be identified and defined so that they are recognizable when they occur. Their identifying description should relate each event to an element of the project/work breakdown structure. Each interface event is "outgoing" for the originator (usually only one) and "incoming" for each receiver (of which there may be several).

The checklist presented in Chapter 10 (Table 10.3) should be helpful to clearly and unambiguously identify such events.

Documentation

On smaller projects, inclusion of well-identified interface events in the project plans and schedules is usually all that is required. However, on large, complex projects formal procedures are required to document and control interface events. These usually provide for three interface event lists:

1. *The Interface Event Coordination List,* covering new events not yet on the other lists.

2. *The Approved Interface Event List,* which includes all such events which have been coordinated with the affected organizations (originators and receivers) and approved by the project manager.

3. *The Interface Event Revision List,* which includes revisions made to the Approved Interface Event List during the past month (or reporting period).

When such formal procedures are required, due to the size or complexity of the project, number of organizations involved, or geographic dispersal of project contributors, the following basic information is provided:

- Codes: An event code number consistent with the network planning procedures in use on the project, plus an identifier indicating that this is an interface event.
- Description of the event.
- Organizations affected:
  —Originator.
  —Receiver(s).
- Project elements and tasks within the breakdown structure related to the event, and the subnetworks in which it appears.

Scheduling

The third step in interface management is to develop a scheduled date for each interface event, reflecting the current integrated project master schedule.

The top-level master project network must include the most important interface events, together with other milestone events of interest to top management. Initial estimates of the time required between the major interface events are made by the persons responsible for each outgoing interface event, and the master project network plan is then analyzed and revised until the key target dates appear to be achievable. At this stage, the second level, more detailed subnets are developed, incorporating the pertinent interface events, and adding detail for the functional tasks involved in each subnet. After each responsible functional manager approves his or her subnets, the results are incorporated into the integrated project network. The subnets can either be integrated into the project network, or the durations between interface events can be entered into the project network on a summary basis. On large projects, integration of all lower level subnets, with all their details, into one integrated project network may prove to be impractical, due to the large volume of information that would have to be updated.

It is not mandatory for lower level schedules to be in the form of network plans, depending on the complexity of the specific tasks involved. In many cases, functional tasks between interface events can be planned and controlled effectively using bar charts, process sheets, or checklists. However, the project manager must assure that the tasks are adequately planned and scheduled, so that there is a reasonable assurance that the future interface event dates that have been promised will, in fact, be met. Weekly or monthly revisions of the estimated time to complete each task (not a percent complete estimate) are required.

On smaller projects, all that may be required is an overall project master schedule that incorporates the key interface events.

Communication

Communication between members of the project team, with the customer and with upper management can be enhanced through the proper use of interface events. By using the interface event lists, with clear identification of each event, omissions, errors, and confusion can be avoided. Properly coded events lend themselves to accurate reference by electronic mail, telex, telefax, or telephone, for discussion, changes in planning, conflict resolution, and progress reporting.

Affected interfaces should be included in task work orders, contracts, subcontracts and purchase orders, with appropriate language to assure that they are properly planned, scheduled, monitored, and controlled.

Monitoring and Controlling the Key Interface Events

Interface events should be emphasized in normal project monitoring and control procedures. Progress reporting should require a statement of the estimated time remaining to reach each future interface, if their previously predicted completion dates have changed.

If all interface events are well controlled, the project will also be well-controlled. Interface event control is achieved through the procedures used to add events to the approved list, to revise them, and through the schedule review and control procedures. Control of the project is achieved jointly by the project and functional managers by:

- Controlling the interface events.
- Work authorization and control procedures and practices.
- Project directives.
- Project evaluation and review procedures.

13.7   CONCLUSION

Good project interface management practices will:

- Clarify roles and responsibilities, and reduce conflicts.
- Define who will provide what to each project team member, enhancing teamwork and communications.
- Improve project planning, scheduling, and control.
- Increase the effectiveness of the project team, thereby improving the changes of project success: Delivery of the specified results on time and within budget.

14

❬ ❭

Evaluating, Directing, and Closing Out the Project

Once a project is set in motion, the project manager must continuously monitor all facets of project activity in conjunction with the contributing functional project leaders. The project manager must evaluate the project in its totality and initiate, with and through the functional project leaders, appropriate directive actions to recover from or prevent undesirable results. This chapter deals with this ongoing process.

14.1   INTEGRATED PROJECT EVALUATION: NEED AND OBJECTIVES

Each area of cost, schedule, and technical performance can be monitored and evaluated separately by one means or another. However, complex interrelationships exist between these three areas. The need is to evaluate the total project in all three areas simultaneously, on an integrated basis. Technical problems cause delays; delays increase cost; budget overruns may adversely affect quality, and so on. Corrective actions in one area of the project may cause unforeseen problems in another area.

The *objectives* of integrated project evaluation are the following:

- To *provide visibility*, as clearly as possible, of the interrelationships between cost, schedule, and technical performance across the entire project.
- To *identify problems before they occur* to the extent possible, so that they can be avoided or their effects minimized.

340

- To *identify opportunities* quickly for schedule acceleration, cost reduction, or technical advance, and to exploit them before the opportunity is lost.

14.2 METHODS AND PRACTICES OF PROJECT EVALUATION

Project evaluation is a continuing process throughout the life cycle of the project. It should not be an occasional panic exercise triggered by sudden awareness of a major problem.

Project Evaluation Process

Project evaluation is a three-step process, repeated at periodic intervals:

1. *Determine status* on a total project basis, of:

   Actual work accomplished.

   Current and anticipated technical results.

   Resources expended (time, labor, money).

2. *Compare status to plan*, for:

   Schedules.

   Budgeted and currently estimated costs.

   Technical specifications to be met, both at the time of comparison and at completion of the project.

3. *Identify variances* between current or future cost, schedule or technical performance, and related plans.

At this point, the evaluation process gives way to project direction, which involves determining and authorizing appropriate actions to eliminate the variances between performance and plan. Further evaluation may be necessary, however, of proposed or alternative actions prior to their implementation.

Basic Methods and Practices

In the following sections, six basic methods and practices for project evaluation are discussed:

1. First-hand observation.
2. Interpretation of verbal and written reports.
3. Graphic displays.

4. Project evaluation review meetings.

5. Project performance reviews.

6. Project control center.

First-Hand Observation

It is vital that the project manager have personal contact with as many contributing functional team leaders and specialists as is possible. Direct observation and contact with the functional team leaders and other project contributors is invaluable to determine physical progress, whether this is related to a design drawing or field installation, and to identify potential problems in those particular fields where the project manager has experience.

There are definite limitations on the effectiveness of first-hand observation, however, especially on large major projects. Geographic dispersal and sheer size and complexity often limit the amount of first-hand observation a project manager can make on a periodic basis. Even under ideal conditions, additional information and evaluation are required.

Interpretation of Verbal and Written Reports

Verbal reports have the great advantage of being current, but they also have a great disadvantage in that they are easily misunderstood, distorted, and forgotten by both parties. Accountability is almost totally absent.

Written reports and documents are valuable, and some are indispensable, for project evaluation. However, these are frequently less effective than they could be because:

- Many reports are poorly designed, too detailed, and difficult to understand.

- With numerical tabular reports, it is difficult to identify significant points of change and trends.

- Written technical progress reports may described in great detail what was done during a given period, but seldom do they present significant information on current or future problem areas and progress toward meeting the ultimate product specifications.

Some steps that can improve the effectiveness of report interpretation include:

- Proper summarization for the purpose at hand (using the project breakdown structure, e.g., to summarize expenditure information, not simply a standard chart of accounts).

- Comparisons and ratios.
- Comparison with previous reports to show trends.
- Selective reporting of only the information of interest to the recipient.
- Conversion to graphic displays.

Graphic Displays

Graphic display of the key elements of information concerning a project improves the manager's ability to evaluate the project on an integrated basis. Properly designed graphic displays are effective because:

- Large amounts of complex information can be presented in pictorial, easily understood form.
- Changes in rates of progress or expenditure are easily identified.
- Different kinds of information (schedule, cost, and technical) can be presented simultaneously for integrated analysis.
- Original plans, past performance, and future predictions are easily shown and compared.
- Open display, if possible, maintains an awareness of the project and its progress on the part of all people concerned.

Graphic display has the following disadvantages:

- Extra effort is required to design, prepare, and maintain various charts and graphs.
- Display of information at too gross a level may mislead management by hiding problems.

Back-up, detailed reports are necessary to prepare and maintain graphic displays and to carry out in-depth analysis of apparent problems indicated by such displays. See Figures 14.1 and 14.2 for examples of useful graphic charts.

One of the important advances in project management information systems over the past decade has been in the graphic presentation of project planning, scheduling, cost, and resource management information. Today the cost of preparing and using graphic displays illustrated throughout this book is too small to be a serious deterrent to their use. This graphic display capability is probably the single most important factor in gaining higher level manager understanding and use of integrated planning and control systems for project management. It is

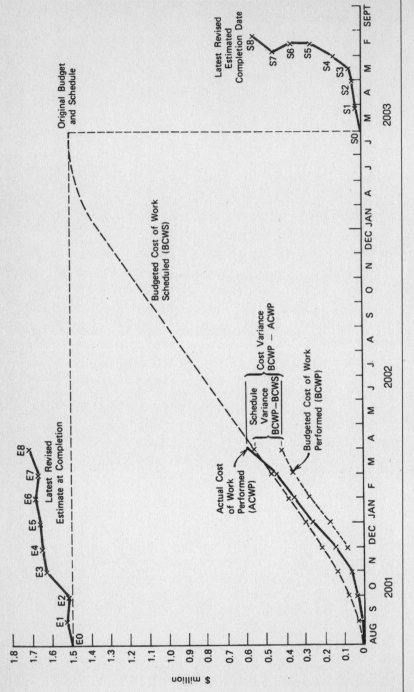

Figure 14.1   Cost and schedule performance chart.

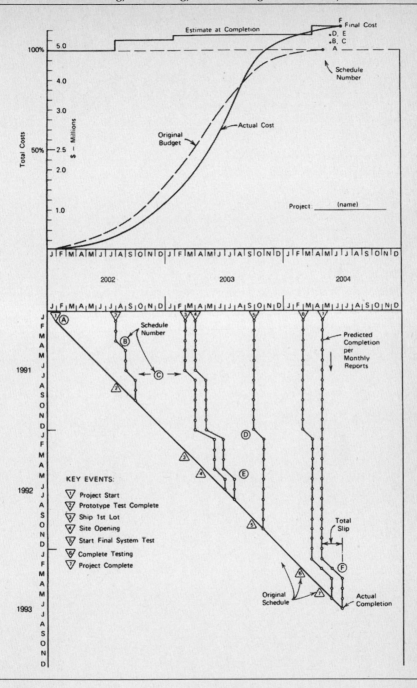

Figure 14.2   Cum-costs milestone slip chart. Shows situation at completion of project.

equally important in gaining acceptance and use of these disciplines by the average project team member.

Project Evaluation Review Meetings

The holding of regular, periodic project evaluation meetings is a recommended practice for all major projects. Here key managers are confronted with the current, integrated analysis of progress against the plan and predictions for the remainder of the project. The primary purposes of project evaluation meetings are:

- To identify problems requiring management action, or opportunities to accelerate schedule or reduce costs.
- To obtain a real agreement among key managers that these problems do exist and require action.
- To identify the manager responsible for action to resolve each problem or exploit each opportunity, and to record action assignments related thereto.
- To follow up on previous action assignments to assure their early completion.

Problems are not usually solved in the review meetings. Separate problem-solving meetings should be held, attended by only those concerned directly with the problem.

Effective project evaluation review meetings require that:

- They be held weekly for most projects, or at other regular intervals on a preestablished schedule, so key participants will plan their schedules accordingly.
- Designated participants personally attend.
- They be brief and follow a prepared agenda.
- Written action assignments, with specific names of people and due dates, be prepared and distributed within 24 hours.

Persons participating should have commitment-making authority and include key members of the project team:

Project manager (usually chair).

Key functional project leaders or managers.

Project engineer.

Project contract administrator.

Project controller.

Project accountant.

Key staff specialists.

This regular, periodic confrontation of all project team members, with personal statements by each on his area of responsibility, can generate a strong team spirit and personal commitment by every team member. If the project manager tries to dominate the meeting, the team members are likely to close off communication and let the manager try to discover what the problems are without their help.

Project Performance Reviews

Another form of project review, similar to a management audit, is conducted by a team of experienced project management professionals who are outside the project team. Such reviews are conducted at critical points in the project life cycle and, if conducted properly, can be beneficial to assuring the ultimate success of the project. Ono and Archibald (1991) describe the experience in AT&T's Business Communications System (BCS)* group with such reviews, whose objectives are:

1. To assist the project team in bringing in the project on time, within budget, and within the defined scope.
2. To determine adherence to AT&T's Project Management Guidelines, with emphasis on project management deliverables and processes.
3. To provide a record for dissemination of the lessons learned.
4. To provide data for validating the effectiveness of AT&T's project management education and training programs.

The results of the evaluation are intended to enhance AT&T BCS Project Management execution and:

- Improve the immediate performance of evaluated projects where required.
- Validate and refine BCS project management standards and guidelines for use with future projects.
- Provide an input for individual performance appraisal.

* Refer to Section 11.3 for a description of the types of projects involved in these reviews.

- Highlight strengths and identify areas for improvement in regard to project activities and the performance of the functional and project organizations.

- Identify innovative techniques that enhance project success and client satisfaction, so they can quickly be transferred to other projects.

- Produce additional understanding of the timing and level of project management resources required to produce the project management deliverables required on each of the AT&T projects.

The AT&T performance review process consists of the following steps:

1. Identify candidate projects and select the next project to be reviewed.
2. Form the Project Review Team and schedule the review.
3. Conduct the project review.
4. Provide immediate on-site assistance as required.
5. Provide verbal feedback and prepare the written evaluation review report.
6. Prepare a success assurance plan, if required.
7. Monitor implementation of the success assurance plan.

The Project Review Team consists of the National Director of Project Management, an area Project Director, and a Project Manager, both from an area outside that of the project under review. The reviews normally require three days of intensive effort, and encompass examination of the project planning documents and interviews with the project manager and other key project participants. Guidelines and lists of interview questions are provided in the BCS Project Management Guidelines.

AT&T concluded that the project evaluation review process is of ongoing value as it (1) identifies projects in trouble with enough time left to correct the problems before a disaster strikes, (2) provides a mapping for the project team to get out of trouble, (3) enhances the adherence to the project management guidelines even for projects not being reviewed, (4) provides the "best training for project managers" (as one of the project managers under review has stated), (5) provides a formalized, regularly scheduled method for continued updating of the project management process and guidelines, and (6) serves to strengthen the reliance on and cross pollination of the informal project management network across the country. Consequently, this review process provides a formal and an informal communications path for lessons learned within the organization.

Project Control Center

The practice of establishing a special room or center for the display and evaluation of project information began in the 1960s, and the effectiveness of this practice is indicated by its continuing adoption by companies in many industries. Control centers are set up for a single large project or program, many projects, or, in some cases, the total company operation.

A project (or management) control center serves the following purposes:

- Provide a single location for concentrated display of relevant information about the project (or projects).
- Serves as a physical representation of the project or projects, reminding all concerned of its existence, status, state of health, and importance.
- Serves as the meeting place for evaluation review meetings and other conferences necessary to the project, providing ready reference to facts pertinent to aspects of the project under discussion.
- Provides through simultaneous displays of graphic, tabular, narrative, and pictorial information a most effective means for the project manager and others to integrate this information mentally, apply judgment and intuition, and identify current or potential problems requiring action.

Suggested facilities to be provided in the project control room include:

- Wall display panels (may be sliding or rack-mounted) to hold charts and graphs.
- Tackboard for temporary display.
- Blackboard or white board (magnetic can be useful for developing network plans or displaying charts).
- Computer terminals and Internet data ports.
- Screen and projector (computer driven, transparency overhead, other).
- Television facilities as appropriate.
- Conference table with seating adequate for the size groups expected.
- Storage facilities.
- Desk and drafting table and facilities for recording proceedings and preparing charts and transparencies (may be in separate room).
- Telephone facilities to support telephone and audiographics teleconferences.

Size of the project and other considerations will dictate how elaborate the facility should be. It is important that such centers be actually used for team meetings, or they will simply become show-places to impress customers or visitors.

14.3 DESIGN REVIEWS AND PRODUCT PLANNING REVIEWS

Design Reviews

At key milestone events, design reviews are conducted to assure that the technical objectives have been or will be met. To be most effective, these reviews are performed by persons outside the project, and even outside the division or company. This assures that an independent audit of the adequacy of the design is obtained. Such reviews are planned and scheduled by the project manager and conducted by an independent chairman not associated with the project.

Engineering inspections of prototypes, mock-ups (full-scale models), pilot plants, or other types of models of the end result are also a valuable means to determine the adequacy of the technical or engineering effort prior to full commitment to the following phases of the project (construction, manufacture, field erection, etc.).

Product Planning Reviews

For major product development projects, the project will have been justified by a product plan, with emphasis on the economic factors, such as product price, market, sales, volume, competition. At key milestone events in the life cycle of the development project, the entire product plan must be reviewed. Such reviews will reflect the progress to date on the project, currently predicted product and project cost, changes in market and competition, and so on. Failure to conduct such reviews after a major project has been authorized has resulted in development of a number of excellent products for which the market has disappeared, either due to product cost increases, delays in project completion, or competition and market changes.

14.4 PROJECT DIRECTION

Integrated project evaluation, as described earlier, is needed so that proper direction of the project can be exercised. Project direction includes all forms of communicating to:

- Change the course of actions that have caused or will cause problems or undesirable cost, schedule, or technical results as follows:

  —Replan to recover to schedule and/or budget.

  —Initiate effort to correct technical difficulties.

  —Reallocate budgets (money, manpower) as required.

- Alleviate the unavoidable undesirable results by the following:

  —Document customer delays.

  —Invoke force majeure where possible.

  —Negotiate new schedules, prices, or budgets.

  —Revise technical objectives.

  —Negotiate changes in scope of work.

The project manager is similar to the pilot at the wheel of a ship or at the controls of an aircraft. She continuously monitors the progress of the project through the evaluation system, watches for indications of present or future difficulty, and communicates to the appropriate functional specialists any need to change plans, schedules, budgets, and performance to reach the project objectives. The "pilot" must also monitor these change signals to be sure they have been received, understood, acted upon, and that they do in fact produce the desired result.

The primary means of giving internal project directing instructions are:

- Action assignments resulting from project review meetings.
- Project directives, special memoranda, or e-mail messages.
- Task work orders, subcontracts, PAR, research and development case, product plan release and revision documents, or contracts and contract amendments.

Verbal directives affecting cost, schedule, technical performance, or scope of work must be documented by one of these means.

Direction through Action Assignments

The primary document produced by the project evaluation and review meetings is the *Action Assignment List.* Each specific identified problem or issue related to cost, schedule, or technical performance is addressed by an action assignment. The project manager defines and records each action assignment, specifying:

- *What* the problem is.
- *How* it is to be solved, in general terms (if possible).

- *Who* has the lead responsibility for the action, and who will contribute.
- *When* the action is scheduled to be completed.

The Action Assignment List is signed by the project manager and distributed within 24 hours after each project review meeting to all key project team members and functional managers. E-mail is very effective here. Accountability is pinpointed, and good coordination is assured since everyone is informed of all action assignments. Any objections to the assignments can be voiced during the review meetings, and acceptance of the assignment in full view of the project team reinforces each person's commitment to complete it as scheduled. Such commitment to peers is much stronger than a one-on-one commitment to the project manager alone.

Continual follow-up must be exerted by the project manager on all outstanding action assignments, to assure their timely completion.

Project Directives

In some situations, it may be desirable to establish a procedure for issuing project directives as a means for documenting and disseminating policies and decisions. Normally these would be signed by the project manager, or for major actions by the project sponsor. Memoranda, letters, or e-mail messages can also be used effectively for giving directive instructions to project team members and contributors.

Directions through Task Work Orders, Contracts, and Similar Documents

Control of funds is, in most cases, the most effective means of directing and revising work scope, schedule, and cost. Approval for release or revision of task work orders, subcontracts, contract amendments, PARs, research and development cases, product plans and similar documents provides a fundamental source of direction giving authority.

Changes to work scope, schedule, cost, or technical objectives resulting from action assignments or project directives, should be documented formally. Procedures are described in Chapter 12 to accomplish this.

14.5   REPORTING TO MANAGEMENT AND THE CUSTOMER

Company management must be informed continually of the overall health and status of the project. Problems that may jeopardize the schedule, profit, or budget must not be withheld from management, and possibly should be communicated with care to the customer. The status reports described here are intended to reveal certain of these problems to make higher level management aware of the actual or potential difficulties, either to assist in their resolution or take appropriate actions to minimize the adverse impact at the multiproject or corporate levels.

When reporting a problem to the project sponsor or to higher management, the project manager should state:

- The problem.
- The cause.
- The expected impact on schedule, budget, profit, or other pertinent areas.
- The action taken or recommended and the results expected of that action.
- What top management can do to help.

Reporting to the customer must be carried out in accordance with the terms of the contract. Careful coordination is required between the project manager, the contract administrator, and the commercial or marketing manager to assure that the content of reports to customers and the means by which they are handled serve the best interests of the company.

Reports to Management

For major projects, as defined in Chapter 2, three levels of management reporting are defined.

	Applicable to	Frequency
Major project register	All major projects	Quarterly or monthly
Monthly progress report	Designated major projects	Monthly
Critical project review	Critical projects	As scheduled

Major Project Register

As mentioned in Chapter 1, this is a summary listing of all major projects meeting the criteria established by appropriate corporate policies (similar to the criteria presented in Chapter 2). Figure 14.3 shows the information listed in a typical major project register. Detailed implementing instructions are needed to assure all reporting organizations comply properly with the policy.

Company:

Product Line:

(1) Serial No	(2) Name and Description	(3) Project Manager	(4) Customer	(5) Value $000	(6) Possible Exposure $000	(7) Contract Award	(8) Contractual Completion	Associated		(11) Management Approval of Proposal Date
						Date of		(9) PARs I.D. No. and $ Amt.	(10) R&D Cases I.D. No. and $ Amt.	

1. Allocate a number, starting at 1 at the beginning of each year; e.g., 93 (1) for the first project in 1993. This number is retained throughout the project life.

2. Project name and brief description of products and services comprising contract.

3. Give name and percent of time devoted to project.

4. Name (and location if export).

5. Gross charges to be billed through full life of project (in U.S. dollars).

6. Maximum penalty, damages, or other exposure in event of default (U.S. dollars).

7. Date of contract award.

8. Contractual date of project completion.

9. Company number and amount of any capital project authorization requests (PAR) judged to be critical to the success of the project—e.g., new manufacturing facilities, test equipment, etc.

10. Company case number and amount of R & D cases, local and general, contributing significantly toward success of project.

11. Date of approval of proposal terms by responsible manager.

Figure 14.3 Typical program/project register.

The major project register performs the following valuable functions:

- Provides an up-to-date inventory of major projects, with related key data for each, for the information and evaluation of top management
- Identifies whether or not a project manager is in place on each major project
- Assists in identification of the projects that have the greatest potential risk and exposure, so that management attention can be focused on these.

Monthly Progress Report

Cognizant executives at various levels may designate major projects requiring monthly progress reports, with appropriate distribution. The following is a suggested outline for such monthly reports:

1. *Summary status*—brief paragraph highlighting current status of the project.
2. *Red flag items*—previous and new red flag items, corrective actions taken, with prediction on resolution and further action required.
3. *Project staffing plan*—showing key or limited resources.
4. *Major achievements and future schedule*—describing actual accomplishments during current reporting period and significant changes in future schedule.
5. *Current and future problem areas*—stating major problems, actions required, and possible impact on the project.
6. *Project cost performance*—commenting on current project cost situation with reference to current cost performance reports.
7. *Exhibits*—(A) Summary Master Schedule (where required), (B) Detailed Project Schedule(s), (C) Project Cost Performance Report.

Many of the report formats described in Chapters 10, 12, and 14 are useful for inclusion in such monthly reports.

Critical Project Review

For specified critical projects, review meetings are held with appropriate executives to assure that the project is progressing as scheduled. These may be monthly, bimonthly, or quarterly, and they may be held on site or at division or higher headquarters levels.

Possible exhibits for projection and distribution in such reviews would include:

1. Project identification data.
2. Summary status, red flags, problem areas.
3. Summary master schedule.
4. Cumulative costs, milestone slip chart.
5. Cost performance report chart.
6. Action assignment summary.
7. Project manpower status.

Reports to the Customer

Good project management requires periodic (usually monthly) reporting to the customer. These reports should be in writing but should be presented personally by the project manager accompanied by appropriate contracts (marketing or commercial) and legal representatives. Such monthly reports provide the opportunity to document delinquencies or requests for change on the customer's side that may affect the project schedule, cost, or scope. Other factors such as strikes, floods, supplier delays, shortages, and the like also can be documented in these monthly reports. Such documentation is vital at project completion to quick settlement of claims, in or out of court. The content and format of such reports depends upon the situation within each project and for each customer.

14.6 PROJECT CLOSE-OUT OR EXTENSION

By definition, a project has a definite end point. However, terminating or closing out a project is more easily said than done. The project manager has the job of literally putting herself and the project team out of business. This is a very demanding assignment and requires considerable discipline to achieve a complete termination on the established date, especially if the manager's next assignment has not yet been identified.

Projects have a tendency, for these and other reasons, to stay alive long after their scheduled completion dates. There may only be a few people remaining on the project, but a long termination period can cause an otherwise successful project to move from financial success to failure. As long as an open work order remains, continuing cost charges are made to the project.

Some companies have found it necessary to replace the project manager near the end of the project with a person who is skilled at closing out projects, to assure that the schedule is met. During termination of a contractual project, the contract administrator plays a very important part.

Close-Out Plan and Schedule

As the final close-out phase approaches, the project manager establishes a specific plan and schedule for project termination. This plan covers at least these major items:

- *Contract.* Delivery and customer acceptance of products and/or service, and completion of all other contractual requirements.
- *Work authorization.* Close-out work orders and assure completion of all subcontracts.
- *Financial.* Collection from customer and closing of project books.
- *Personnel.* Reassignment or termination of people assigned to project office or project team.
- *Facilities.* Close office and other facilities occupied by the project office and team.
- *Records.* Deliver the project file and other records to the appropriate responsible manager.

Responsibilities during Close-Out Phase

The project manager and the project contract administrator have prime responsibilities during the close-out phase, as indicated in Chapter 9. These responsibilities are repeated here for emphasis.

Project Manager
- Ensure that all required steps are taken to present to the customer adequately all project deliverable items for acceptance, and that project activities are closed out in an efficient and economical manner.
- Assure that the acceptance plan and schedule comply with the customer contractual requirements.
- Assist the legal, contract administration and marketing, or commercial departments in preparation of a closeout plan and required closeout data.
- Obtain and approve closeout plans from each involved functional department.
- Monitor closeout activities, including disposition of surplus materials.
- Notify finance and functional departments of the completion of activities and of the project.
- Monitor payment from the customer until all collections have been made.

Project Contract Administrator

- At the point where all contractual obligations have been fulfilled, or where all but longer term warranties or spare parts deliveries are complete, assure that this fact is clearly and quickly communicated in writing to the customer.

- Assure that all formal documentation related to customer acceptance as required by the contract is properly executed.

- Expedite completion of all actions by the company and the customer needed to complete the contract and claim final payment.

- Initiate formal request for final payment.

- Where possible, obtain certification from the customer acknowledging completion of all contractual obligations and releasing the company from further obligations, except those under the terms of guaranty or warranty, if any.

Project Extensions

In many projects, such as new products, system development, and commercial projects of various kinds, the project manager may have a very important responsibility to obtain legitimate, funded extensions to the project, in cooperation with the marketing department. These would be to develop a new feature or otherwise perform work beyond the scope of the original project. It must be clearly recognized that such extensions do change the original scope, and in fact represent new, probably smaller, projects springing out of the original one. Each extension must be planned, scheduled, and controlled—and closed-out efficiently when the new scope of work is complete. Any request by the customer for a change may become a source of new business or extension of the project. Strict monitoring and control of the contract scope, as discussed in Chapter 12, will protect the financial objectives of the project and provide opportunities for legitimate project extensions.

Postcompletion Evaluation or Audit

An often neglected but important final step in effective project management is the postcompletion evaluation. It is frequently said that we learn by experience. However, the first things we forget are the unpleasant, bad experiences. This is very good for our individual sanity, but not very good for improvements in managing future projects.

Unless a formal postcompletion evaluation is made on each major project (or representative smaller ones), we will not learn by experience, but will repeat the same mistakes a number of times, to the detriment of our organization. Looking back on a project without a thorough postcompletion evaluation, it is quite easy to come to a general conclusion that, "Well, it didn't really go too badly, after all."

Mistakes are made on every project. Some are large, some small. Postcompletion evaluation is required to:

- Identify the mistakes.
- Determine their impact.
- Determine how they can be avoided on future projects.
- Initiate appropriate changes and improvements in project management and functional policies and procedures.

In Chapter 3, some symptoms and probable causes of poor performance on projects are described. These provide a starting point for identification of problems and improvement opportunities during the postcompletion evaluation. Such an evaluation should be conducted a reasonable time after completion, allowing enough time to elapse to be able to judge the ultimate success of the project, but not so much time that records are lost and memories fade completely. Perhaps one to three months after completion is the proper interval. The evaluation should be conducted by a person outside the project, to ensure objectivity. However, the person must be familiar with the project and the organization, and must have access to key project team members.

The general procedure for a postcompletion evaluation is:

1. Determine the original and final objectives, in terms of performance (end product), cost, and schedule.
2. Determine whether these objectives were met.
3. Where things went right, determine what factors contributed to the success.
4. Where things went wrong, determine the basic causes.
5. Develop policy and procedure changes to eliminate causes of missed objectives or other problems.
6. Implement the changes.

Actually, this effort can be considered a management project itself, and therefore should be managed using the principles presented in this book.

Appendix

❰ ❱

Integrated Scope, Schedule, Resource, Financial, and Risk Management for Projects

This appendix presents an important concept for effective project management based on successful experience in using advanced planning and analysis methods coupled with an advanced project management computer software application package. The described methods

Coauthor of this appendix, Vladimir Liberzon, PMP, MSc., is general director of Spider Management Technologies, a leading Russian project management consulting company and the vendor of Spider Project, the most widely used Russian professional project management software package. Liberzon is the architect and manager of Spider Project development. He has broad experience in managing many large-scale projects in construction, oil and gas, aerospace and defense, and shipbuilding, and in implementing enterprise-wide PM methodology and tools in many Russian companies.

Liberzon is a project management consultant, advisor, and trainer for the largest Russian enterprises in those industries plus banking, telecommunications, software development, metallurgy, and others. He is a lecturer on project management at the Moscow State University Business School, author of three books on project management (in Russian) including *The Outlines of Project Management* (the Russian counterpart of the PMI *A PMBOK® Guide*) and more than 100 papers. He is president of the Moscow, Russia, PMI chapter, and is the author of Moscow PMI training courses. Liberzon has presented papers at annual PMI conferences in 1994, 1996, 1998, 1999, and European PMI conferences in 2000, 2001, plus the IPMA congress in 1996 and many Russian regional project management symposia. For additional information on the Spider Project software package visit www.spiderproject.ru or contact Vladimir Liberzon at spider@mail.cnt.ru.

are illustrated with a simple case example project, and comparisons are made between resource analysis, success probability analysis, and earned value analysis by simulating the execution of the case project. Recommendations are given for implementing these integrated management methods to achieve success-driven project management. Finally, this approach is compared briefly with the critical chain method of project planning and control.

NEED FOR INTEGRATED INFORMATION

Effective project planning and control requires that the information regarding project scope, schedules, resources, finances, and related risks be integrated at detailed and summary levels. This requirement has been recognized for many years but it has not often been achieved in practice. As we will show, the methods used by most of the currently available project management application packages do not provide truly integrated management information. In particular, critical path calculations usually do not include the impact of resource constraints when calculating float values and the critical path. The methods described here, which do include all of these constraints, reflect over 10 years of practical application and experience in Russia and other European countries.

INTEGRATION METHODS

Integrated scope, schedule, financial, and risk management for projects is achieved using these methods:

1. Scope is defined systematically using appropriate breakdown structures that interrelate all project information. The work scope or volume is estimated for each task, work package, or activity, together with the types of resources required and the planned rate of usage or resource productivity for each activity.

2. Sequential, logical dependencies of work and deliverables are defined using appropriate network planning methods.

3. Resources are:

   a. Defined as consumable, renewable, and created;

   b. Estimated as independent units, units in teams or crews, or interchangeable units within assignment pools;

   c. Assigned to project activities; and

   d. Considered as constraints when their limits of availability are reached in calculating the project critical path, in both forward and backward pass calculations.

4. Activity durations are calculated, when appropriate, by combining work scope or volume with resource usage or productivity rates.

5. Risks are calculated by simulating risk events and using a range of three estimates where appropriate for work scope and volume, resource usage and productivity rates, activity duration when estimated directly, and calendar variation for weather and other factors, to produce predicted probabilities of meeting the desired target schedule dates and budgets.

6. Project schedules are produced in the usual manner by processing the network plans, but most importantly the true critical path is calculated to reflect logical and all schedule constraints, including resources, in both the forward and backward pass calculations of the network plans. This has become known as the resource critical path/RCP to emphasize that resource constraints have been used in determining which activities are truly critical to project completion, and in the calculation of available float or allowable delay.

7. Actual expenditures of time, money, and resources are compared with plans, schedules, and budgets to enable effective project monitoring and control.

8. The current probabilities of success in all areas (schedules, resources, financial) are calculated, and their trends are determined and presented graphically through analysis of frequently revised and retained project plans. Initially the desired targets for project dates, costs, and material or other resource requirements are calculated based on the desirable probabilities set by the project manager and planner. If the target data are preset then project planner calculates the probability of their successful achievement.

Each of these methods is discussed in more detail in the following paragraphs, and their application to a simple case project is then described.

1. SYSTEMATIC PROJECT SCOPE DEFINITION

The well-established concept of systematically breaking down a project by life cycle phase, end item deliverables, products, processes, resources, and responsibilities provides the primary means for correlating project scope, schedule, resource, cost, and risk information and summarizing it for analysis and management purposes. Rather than attempting to produce only one project/work breakdown structure that serves every purpose on a given project, the approach described here allows the use of a number of different structures, each designed for a specific purpose. These are used to break down and summarize project information in a variety of ways, such as by life-cycle phase, deliverables, physical area, assignment of responsibilities, functional type of work, cost account, contract or subcontract, and others.

The work scope or volume is estimated for each activity, together with the types of resources required and the planned rate of usage and productivity for each.

2. DEFINING LOGICAL, SEQUENTIAL DEPENDENCIES WITH NETWORK PLANS

All logical, sequential dependencies between project deliverables, task, work packages, and activities are defined using the most appropriate network planning method (PERT/CPM/PDM or similar planning techniques).

3. RESOURCE INFORMATION AND ANALYSIS

Resource types include:

- Consumable: materials, supplies, and other expendables.
- Renewable: labor, equipment, facilities.

The resources required to execute each activity are identified and estimated in units (individual people with specified skills and/or experience levels, equipment, machines, etc.), teams or groups of particular resource units, or assignment pools of interchangeable resource units.

Projects are often planned (especially in construction and manufacturing) using federal, local, industrial or corporate *norms* and *standards*. These norms usually refer to *resource productivity* for certain activity types, with costs and materials per unit of *activity volume of work*. Usage of these norms affects the planning and definition of project activities.

4. ACTIVITY DURATION CALCULATION OR ESTIMATION

Activity volume can be measured in meters, tons, and so on, planned work hours, percents, or any other measurable units. Volume is often used as the initial activity information instead of estimated activity duration. If the assigned resource productivity is defined in volume units per hour, then the activity duration can be calculated during project scheduling. Activity volume does not depend on assigned resources but the duration obviously does.

Calculation of activity duration based on assigned resource productivity has many advantages. We have already mentioned the possibility of applying corporate norms. By changing the expected resource productivity, we can change the planned duration of all activities of a specified type. This is especially useful to forecast uncertainties related to the project duration. When it is not feasible or appropriate to calculate activity duration based on work volume, it is estimated directly in time units.

5. RISK SIMULATION AND SUCCESS PROBABILITY ANALYSIS

Our experience of project planning shows that the probability of successful implementation of *deterministic project schedules* and budgets based on single estimates of the most probable activity duration, material requirements, and costs is very low. Therefore, project planning technology should always include risk simulation to produce reliable results. As an example of how this can be accomplished, we will describe the approach to project planning and risk simulation that is supported by Spider Project, a widely used software package developed in Russia over the past 10 years.

The project planner obtains three estimates (optimistic, most probable, and pessimistic) for all initial project data. These data are used to calculate optimistic, most probable and pessimistic project schedules and budgets. The most probable and pessimistic project versions will often contain additional activities and costs and may employ other resources and different calendars than the optimistic schedule. Based on optimistic, most probable and pessimistic project (phase) data, the probability distribution is created for the project (phase) finish date, cost, and material requirements. For a single activity beta distribution is used, and for a number of activities the curve is adjusted in accordance with the total number of project (phase) activities and the number of resource critical activities. This approach permits calculation of all the necessary data very quickly, although it does not guarantee the accuracy of the risk estimations. But the errors are not large and do not weigh much compared with the accuracy of the initial information. Besides the trends of the calculated parameters are much more valuable for decision making than their initial estimates.

The planner defines the *desirable probabilities* of meeting target dates, costs, and material consumption rates for the main elements of the primary project work breakdown structure. Based on these probabilities, the package calculates corresponding *desired project target dates, costs, and material requirements.* These desired data form the basis for contract or other authorizing negotiations and decision making.

Negotiations may result in establishing new *target data*. Project risk simulation results help the negotiations by answering the questions on probability to meet any restrictions on time and on budget. The probability of meeting target data (cost, time, quantity) is called the *success probability*. Success probability is the best indicator of the current project status during project execution.

In addition, the package calculates the *target schedule*. The target schedule is the backward project resource constrained schedule using the most probable activity duration, resource and material requirements, costs, and target dates of the project phase completion.

An alternative method of risk simulation uses the Monte Carlo technique, which randomly assigns various values throughout the project plan and then recalculates the project schedule, resource and cost estimates many times. Even with today's computing capabilities, the time required to produce reliable simulations using this method prevents it from being of practical value. For this reason, we consider the described probabilistic approach to be far more practical than using the Monte Carlo method, although Monte Carlo simulation may be incorporated in the suggested methodology if the simulation results can be produced in a reasonable time.

6. PROJECT SCHEDULES AND THE RESOURCE (OR TRUE) CRITICAL PATH/RCP

Project schedules are produced by processing the network plans and the true critical path is calculated to reflect both logical and resource constraints in both the forward and backward pass calculations. As previously mentioned, this has become known as the *resource critical path* to emphasize that resource constraints have been used in determining which activities are truly critical to project completion, and in the calculation of available float or allowable delay.

A Guide to the Project Management Body of Knowledge® (PMI, 2000, p. 200) defines the *critical path* as those activities with float less than or equal to a specified value, usually zero. *Float* is the amount of time that an activity may be delayed from its early start without delaying the project finish date. *Early start* is the earliest possible point in time at which the uncompleted portions of an activity (or the project) can start, based on the network logic and any schedule constraints.

The true critical path must be based on all schedule constraints. Project schedule constraints include resource constraints, finance and supply constraints, calendar constraints and imposed dates. Activity float should be calculated with all of these schedule constraints as well as the network logic taken into account. However, most project management software packages calculate float based on the network dependencies while completely ignoring the availability of resources. The result is not the true activity float as defined by the PMBOK Guide. When all schedule constraints are included in the critical path calculation we call the result the *resource critical path* (RCP) to distinguish it from the traditional interpretation of the critical path definition that ignores these resource and other constraints.

The calculation of the RCP is similar to the calculation of the traditional critical path with the exception that both the early and the late dates are calculated during forward and backward resource (and material and cost) leveling. This leveling is simply the imposition of resource limits by specified time period. It appears that by adding financial and supply constraints to the critical chain definition as well as the method of calculating the critical chain, the result will be something very similar to the RCP. The RCP can consist of activities that are not linked logically to each other in the network plan. The traditional critical path approach assumes that this may be due to the different activity calendars and imposed dates. In calculating the RCP, it can also be due to resource constraints and financial and supply limitations.

Activity resource float has one major advantage over the total float calculated by most PM software. This advantage is feasibility. Traditional total float shows the period for which the execution of an activity may be postponed if project resources are unlimited. *Activity resource float* shows the period for which activity execution may be postponed within the current schedule with the set of resources available to this project at that particular time.

Contingency reserves or buffers (for money, labor, material, or other resources) are calculated as the difference between activity start times (cost, material requirements, etc.) in the optimistic and target schedules.

Illustration of the Resource Critical Path Concept

Let's illustrate this concept using a project consisting of only three independent activities and two resources. The project data are:

Activity Name	Activity Volume	Assigned Resource	Resource Productivity	Resource Hour Cost
Activity 1	120	Resource 1	0.5	50
Activity 2	60	Resource 2	0.3	30
Activity 3	60	Resource 2	0.3	30

The project schedule before resource leveling and the legend that shows the symbology used in this and following pictures is shown at Figure A.1. Activity 1 is critical, and the other activities have 5 days of float.

Name	Prod uctiv ity	Volume	Duration, Days [Schedul	Float, Days	Total Cost	Mar 2003					Apr 2003				May 2C	
						3	10	17	24	31	7	14	21	28	5	12
Sample Project			30.00		24000.00							Project bar			
Activity 1		120.00	30.00		12000.00							Critical Activity			
Resource 1	0.50	120.00	30.00		12000.00							Assignment bar			
Activity 2		60.00	25.00	5.00	6000.00							Non-critical activity			
Resource 2	0.30	60.00	25.00	5.00	6000.00										
Activity 3		60.00	25.00	5.00	6000.00										
Resource 3	0.30	60.00	25.00	5.00	6000.00										

Figure A.1   Sample project schedule before resource leveling.

After resource leveling activities 2 and 3 became *resource critical* while activity 1 has 20 days of float (*resource float*). So the RCP consists of activities 2 and 3 (Figure A.2).

7. TRACKING ACTUAL EXPENDITURES

Actual expenditures of time, money, and other resources are reported in the usual fashion and compared with plans, schedules and budgets to enable effective project monitoring and control using resource analysis and success probability analysis.

8. SUCCESS PROBABILITY ANALYSIS

The current probabilities of success in all areas (schedules, resources, financial) are calculated, and their trends are determined and presented graphically through analysis of frequently revised and retained project

Name	Prod uctiv ity	Volume	Duration, Days [Schedul	Float, Days	Total Cost	Mar 2003					Apr 2003				M
						3	10	17	24	31	7	14	21	28	5
Sample Project			50.00		24000.00										
Activity 1		120.00	30.00	20.00	12000.00										
Resource 1	0.50	120.00	30.00	20.00	12000.00										
Activity 2		60.00	25.00		6000.00										
Resource 2	0.30	60.00	25.00		6000.00										
Activity 3		60.00	25.00		6000.00										
Resource 3	0.30	60.00	25.00		6000.00										

Figure A.2   Sample project schedule after resource leveling.

plans. Initially the desired targets for project dates, costs, and material or other resource requirements are calculated based on the desirable probabilities set by the project manager and planner. If this or other target data are pre-set then project planner calculates the probabilities of their successful achievement (which we call success probabilities).

Application to the Sample Project

To illustrate the application of this approach to our sample project we will make these simple assumptions:

- The optimistic productivity of assigned resources is 20 percent higher and the pessimistic is 20 percent lower than the most likely estimates.
- We have no other risks.

The resource productivity estimates are:

Resource Name	Most Probable Resource Productivity	Optimistic Resource Productivity	Pessimistic Resource Productivity
Resource 1	0.5	0.6	0.4
Resource 2	0.3	0.36	0.24

Target Probabilities. We have decided for this example that we want to be on time with 70 percent probability and under budget with 75 percent probability. The package will identify the desired finish date and the required project budget for each of these values:

Parameter Name	Most Probable Value	Desired Probability	Desired Finish Date/ Project Budget
Finish Date	9 May 2003	70	14 May 2003
Project Budget	$24,000.00	75	$25,613

Figure A.3 shows the resulting target project schedule together with the optimistic schedule.

Let's assume that after negotiating the contract we established the project target finish date as May 14, 2003, and the target budget as $25,000. The package will calculate the probability of meeting the target

Name	Finish [Desired]	Total Cost [Desired]	Start Buffer	Cost Buffer	Mar 2003				Apr 2003				May	
					3	10	17	24	31	7	14	21	28	5	1:
Sample Project	**14.05.2003 14:08**	**25612.90**	**2.77**	**5612.90**										
Activity 1	14.05.2003 14:08	12806.45	22.77	2806.45										
Activity 2	14.05.2003 14:08	6403.23	6.93	1403.23										
Activity 3	09.04.2003 14:08	6403.23	2.77	1403.23										

Figure A.3   Sample project target schedule.

parameters and we will see that we are in fairly good shape with the schedule but should be very cautious with the project budget:

Parameter Name	Target Value	Success Probability
Finish Date	14 May 2003	72.10
Project Budget	$25,000	63.71

For comparison, if we assume that the most probable version of our project was defined as the project baseline then the probabilities of meeting the most probable project parameters are not very good, and in fact are unacceptably low:

Parameter Name	Target Value	Success Probability
Finish Date	9 May 2003	40.93
Project Budget	$24,000	40.93

Sample Project Execution

Now we will simulate the sample project execution. Let's assume that the actual productivity for resource 1 was 10 percent higher than expected (0.55), while the actual productivity for resource 2 was 10 percent lower (0.27), and the productivity of these resources did not change during project execution. Our task is to analyze project performance, to forecast future project results, and to decide if corrective action is necessary. We will use resource analysis, success probability analysis, and earned value analysis. We assume that estimates were done each week and will analyze the trends, comparing against our project target parameters and baseline cost of:

Target project finish date   May 14, 2003

Target project cost $25,000

Most probable project cost $24,000

Resource Analysis

First week performance analysis and adjustments. Using resource analysis, we will decide if the actual deviations in resource productivity are accidental or if the planned productivity should be adjusted. After analysis we decide to adjust them raising the productivity of resource 1 by 5 percent (half of the difference between planned and actual productivity to 0.525) and lowering the productivity of resource 2 by the same 5 percent (to 0.285) (Figure A.4). Our new forecast (estimate at completion) becomes:

Project Finish   May 14, 2003

Project Cost $24,028

Advice: The project will most likely be 5 days late against baseline finish and slightly over baseline budget.

Second week performance analysis and adjustments. New performance data for the second week show that the planned resource productivity should be adjusted again. Let's adjust them raising productivity of resource 1 to 0.5375 and lowering the productivity of resource 2 to 0.2775. Our second forecast (estimate at completion):

Project Finish   May 16, 2003

Project Cost $24,108

Advice: The project will be delayed another two days with a slightly larger budget overrun.

Name	Volume	Produ ctivity	Rem Duratio n, Days	Finish	Total Cost	Mar 2003				Apr 2003				May	
						3	10	17	24	31	7	14	21	28	5	1:
Sample Project			47.895	14.05.2003	24028.089										
Activity 1	98.000		23.333	10.04.2003	11333.347										
Resource 1	98.000	0.525	23.333	10.04.2003	11333.347										
Activity 2	60.000		26.316	14.05.2003	6315.792										
Resource 2	60.000	0.285	26.316	14.05.2003	6315.792										
Activity 3	49.200		21.579	08.04.2003	6378.950										
Resource 3	49.200	0.285	21.579	08.04.2003	6378.950										

Figure A.4   First week forecast by resource analysis.

Third week performance analysis and adjustments. New performance data show that the planned resource productivity should be made equal to the actual because they did not change from the project start. Productivity forecast for resource 1 is now 0.55 and for resource 2 it is 0.27 (Figure A.5).

Our third forecast (estimate at completion) is:

Project Finish	May 19, 2003
Project Cost	$24,242

Advice: The project probably will be delayed five days against target finish and 10 days against baseline finish with a budget overrun of $242.

Success Probability Analysis

Success probability shows current project status, and success probability trends show the project manager if corrective action is needed. These trends for our sample project are shown in the Figure A.6.

The success probability trends in Figure A.6 show us that the project will certainly be late, probably over the baseline budget of $24,000, but certainly under target cost of $25,000. The problems with the project on-time completion were shown from the very beginning, but the problems with meeting the baseline cost became obvious only after actually finishing activity 1.

Current success probability may change not only due to performance deviations but also because risk estimates were changed, causing changes in the pessimistic and most probable project versions. This can cause changes in the probability distribution curves and thus changes in current success probability data. Using success probability trends as

Name	Volume	Prod uctiv ity	Rem Duration, Days	Total Cost	Finish	Mar 2003 3 10 17 24	Apr 2003 31 7 14 21 28	May 20 5 12
Sample Project			40.56	24242.44	19.05.2003			
Activity 1	54.00		12.27	10909.10	09.04.2003			
Resource 1	54.00	0.55	12.27	10909.10	09.04.2003			
Activity 2	60.00		27.78	6666.67	19.05.2003			
Resource 2	60.00	0.27	27.78	6666.67	19.05.2003			
Activity 3	27.60		12.78	6666.67	09.04.2003			
Resource 3	27.60	0.27	12.78	6666.67	09.04.2003			

Figure A.5   Third week forecast by resource analysis.

Name	Start	Optimistic Finish	Finish [Target]	Total Optimistic Cost	Mar 2003				Apr 2003				May 2	
					3	10	17	24	31	7	14	21	28	5	12
Sample Project	03.03.2003	16.05.2003	14.05.2003	23909.1										
Activity 1	03.03.2003	09.04.2003		10909.1										
Activity 2	09.04.2003	16.05.2003		6333.3										
Activity 3	03.03.2003	09.04.2003		6666.7										

Sample Project (evalue) - Success Probability Trends	Cost (24000) ▪ Total Cost (CostTotal) ▪ Finish (Fin) ▪	100 — 80 — 60 — 40 — 20 — 0 —	Total Cost · · · Cost (24000) · Finish

Figure A.6   Success probability trends for the sample project.

the estimate of project performance, senior management encourages project managers to resolve uncertainties as early as possible. Solving uncertainties can increase current success probabilities even when this involves finish delays and cost overruns. Postponing execution of problem activities leads to negative trends in success probabilities. This attribute of success probability trends as the performance measure is especially useful in new product development project management.

EARNED VALUE ANALYSIS/EVA

The results of applying earned value analysis to the sample project are shown in Table A.1.

You will notice that the problems with the sample project schedule and budget are hidden until the finish of activity 1 and even later. It is necessary to analyze the trends very carefully to discover that the problems exist. The difficulty in finding these problems using EVA can be explained by the fact that EVA does not consider project logic dependencies. Thus the successful execution of activities that don't belong to the resource critical path may produce good earned value parameters despite the poor forecast of project completion date and budget. We recommend applying EVA to the critical path activities of each project life-cycle phase to forecast the phase duration and budget. You cannot use earned value data from one phase to forecast the execution of another phase if the resources used on these phases are different.

Table A.1. Earned Value Management Data Trends for the Sample Project

| | | | | | | Date | | | |
Parameter	03.03.03	10.03.03	17.03.03	24.03.03	31.03.03	07.04.03	14.04.03	21.04.03	28.04.03
AC	3,200	6,400	9,600	12,800	16,000	18,109.1	19,309.1	20,509.1	21,709.1
EV	3,280	6,560	9,840	13,120	16,400	18,480	19,560	20,640	21,720
PV	3,200	6,400	9,600	12,800	16,000	19,200	20,400	21,600	22,800
CV	80	160	240	320	400	370.89	250.89	130.89	10.89
SV	80	160	240	320	400	-720	-840	-960	-1,080
CPI%	102.5	102.5	102.5	102.5	102.5	102.05	101.3	100.64	100.05
SPI%	102.5	102.5	102.5	102.5	102.5	96.25	95.88	95.56	95.26

IMPLEMENTING INTEGRATED INFORMATION METHODS TO ACHIEVE SUCCESS-DRIVEN PROJECT MANAGEMENT

Here are several recommendations for consideration when implementing the integrated information methods described. We call this approach *success-driven project management* to emphasis that the focus is on the actions needed to successfully complete the project on schedule and within budget.

1. *Use range estimates (optimistic, most likely, pessimistic) for activity duration and volume, resource productivity and quantity, activity and resource cost, and calendars, to enable risk assessment and management.* Estimates are usually based not only on expert judgments buy also on regulatory or corporate norms. These range estimates enable creation and evaluation of optimistic, most likely and pessimistic resource and cost constrained project schedules and budgets.

2. *Use success probabilities to negotiate realistic target finish dates and budgets.* Determine acceptable, realistic target dates and budgets that reflect reasonable success probabilities, and reach agreement and understanding with the approving authorities regarding these dates, budgets, and probabilities.

3. *Set optimistic targets and manage the contingency reserves.* We recommend using the optimistic project version for setting task schedules and budgets for the project implementers. The calculated contingency reserves or buffers (for labor, cost, materials, and schedule) are used by the project manager as required to overcome possible problems.

4. *Use probability trends as the most valuable indicator of project success.* Trends in the success probabilities show the project manager where and when corrective actions are needed. These trends show current project status better than any other parameter. Figure A.7 illustrates the optimistic and target data, and other available scheduling and risk analysis information for our sample project.

5. *Control risks and regularly recalculate project schedules, buffers, and success probabilities.* Combine actual progress and resource expenditure data with any corrective planning changes made, and recalculate their impact on the remainder of the project. Analyze the resulting success probabilities to determine where further planning changes are required to prevent or overcome predicted problems.

Name	Finish	Finish [Target]	Target Finish Probability	Start Buffer	Optimistic Cost	Total Cost [Target]	Total Cost [Proba	Cost Buffer	Mar	Apr	May
Sample Project	29.04.2003	14.05.2003	72.1	3.0	20000.0	25000.0	63.7	5000.0			
Activity 1	04.04.2003			23.0	10000.0			2500.0			
Activity 2	29.04.2003			7.2	5000.0			1250.0			
Activity 3	31.03.2003			3.0	5000.0			1250.0			

Figure A.7   Initial data for the sample project.

6. *Apply these management tips for project control:*
   - Plan day-to-day activities using the optimistic estimates but pay special attention to resource floats and to contingency reserves.
   - Include the causes of delays in activity completion and cost over-runs in performance reports.
   - Regularly update and analyze the estimates in the optimistic, most probable and pessimistic project schedules.
   - Regularly recalculate the success probabilities and analyze trends.
   - If trends are negative then there is a need for corrective actions regardless of the current level of success probabilities.

COMPARISON OF THIS INTEGRATED APPROACH WITH THE CRITICAL CHAIN METHOD

The described integrated approach and the critical chain (Goldblatt, 1997) method obviously have a lot in common:

- The resource critical path is the same as the critical chain.
- Therefore the critical chain "project buffer" may be regarded as an analogue of the "contingency time reserve."
- The critical chain "feeding buffers" are similar to our "resource floats."
- Both approaches recommend using optimistic estimates for setting the task schedules for project implementers.

Success probability trends show if the project time and cost reserves for a given phase were spent faster or slower than expected. This is believed to be more effective than trying to estimate qualitatively whether or not the critical chain project buffers were properly utilized.

But there are differences, too. We cannot agree with the critical chain theory's assumption that *one should always avoid multitasking*. Usually there are many sub-critical activities belonging to the different network paths and even minor delays in the execution of sub-critical activities can lead to the changes in the RCP. This comes into conflict with the critical chain theory's assumption that the *critical chain never changes* during the project execution. The assumption that only *one project drum* (in our terminology—critical) *resource* exists is also dubious. Our experience shows that critical resources are different during the different phases of a project's lifecycle.

Bibliography

A *Guide to the Project Management Body of Knowledge®*. Newtown Square, PA: Project Management Institute, 2000.

APM-BoK Project Management Body of Knowledge, 4th ed. High Wycombe, U.K.: Association for Project Management, 2000. ISBN 1-903494-00-1. See also *British Standard BS6079–1:2000. Project Management—Part 1: Guide to Project Management.* British Standards Institute, U.K. ISBN 0-580-25594-8.

Archibald, Russell D., and Alan Harpham. "Project Managers Profiles and Certification Workshop Report." *Proceedings of the 14th International Expert Seminar,* Zurich, Switzerland: International Project Management Association (IPMA), March 15–17, 1990.

Archibald, Russell D., and Richard L. Villoria. *Network-Based Management Systems (PERT/CPM).* New York: Wiley, 1967.

Belanger, Thomas C. "Choosing a Project Life Cycle." *Field Guide to Project Management,* edited by David I. Cleland. New York: Wiley, 1998, 61–73.

Block, Thomas R. "The Project Office Phenomenon." *PM Network* (March 1998).

Boznak, Rudolph G. "Master Business Planning—The Art of Controlling Project Management in a Multi-Project Environment." *Proceedings of the Project Management Institute Seminar Symposium,* Newtown Square, PA: Project Management Institute, October 1987, 143–158.

Bridges, Dianne N., and J. Kent Crawford. "How to Start Up and Rollout a Project Office." *Proceedings of the Project Management Institute Annual Seminars & Symposium,* Newtown Square, PA: Project Management Institute, September 7–16, 2000.

Briner, Wendy, Michael Geddes, and Colin Hastings. *Project Leadership.* New York: Van Nostrand, 1990.

Buchanan, B. "Building Organizational Commitment: The Socialization of Managers in Work Organizations." *Administrative Science Quarterly,* 19 (1974): 533–546.

Buchanan, B. "To Walk the Extra Mile: The Whats, Whens and Whys of Organizational Commitment." *Organizational Dynamics* (spring, 1985).

Burke, R. J. "Methods of Resolving Interpersonal Conflict." *Personnel Administration* (July/August, 1969).

Burnett, Nicholas R., and Robert Youker. "Analyzing the Project Environment," The World Bank Institute Course Note Series. Washington, DC: The World Bank Institute, CN-848, July 1980.

Buss, Martin D. J. "How to Rank Computer Projects." In *Project Portfolio Management, Selecting and Prioritizing Projects for Competitive Advantage,* edited by Lowell D. Dye and James S. Pennypacker. West Chester, PA: Center for Business Practices, 1999, 183–192.

Center for Business Practices Research Report: *The Value of Project Management.* 316 W. Barnard St., West Chester, PA 19382: PM Solutions' Center for Business Practices, January 2001.

Cleland, David I. "The Discipline of Project Management." *Project Management for the Business Professional,* edited by Joan Knutson. New York: Wiley, 2001.

Cleland, David I., and William R. King. "Linear Responsibility Charts in Project Management." *Project Management Handbook,* 2nd ed., edited by David I. Cleland and William R. King. New York: Van Nostrand Reinhold, 1988.

Cloninger, Ellodee A. *Project Management Software Buyer's Guidelines.* Cupertine, CA: Pmnet, 1988.

Combe, Margaret W., and Gregory D. Githens. "Managing Popcorn Priorities: How Portfolios and Programs Align Projects with Strategies." *Proceedings of the PMI 1999 Seminars & Symposium.* Philadelphia, PA, Newtown Square, PA: Project Management Institute, October 10–16, 1999.

Combe, Marge. "Making the Link from Strategy to Projects—What's the Payoff?" *Proceedings of the 2000 Seminars & Symposium,* Houston, TX, Newtown Square, PA: Project Management Institute, September 7–16, 2000.

Cooke-Davies, Terry, John Schlichter, and Christophe Bredillet. "Beyond the *PMBOK® Guide,*" *Proceedings of the PMI 2001 Seminars & Symposium,* Nashville, TN, Newtown Square, PA: Project Management Institute, November 1–10, 2001.

Cooper, Robert G. "Selecting Winning New Product Projects: Using the NewProd System." *Journal of Product Innovation Management,* 2 (1985): 34–44.

Cooper, Robert G., Scott J. Edgert, and Elko J. Kleinschmidt. *Portfolio Management for New Products.* Cambridge, MA: Perseus Publishing, 1998. Contact: www.perseuspublishing.com.

Cooper, Robert G., Scott J. Edgett, and Elko J. Kleinschmidt. *Portfolio Management for New Products,* 2nd ed. Cambridge, MA: Perseus, 2001. Publishing, http://www.perseuspublishing.com.

Cooper, Robert G., Scott J. Edgett, and Elko J. Kleinschmidt. "Portfolio Management in New Product Development: Lessons from the Leaders, Phase I." In *Project Portfolio Management—Selecting and Prioritizing Projects for Competitive*

Advantage, edited by Lowell D. Dye and James S. Pennypacker. West Chester, PA: Center for Business Practices, 1999, 97–116.

Cooper, Robert G., Scott J. Edgert, and Elko J. Kleinschmidt. "Portfolio Management in New Product Development: Lessons Learned from the Leaders, Phase II." In *Project Portfolio Management—Selecting and Prioritizing Projects for Competitive Advantage,* edited by Lowell D. Dye and James S. Pennypacker. West Chester, PA: Center for Business Practices, 1999, 23–38.

Cooper, Robert G., and Elko J. Kleinschmidt. "Stage-Gate Systems for New Product Success." *Marketing Management,* 1, no. 4 (1993): 20–29. See www.prod-dev.com.

Crawford, J. Kent, and James S. Pennypacker. "The Value of Project Management: Proof at Last." *Proceedings of the PMI 2001 Seminars & Symposium.* Nashville, TN, Newtown Square, PA: Project Management Institute, November 1–10, 2001.

Crawford, J. Kent, and James S. Pennypacker. "The Value of Project Management: Why Every Twenty-First Century Company Must Have an Effective Project Management Culture." *Proceedings of the PMI 2000 Seminars & Symposium.* Houston, TX, Newtown Square, PA: Project Management Institute, September 7–16, 2000.

Desaulniers, Douglas H., and Robert J. Anderson. "Matching Software Development Life Cycles to the Project Environment." *Proceedings of the Project Management Institute Annual Seminars & Symposium.* Nashville, TN. Newtown Square, PA: Project Management Institute, November 1–10, 2001.

Dinsmore, Paul C. *Winning in Business with Enterprise Project Management.* New York: Amacom American Management Association, 1999.

Dye, Lowell D., and James S. Pennypacker (Eds.). *Project Portfolio Management— Selecting and Prioritizing Projects for Competitive Advantage.* 316 W. Barnard St., West Chester, PA: PM Solutions' Center for Business Practices, 1999.

Dye, Lowell D., and James S. Pennypacker. "Project Portfolio Managing and Managing Multiple Projects: Two Sides of the Same Coin?" *Proceedings of the 2000 PMI Seminars & Symposium.* Newtown Square, PA: Project Management Institute.

Eden, D. "Self-Fulfilling Prophecy as a Management Tool: Harnessing Pygmalion." *Academy of Management Review,* vol. 9, no. 1 (1984).

Elmes, M., and D. Wilemon. "Organization Culture and Project Leader Effectiveness." *Project Management Journal,* 19, 4 (1988).

Eskelin, Allen. "Managing Technical Acquisition Project Life Cycles." *PM Network* (March 2002).

Fangel, Morten. (Ed.). *Handbook of Project Start-Up.* Hilleroed, Denmark: International Project Management Association, Saettedammen 4, 1989. Contact: Morten@fangel.dk.

Fleming, Quentin W., and Joel M. Koppelman. *Earned Value Project Management,* 2nd ed. Newtown Square, PA: Project Management Institute, 2000.

Frame, J. Davidson. "Selecting Projects That Will Lead to Success." In *Project Portfolio Management, Selecting and Prioritizing Projects for Competitive Advantage,* edited by Lowell D. Dye and James S. Pennypacker. West Chester, PA: Center for Business Practices, 1999, 169–182.

Galbreath, Robert D. "Working with Pulses, Not Streams: Using Projects to Capture Opportunity." In *Strategic Planning and Management Handbook,* edited by William R. King and David I. Cleland. New York: Van Nostrand Reinhold, 1987.

Gillis, Robert. "Strategies for Successful Project Implementation." In *Handbook of Project Start-Up,* edited by Morten Fangel, 1989. See Fangel 1989.

Goldratt, E. M. *Critical Chain.* Great Barrington, MA: North River Press, 1997.

Goldratt, E. M. *Theory of Constraints.* Great Barrington, MA: North River Press, 1994.

Goldratt, E. M. *What Is This Thing Called Theory of Constraints, and How Should It Be Implemented?* Croton-on-Hudson, New York: ASQC Quality Press, 1997.

Griffin, Abbie. "PDMA Research on New Product Development Practices: Updating Trends and Benchmarking Best Practices." *PDMA Journal of Product Innovation Management,* 14 (1997): 429–458.

Hastings, Colin, Peter Bixby, and Rani Chaudhry-Lawton. *The Superteam Solution.* San Diego: University Associates, 1987.

Hosley, William N. "Managing High-Technology Research Projects for Maximum Effectiveness." *The AMA Handbook of Project Management,* edited by Paul C. Dinsmore. New York: AMACOM American Management Association, 1993, 377–387.

Ibbs, C. William, and Young-Hoon Kwak. *The Benefits of Project Management: Financial and Organizational Rewards to Corporations.* Newtown Square, PA: Project Management Institute, 1997.

Ibbs, C. William, Justin Reginato, and Peter W. G. Marris. "Calculating the $$$ Value of Project Management." *Proceedings of the PMI 2001 Seminars & Symposium.* Newtown Square, PA: Project Management Institute, November 1–10, 2001.

Kerzner, Harold. *Strategic Planning for Project Management Using a Project Management Maturity Model.* New York: Wiley, 2001.

Kezsbom, Deborah S., and Katherine A. Edward. *The New Dynamic Project Management—Winning Through Competitive Advantage.* New York: Wiley-Interscience, 2001.

Knutson, Joan. "Measurement of Project Management ROI: Making Sense to Making Cents." *Proceedings of the PMI 1999 Seminars & Symposium.* Philadelphia, PA, Newtown Square, PA: Project Management Institute, October 10–16, 1999.

Knutson, Joan. "Project Office: An Evolutionary Implementation Plan." *Proceedings of the 30th Annual Project Management Institute 1999 Seminars & Symposium,* Newtown Square, PA: Project Management Institute, October 10–16, 1999.

Knutson, Joan. *Succeeding in Project-Driven Organizations: People, Processes and Politics.* New York: Wiley, 2001.

Lambert, Lee R. "R&D Project Management: Adapting to Technological Risk and Uncertainty." *The AMA Handbook of Project Management,* edited by Paul C. Dinsmore. New York: AMACOM American Management Association, 1993, 388–397.

Lawrence, P., and J. Lorsch. "New Managerial Job: The Integrator." *Harvard Business Review* (November–December, 1967).

Leach, Lawrence P. *Critical Chain Project Management.* Norwood, MA: Artech House, 2000.

Lewin, Marsha D. *Better Software Project Management—A Primer for Success.* New York: John Wiley & Sons, 2002.

Liberzon, Vladimir. "Project Management Development in Russia—Achievements and Lessons Learned." *Proceedings of the 1st International Project Management Conference in Portugal:* "Global Trends in Project Management for the XXI Century." Lisbon, Portugal: PMI-Portugal Chapter, November 22–24, 2000. Contact: www.pmi.org.

Liberzon, Vladimir. "Resource Critical Path Approach to Project Schedule Management." *Proceedings of the PMI Europe Conference.* Newtown Square, PA: Project Management Institute, June 6–7, 2001.

Liberzon, Vladimir, and Igor Lobanov. "Advanced Features of Russian Project Management Software." *Proceedings of the 3rd PMI Europe Project Management Conference,* Jerusalem, Israel, Newtown Square, PA: Project Management Institute, June 12–14, 2000.

Lichtenberg, Steen. "Experiences From a New Logic in Project Management." *Dimensions in Project Management.* Heidelberg: Springer-Verlag, 1990.

Lichtenberg, Steen. *Proactive Management of Uncertainty Using the Successive Principle—A practical way to manage opportunities and risk.* Lyngby, Denmark: Polyteknisk Press, 2000. Contact: www.polyteknisk.dk.

Lichtenberg, Steen, and Russell D. Archibald. "Experiences Using Next Generation Management Practices." *Proceedings of INTERNET '92.* Florence, Italy. Zurich: International Project Management Association, 1992.

McMahon, Patricia, and Ellen Busse. "Surviving the Rise and Fall of a Project Management Office." *Proceedings of the Project Management Institute Annual Seminars & Symposium.* Nashville, TN, Newtown Square, PA: Project Management Institute, November 1–10, 2001.

Morris, Peter W. G. "Initiating Major Projects—The Unperceived Role of Project Management." *Proceedings of INTERNET '88.* Glasgow, Zurich: The International Project Management Association, 1988.

Morris, Peter W. G. *The Management of Projects.* London: Thomas Telford, 1994.

Morris, Peter W. G. "Updating the Project Management Bodies of Knowledge." *Project Management Journal,* 32, no. 3 (September 2001).

Mowdray, R., L. Porter, and R. Steers. *Employee-Organizational Linkages: The Psychology of Commitment, Absenteeism, and Turnover.* New York: Academic Press, 1982.

Mower, Judith, and David Wilemon. "A Framework for Developing High-Performing Technical Teams." *Engineering Team Management,*" edited by David I. Cleland and Harold Kerzner. New York: Van Nostrand, 1986.

Muench, Dean, et al. *The Sybase Development Framework.* Oakland, CA: Sybase, 1994.

Mulvaney, John. *Analysis Bar Charting, A Simplified Critical Path Analysis Technique.* Bethesda, MD: Management Planning and Control Systems, 1969.

Murphy, Patrice L. "Pharmaceutical Project Management: Is It Different?" *Project Management Journal* (September 1989).

NASA 2002, "The PBMA Life Cycle and Assurance Knowledge Management System (KMS)"; www.hq.nasa.gov/tutorial/Details/implement.

Nicholson, R. F., and E. M. Sieli. "Integrating Process Management with Project Management." *Proceedings of the Project Management Institute Seminar/Symposium.* Newtown, PA: Project Management Institute, October 1990.

O'Brien, James J. *CPM In Construction Management,* 3rd ed., New York: McGraw-Hill, 1984.

Ondov, Rhoda. "Managing Software Projects at AT&T: Common Risks and Pitfalls." *Proceedings of the Project Management Institute Annual Seminars & Symposium.* Nashville, TN. Newtown Square, PA: Project Management Institute, November 1–10, 2001.

Ono, Daniel P., and Russell D Archibald, "Achieving Quality Teamwork through Project Performance Reviews." *Proceeding of the Project Managment Institute Annual Seminar/Symposium.* Dallas, TX. Newtown Square, PA: Project Management Institute, 1991.

Owens, Stephen D. "Project Management and Behavioral Research Revisited." *Project Management Institute Proceedings.* Toronto, Canada, Newtown Square, PA: The Project Management Institute, 1982.

Parkinson, C. Northcote. *Parkinson's Law.* Boston: Houghton Mifflin, 1957.

Patrick, Francis S. "Buffering Against Risk—Critical Chain and Risk Management." *Proceedings of the Project Management Institute Annual Seminars & Symposium.* Nashville, TN, Newtown Square, PA: Project Management Institute, 2001.

Patterson, Dan. "The Necessity of a Collaboration Tool in Today's Projects—A Welcom White Paper," available at www.welcom.com, 2002. Cited references include "Executive Summary-Distributed Project Management: A Marketplace and Software Vendor Analysis," 2000; and Executive Summary-Distributed Project Management: Update 2001;" Collaborative Strategies LLC; available at www.technography.com/CS-PM.

PC Magazine Internet Business. (June 12, 2001). Source: Accenture and The Conference Board.

Peterson, Craig D., and C. Leigh Filiatrault. "Earned Value vd. Critical Chain Project Management." *Proceedings of the Project Management Institute Annual Seminar & Symposium.* Houston, TX, Newtown Square, PA: Project Management Institute, September 7–16, 2000.

Pilcher, Roy. *Appraisal and Control of Project Costs*. London: McGraw-Hill, 1973.

Pincus, Claudio. "A Workshop Approach to Project Execution Planning, Project Management, A Reference for Professionals," edited by Robert L. Kimmons and James H. Loweree. New York: Marcel Dekker, 1989, 349–355.

Piney, Crispin (Kik). "Critical Path or Critical Chain—Combining the Best of Both." *PM Network* (December 2000).

PMI *PMBOK® Guide: A Guide to the Project Management Body of Knowledge*. Newtown, PA: Project Management Institute 2000. Can be downloaded (but not printed) free by PMI members from www.pmi.org

PMI *Practice Standard for Work Breakdown Structures*. Newtown, PA: Project Management Institute, 2000.

PMI® Project Management Software Survey. Newtown Square, PA: Project Management Institute, 1999.

Rosenstock, Christian, Robert S. Johnson, and Larry M. Anderson. "Maturity Model Implementation and Use: A Case Study." *Proceedings of the PMI 2000 Seminars & Symposium*. Houston, TX, PMI Newtown Square, PA, September 7–16, 2000.

Salancik, G. "Commitment and the Control of Organizational Behavior and Belief." In *New Directions in Organizational Behavior*, edited by B. M. Staw and G. Salancik. Chicago: St. Clair, 1977.

Sathe, V. *Culture and Related Corporate Realities*. Homewood, IL: Richard D. Irwin, 1985.

Schlichter, John, "The Project Management Institute's Organizational Project Management Maturity Model—An Update of the PMI's OPM3 Program." http://www.pmforum.org/library/opm3update1.htm, October 2002.

Schneidmuller, James J., and Judy Balaban. "An Invaluable Tool: A Proven Project Management Review Process." *Proceedings of the Project Management Annual Seminar & Symposium*. Nashville, TN, Newtown Square, PA: Project Management Institute, November 1–10, 2001.

Schwalbe, Kathy, and Vijay Verma. "Case Studies in Project Management: Theory Versus Practice." *Proceedings of the Project Management Annual Seminar & Symposium*. Nashville, TN, Newtown Square, PA: Project Management Institute, November 1–10, 2001.

Sharpe, Paul, and Tom Keelin. "How SmithKline Beecham Makes Better Resource-Allocation Decisions." *Harvard Business Review* (March/April 1998): 5–10.

Souder, William E. "Selecting Projects That Maximize Profits," Chapter 7, *Project Management Handbook*, 2nd ed., edited by David I. Cleland and William R. King. New York: Van Nostrand Reinhold, 1988.

Stratton, J. Michael. "First, Functional and Facilitator for the Future: The Program Management Office Role in IT Operations Engineering Implementation." *Proceedings of the Project Management Institute Annual Seminar & Symposium*. Nashville, TN. Newtown Square, PA: Project Management Institute, November 1–10, 2002.

Thamhain, Hans J. "Accelerating Product Developments via Phase-Gate Processes." *Proceedings of the Project Management Institute Annual Seminars & Symposium.* Houston, TX, Newtown Square, PA: Project Management Institute, September 7–16, 2000.

Thamhain, Hans J., and David L. Wilemon. "Conflict Management in Project Life Cycles." *Sloan Management Review* (summer, 1975).

Thamhain, Hans J., and David L. Wilemon. "Criteria for Controlling Projects According to Plan." *Project Management Journal* (June 1986).

Timmons, John. "Web-Enabled Project Management—Your Ticket to Success." *Proceedings of the Project Management Institute Seminars & Symposium.* Houston, TX. Newtown Square, PA: Project Management Institute, September 7–16, 2000.

Tuman, John, Jr., "Development and Implementation of Project Management Systems," Chapter 27, *Project Management Handbook,* 2nd ed., edited by David I. Cleland and William R. King. New York: Van Nostrand Reinhold, 1988.

U.S. DOD Department of Defense Instruction 5000.2. Washington DC: U.S. Government Printing Office (Final Coordination Draft, April, 2000).

U.S. DOD: *Department of Defense Handbook: Work Breakdown Structure.* MIL-HDBK-881. Washington, DC: U.S. Government Printing Office, January 15, 1998.

U.S. DOD: *Military Standard, Defense System Software Development.* DOD-STD-2167A. Washington, DC: U.S. Government Printing Office, February 29, 1988.

U.S. DOE: *Work Breakdown Structure Guide.* U.S. Department of Energy, DE87–007606.Washington, DC: U.S. Government Printing Office, February 6, 1987.

Valencia Franco, Ing. Hector. "Procediento para la Preparation y Arranque de un Nuevo Proyecto," *Proceedings of the PMI Foro Nacional.* México City: Project Management Institute México City Chapter, Ponencia 17, November 13–14, 1997, (www.pmi.org).

Vargas, Ricardo Viana. "A New Approach to PMBOK® Guide 2000." *Proceedings of the Project Management Institute Seminar & Symposium.* Nashville, TN, Newtown Square, PA: Project Management Institute, November 1–10, 2001.

Voropajev, Vladimir I. *Project Management in Russia—Basic Notions, History, Achievements, Perspectives.* Newtown Square, PA: Project Management Institute, 1997.

Ward, Gregory F. "The WBS Dictionary—Extending the Work Breakdown Structure." *Proceedings of the Project Management Institute Annual Seminars & Symposium.* Newtown Square, PA: Project Management Institute, Nashville, TN, 2001.

Whitten, Neal. *Managing Software Development Projects.* New York: Wiley, 1995.

Wideman, R. Max. *Wideman Comparative Glossary of Project Management Terms.* 2002. Available online at http://www.maxwideman.com/pmglossary/index/htm.

Wilemon, David L., and Gary R. Gemmill. "Interpersonal Power in Temporary Management Systems." *Journal of Management Studies* (October 1971).

Winograd, T., and F. Flores. *Understanding Computers and Cognition.* Norwood, NJ: Ablex, 1986.

World Bank Institute, Knowledge Products and Outreach Division. *Managing the Implementation of Development Projects, A Resource Kit on CD-ROM for Instructors and Practitioners, 2002.* The World Bank, Room J-2–105, Washington, DC, 20433 United States. Contact John Didier at Jdidier@worldbank.org.

Youker, Robert. "Organizational Alternatives for Project Management." *Project Management Quarterly,* 8, no. 1 (March 1975).

Youker, Robert. "A New Look at Work Breakdown Structure (WBS) (Project Breakdown Structure—PBS)." *Proceedings of the Project Management Institute Seminar/Symposium.* Calgary, Alberta, Canada, Project Management Institute, Drexel Hill, PA, October 1990.

Youker, Robert. "The Difference Between Different Types of Projects." *Proceedings of the PMI 1999 Seminars & Symposium.* Philadelphia, PA, Newtown, PA: Project Management Institute, October 10–16, 1999.

‹ ›

Index